The most radical gesture

M
T

Most Radical Gesture is the first major study of the Situationist rnational, a revolutionary movement of extraordinary ambition influence whose reflections on art, everyday life, pleasure, ntaneity, the city, and the spectacle have ensured it a vital, but ely hidden, role in the development of twentieth-century ure and politics. Revealing the extent to which situationist ideas tactics have influenced subsequent political theory and cultural ation, this book discusses a variety of specific movements and ments of contestation, including Dada, surrealism, the events of y '68, the Italian autonomists, the Angry Brigade, and punk, cing the situationists in a line of impassioned anti-authoritarian sent which also informs the work of writers like Lyotard and leuze and underwrites contemporary debates on postmodernism suggests that Baudrillard's reflections on hyperreality are poverished reworkings of the situationists' critical analysis of pitalist society as a spectacle, and challenges postmodern denials f meaning, reality, and history by showing that postmodernism self depends on a tradition which completely undermines the urposeless pessimism it promotes.

In addition to its unprecedented treatment of situationist theory, *The Most Radical Gesture* is therefore also the first book to situate postmodern ideas in this vital historical, cultural, and political context. The product of a long-standing engagement with situationist ideas, it uses theoretical reflection, polemical speculation, and accounts of particular moments of cultural and political excitement to tell a fascinating and accessible tale with wide appeal to the general reader and those interested in all aspects of twentieth-century culture. *The Most Radical Gesture* will also be welcomed by those engaged with radical artistic, cultural, and political interventions, and debates around Marxism, poststructuralism, and postmodernism.

Sadie Plant is Lecturer in Cultural Studies at the University of Birmingham.

The most radical gesture

The Situationist International in a postmodern age

Sadie Plant

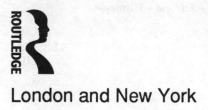

London and New York

First published in 1992
by Routledge
11 New Fetter Lane, London EC4P 4EE

Simultaneously published in the USA and Canada
by Routledge
a division of Routledge, Chapman and Hall Inc.
29 West 35th Street, New York, NY 10001

© 1992 Sadie Plant

Typeset by LaserScript, Mitcham, Surrey
Printed and bound in Great Britain by
Mackays of Chatham PLC, Chatham, Kent

British Library Cataloguing in Publication Data
Plant, Sarah-Jane, *1964–*
The most radical gesture: the Situationist
International in a postmodern age.
I. Title
700.9045

Library of Congress Cataloging in Publication Data
Plant, Sadie, 1964–
The most radical gesture: the Situationist International in a
postmodern age/Sadie Plant.
    p. cm.
    Includes bibliographical references and index.
    1. Internationale situationniste. 2. Arts, Modern – 20th century –
Europe. 3. Avant-garde (Aesthetics) – Europe – History –
20th century. I. Title.
NX542.P5 1992
700'.1'03 – dc20   91-32553
                                                                CIP

ISBN 0–415–06221–7 (hbk)
ISBN 0–415–06222–5 (pbk)

To my parents and my cosmic twin.

Thanks, in place of acknowledgements,
to everyone who helped.

Contents

Preface

The situationist analysis of contemporary capitalist society was simple and effective. Its express purpose was to transform this society, and it remains invaluable to those who share its revolutionary aims. Removed from this context, it can be like a series of instructions about swimming: interesting to the non-swimmer, but unable to express the wetness of water. Much of its meaning is therefore lost in the course of this discussion, which does not use the situationist thesis, but describes it in comparison to other analyses. Situationist theory can be made to perform in the big top of critical theory to great effect: it can expose the complacency and superficiality of much contemporary thought, jump through the same intellectual hoops and stand up to academic scrutiny. But unlike those theories to which it can be compared, it is merely playing in this role. It demands practical realisation, and is a theory which was only made possible by the acts of rebellion, subversion, and negation which foreshadowed it and continue to assert the discontent and disrespect inspired by the economic, social, and discursive relations which define contemporary capitalism. Nevertheless, the Situationist International has been ignored by its detractors and protected by those attracted to it for too long. There is no longer any damage to be done to its ideas by introducing them into the profoundly non-revolutionary milieu of contemporary intellectual debate. And its practices, which never, of course, belonged to it at all, are quite safe in the hands of those whose need them.

Chapter 1

'Now, the SI'

The Situationist International was established in 1957 and published twelve issues of a journal, *Internationale Situationniste*, until 1969. Many aspects of its theory can be found in Marxist thought and the tradition of avant-garde artistic agitation which includes movements like Dada and surrealism. But the movement also stands in a less distinct line of pleasure-seeking libertarianism, popular resistance, and autonomous struggle, and its revolutionary stance owes a great deal to this diffuse tradition of unorthodox rebellion. With its beginnings in an artistic milieu, the SI finally developed a more overtly political position from which its members gave full expression to their hostility to every aspect of existing society.

The situationists characterised modern capitalist society as an organisation of spectacles: a frozen moment of history in which it is impossible to experience real life or actively participate in the construction of the lived world. They argued that the alienation fundamental to class society and capitalist production has permeated all areas of social life, knowledge, and culture, with the consequence that people are removed and alienated not only from the goods they produce and consume, but also from their own experiences, emotions, creativity, and desires. People are spectators of their own lives, and even the most personal gestures are experienced at one remove.

The situationist project was not, however, ridden with pessimism, and while the first chapter of this book dwells on the darker implications of defining modern society as a spectacle, reams of situationist exuberance and delight come quickly on its tail. For although the situationists suggested that the whole of life as it is experienced under capitalism is in some sense alienated from itself, they postulated neither the inevitability of this alienation nor the impossibility of its critique. Even though the ability to control one's own life is lost in the midst of all-pervasive capitalist relations, the demand to do so continues to assert itself, and the situationists were convinced that this demand is encouraged by the increasingly obvious discrepancy between the possibilities awoken by capitalist development and the poverty of their actual use. The ethos of need, labour, and sacrifice is unnecessarily perpetuated, serving only to maintain the capitalist system; the idea that we must continue to struggle to survive hinders human development and precludes the possibility of a life of playful opportunity in which the satisfaction of desires, the realisation of pleasures, and the creation of chosen situations would be the principal activities. Long a utopian dream realisable only on canvas or in poetry, capitalist development has brought us to the point at which the end of alienated experience is a real possibility. The situationists saw the dissemination of propaganda to this effect as the central task of a revolutionary organisation.

The situationists were, of course, writing at a time of great affluence and technological achievement. At its peak, the capitalism of the 1950s and 1960s could promise and deliver more than ever before. A buoyant economy offered unprecedented levels of income, social security, education, and technological development. Political, sexual, and artistic freedoms were encouraged, blatant inequalities were reduced, anything could be bought and more people had the money to buy. Leisure, tourism, and consumer choice extended the variety, opportunity, and comfort afforded by capitalist society, and the possibility of economic crisis, still less social revolution, seemed remote. Some theorists proclaimed the disappearance of the working class, and many even declared capitalism to have been transformed by its own success into the progressive society free from class and ideological conflict it had always claimed to be. Others, however, including the situationists, considered such complacency superficial and premature. Recognising that capitalist society had indeed changed since Marx's mid-nineteenth-century critique, they claimed that its economic structure remained fundamentally the same. The misery of material poverty may have diminished, but life in capitalist society was still made miserable by the extension of alienated social relations from the workplace to every area of lived experience. The leisures and luxuries gained from capitalism can only be consumed: there is more free time, choice, and opportunity, but the commodity form in which everything appears serves only to reproduce the alienated relations of capitalist production.

The introduction of the radical demands of the imagination, creativity, desire, and pleasure to their revolutionary project is indicative of the situationists' distance from orthodox Marxism. It also reflects the influence of Dada and surrealism, whose provocative style, demands for immediacy, and cravings for autonomy were carried into the situationist project. These movements extended their initial artistic concerns to attacks on the whole gamut of cultural and social relations, arguing that capitalism circumscribes even the possibilities of expressing subjective experience. While Dada railed against every constraint, the surrealists developed a more coherent and dialectical critique of existing society which demanded the complete reconciliation of subject and object, the individual and the world, reason and the imagination. Drawing on what they considered to be the most useful aspects of these movements, the situationists developed their recognition that language and artistic expression were implicated with all other social relations, their hostility to the separation of art and poetry from everyday life, and their demands for experiences disallowed by existing society. Dada and surrealism had interrupted and subverted the language and images with which they worked, invoking a wider world of meanings which challenged conventional arrangements of reality. And in their challenges to the inevitability and immutability of the spectacle, the situationists pursued this same attempt to conjure a totality of possible social relations which exceeds and opposes the totality of spectacular relations. They took the words, meanings, theories, and experiences of the spectacle, and placed them in an opposing context; a perspective from which the world was given a fluidity and motion with which the static mediocrity of the spectacle could be negated. Introducing a sense of historical continuity by showing that the spectacle, in spite of its seamless appearance, carries the seeds of an emancipated and pleasure-filled world, the situationists showed that what could become real is more meaningful and desirable than that which is in being. The spectacle circumscribes the reality it presents, but it does not preclude the possibility of identifying a bigger and better world of chosen relations and experiences beyond its constraints.

For the situationists, freedoms of thought and action were not to be sacrificed to the future: theirs was a programme of immediate demands to be lived in the present as both the means and ends of revolutionary activity. Scorning all mediation and representation, they demanded autonomy for themselves and the proletariat in whose hands the possibility of social transformation lay. Capitalist social relations arise in every area and must be exposed and contested by those who experience them, and in their advocacy of workers' councils, the situationists joined a revolutionary tradition hostile to the hierarchy and bureaucracy of those who would educate, represent, and lead the people to revolution. Yet in a sense, the situationists formed a vanguard movement themselves, claiming theoretical superiority and tactical supremacy. They alone could sense the cravings of even the well-fed; of all radical currents, they had revealed the spectacular nature of capitalist society and could maintain a position in contradiction to it. But their libertarianism placed them in the role of propagandists and provocateurs rather than leaders or organisers. And in this role they continuously undermined complacency wherever it arose, particularly among the radical milieu. Situationist texts make uncomfortable reading for anyone with an interest in the maintenance of the status quo, and in their terms this includes even many of those committed to its negation.

This antagonistic stance has undoubtedly contributed to the scarcity of serious discussion of situationist theory, something which has not always been to the detriment of its ideas and practices. Those in sympathy with the movement's goals and tactics have been able to proceed without the unwelcome attentions of academics, and there has been none of the mystification or stasis usually associated with the introduction of revolutionary discourse to the academy. For many, situationist theory is already mysterious, and the apparent obscurity of many of the texts has also contributed to their neglect. However, their basic thesis is plain enough. And what has really written the situationists out of intellectual history is their own determination to avoid recuperation within existing channels of dissent and critical theory. Shunning the academy, the media, and orthodox conceptions of art and politics, they defined themselves as the last specialists: in the post-revolutionary world, there would be no need for elite groups of revolutionaries, and art, politics, and all other disciplines would no longer exist as separated areas of thought. Situationist theory, the unified study of spectacular society, was therefore to be the last discipline too, the last great project, the final push towards the transformation of everyday life from a realm of bland consumption to free creation. Poetry, political theory, adventure, scandal: anything which disturbed the old world and revealed the possibilities of the new was collected and woven into situationist theory, and every hint of compromise with the spectacle smacked of complicity with its relations and promised certain defeat.

Of course, the situationists' attempt to transform everyday life has been defeated, although their involvement with the upheavals of 1968 made them believe they had succeeded in helping it on its way. Neither have there been any further projects of the scale of that perpetrated by the SI and, in the present *fin de millénium* atmosphere of postmodernity, such all-encompassing revolutionary theories are said to be no longer possible. They bear the illegitimate arrogance of political totalitarianism, depending on unsupportable beliefs and assuming the possibility of ascertaining the way the world really is, regardless of the vicissitudes of appearance or the ambiguities of meaning. On this reading, the situationists' attempt to construct a unified theory of capitalism merely brought them within the totality they thought they were opposing. But in spite of the radical opposition of situationist and postmodern thought, all theoretisations of postmodernity are underwritten by situationist theory and the social and cultural agitations in which it is placed. The situationist spectacle prefigures contemporary notions of hyperreality, and the world of uncertainty and superficiality described and celebrated by the postmodernists is precisely that which the situationists first subjected to passionate criticism.

This continuity is not coincidental. The philosophers most closely associated with postmodern thought, Jean-François Lyotard and Jean Baudrillard, both emerged from the same political milieu as the situationists. Baudrillard's work is informed by his contacts with the situationist Guy Debord, and Lyotard was involved with *Socialisme ou Barbarie* and the *mouvement du 22 mars*, probably the groups whose political ideas and activities were closest to those of the SI. Allusions to the situationists are to be found in the work of both authors, and although postmodernism turns situationist theory against itself, the traces, even the tyre-tracks of the style, vocabulary, and scope of the situationist project run across postmodernism. Poetry, pleasures, cities, and subversions are themes common to both frameworks, and in their hostility to the Left, their attacks on the complacency and complicity of established forms of radicalism, their desire to collapse distinctions between the aesthetic and the everyday, and their search for the loci of social power in relations of language, knowledge, and everyday experience, the situationists provided postmodernism with much of the ammunition for its attacks on established genres of thought and social organisation. Moreover, the tactics with which postmodernism makes these attacks were already present in the situationist armoury: pastiche and deconstruction, subversive violence from within systems of social organisation or thought, playful irreverence towards respected theories, and the exposure of every hidden allusion and resonance.

Postmodernism uses all this to convey our departure from the modern period in which we experienced ourselves as autonomous subjects capable of making judgements, expressing desires, and acting upon the world. In Jean Baudrillard's work, it suggests that modern society has become hyperreal, a world in which the spectacle defines, circumscribes, and becomes more real than reality itself. Baudrillard describes the seductive power of images which fool us into believing a reality persists beyond this hyper-reality, and suggests that subjectivity is produced by a host of networks of social relations and discursive constructions so complex that it cannot be unravelled to reveal causes, directions, or meanings. There is no such thing as a social whole or a theoretical unity: the notion of society is a myth belying the essential discontinuity of social relations, and the development of theory is the totalitarian exercise of power on the world's dynamic fragments. The individual and the world are decentred: there is no core, no soul, no God, and no economic imperative. Alienation is not a problem peculiar to capitalism, but an inevitable feature of life to which we might as well develop a positive attitude, and the search for authenticity betrays a hopeless nostalgia for a unity which never existed in the first place. We live in the midst of codes, messages, and images which produce and reproduce our lives. These may have had their origins in commodity production, but have since won their independence and usurped its role in the maintenance of social relations. All that remains is the pleasure of playing in the fragments, the disruption and resistance of the codes in which we live, the *jouissance* of realising that the search for meaning is endlessly deferred and has no point of arrival and, in the absence of new movements, styles, or genres, the continual reiteration of those of the past. In the postmodern imagination, alienation is everywhere and is therefore nowhere; power is dispersed and so impossible to seize. We will only ever feel at home, liberated, and content if we give up looking for a world more real, a social organisation more free, and a happiness more profound than those provided for us. There is no subject of history digging capitalism's grave, and no Elysian field on the other side of the barricade.

Considered in these terms, postmodernism is a manual for survival, and a very good one, in a capitalist world which seems immune to transformation. Building on the failure of the social revolution which has been just around every twentieth-century corner, it cultivates an attitude which enables one to cope with the continual refurbishment of buildings, opinions, cities, and fashions, and its reassurance that it is quite natural to feel lost, confused, and uncertain of the solidity of the ground beneath one's feet is welcome news to the shaky survivor of the late twentieth century. But, full of advice about surviving in the here and now, it tells us little about the possibilities of transforming it: of metaphorically and literally leaving the twentieth century behind. And this was the intention of the situationist analysis, which was not a treatise on survival, but an indication of the possibilities of living in a world for which the imperatives of survival have long since disappeared. It was not an account of how to have as much fun as possible in this social environment – although in this respect it rivals postmodernism – but the theoretical transcription of attempts to have as much fun as possible changing it.

The articles published in *Internationale Situationniste* are indicative of the scope of the movement's interests. Questions of town planning and artistic intervention were joined by critiques of the cinema, language, and political organisation; the Algerian War, the Middle East, Vietnam, the situation in China and, in later issues, the beginnings and aftermath of the events of 1968, were all given serious consideration. The SI's conferences, its internal wrangles, and its reception in mainstream discourse were widely covered, and a variety of telling tales of everyday life were reported in support of the situationists' theoretical stance. Like the metallic colours of its covers, the collective editorship of the journal changed with each issue. An extraordinary number and variety of people passed through the ranks of the Situationist International, but the majority had brief and ignominious careers, with exclusion or resignation sealing the fate of most participants. Two major books emerged from this chaos, one by Raoul Vaneigem, who joined the SI in 1962, and the other, *The Society of the Spectacle*, by the somewhat self-styled leader of the group, Guy Debord.

The Society of the Spectacle appeared a decade after the establishment of the Situationist International. The book by no means encompasses the wealth of situationist theory and read in isolation from the movement's other texts, it is dry and uninspiring, with the only hints of situationist provocation and extravagance appearing in the wealth of italicised enthusiasm and the stolen goods it collects. In line with the movement's tactical subversions of existing texts and materials, much of the book consists of passages plagiarised and subtly rewritten; as a consequence, it is full of Hegelian turns of phrase and vaguely familiar transpositions of the work of Marx and Lukács. But the condensed form in which its arguments are presented makes *The Society of the Spectacle* a rich source for a number of situationist themes, particularly those which define modern capitalist society as a spectacle and identify its internal contradictions.

Vaneigem's book, *The Revolution of Everyday Life*, was published in the same year as *The Society of the Spectacle* and presented a rather more anecdotal, extravagant, and subjective work of propaganda to accompany Debord's theoretical investigations. Vaneigem's rejection of the spectacle was a moral, poetic, erotic, and almost spiritual refusal to co-operate with the demands of commodity exchange. It unleashed witty and compelling tirades against the myths and sacrifices of consumer society, asserting a radical subjectivity which could fire pleasures, spontaneity, and creativity at the all-encompassing equivalence and emptiness of modern life. Above all, it contested the system of social relations which forces us to exist as survivors shackled by needs and forced into labour when all the possibilities of a rich, desiring life are constantly displayed. But although *The Revolution of Everyday Life* expressed the situationists' enduring appeal for life, intensity, passion, and play, it also displayed an impatience with theory and the rather more serious political commitment demanded by Debord. Nobody thought it was very funny when Vaneigem went off on holiday as the great events of 1968 began to unfold, and the tension between

having fun in the present and saving it up until after the revolutic
was an enduring problem which played no small part in the fin;
collapse of the SI.[1]

It was in rather more sober tones, therefore, that Debord
presented *The Society of the Spectacle*. More than a decade after its
publication, he wrote:

> In 1967 I wanted the Situationist International to have a book
> of theory. The SI was at this time the extremist group which
> had done the most to bring back revolutionary contestation to
> modern society; and it was easy to see that this group, having
> imposed its victory on the terrain of critical theory, and having
> skilfully followed it through on that of practical agitation, was
> then drawing near the culminating point of its historical
> action. So it was a question of such a book being present in the
> troubles that were soon to come, and which would pass it on
> after them to the vast subversive sequel that they could not fail
> to open up.[2]

The 'troubles' of 1968 which were indeed 'soon to come' were
regarded by the situationists as the mass demonstration of their
theory, and if Debord had a single message to convey, it was
without doubt the conviction that the 'days of this society are
numbered; its reasons and merits have been weighed and found to
be lacking; its inhabitants are divided into two parties, one of
which wants this society to disappear'.[3] His book contended that
although the class and economic structure of capitalist society had
suffered no qualitative change since its analysis by Marx, the extension of commodity relations to all aspects of life and culture,
accelerated by new systems of technology, information, and communication, required the development of a new paradigm within
which contemporary society could be understood. The spectacle
provided the perfect framework. It captured the contemplative
and passive nature of modern life and accounted for the boredom
and apathetic dissatisfaction which characterised social experience. It could move beyond the basic categories of orthodox
Marxism while at the same time preserving the possibility of a
revolutionary critique and providing a perspective from which
every aspect of contemporary discourse, culture, social organisation, and daily existence could be challenged. And although the
SI's analysis was not just a response to the increasing role of the
mass media, information, and advertising, the notion of the spec-

tacle also facilitated a valuable analysis of the ubiquitous messages, signs, and images which conspire to confuse appearance with reality and throw into question the possibility of distinguishing true experience, authentic desire, and real life from their fabricated, manipulated, and represented manifestations. Above all, the notion of the spectacle conveyed the sense in which alienated individuals are condemned to lives spent effectively watching themselves. It suggested that, far from being inevitable attributes of the human condition, the boredom, frustration, and powerlessness of contemporary life are the direct consequence of capitalist social relations.

In common with other situationist texts, therefore, *The Society of the Spectacle* painted a picture of a society which believes itself capable of providing everything, satisfying all desire, relieving every burden, and fulfilling every dream. But this is also a world which insists that every moment of life must be mediated by the commodity form, a situation which makes it impossible to provide anything for oneself or act without the mediation of commodities. A spectacle can only be watched and enjoyed at a distance, from where it appears glamorous and desirable; participation may be possible, but its form and extent will be predetermined by the context in which it appears. The promises of self-fulfilment and expression, pleasure and independence which adorn every billboard are realisable only through consumption, and the only possible relation to the social world and one's own life is that of the observer, the contemplative and passive spectator. The commodity form places everything in the context of a world organised solely for the perpetuation of the economic system; a tautological world in which the appearance of real life is maintained in order to conceal the reality of its absence. Bombarded by images and commodities which effectively represent their lives to them, people experience reality as second-hand. Everything has been seen and done before; quests for fulfilment are always frustrated, and just as workers find no satisfaction in the products of their labour, so 'no one has the enthusiasm on returning from a venture that they had on setting out on it. My dears,' said Debord in one of his films, 'adventure is dead.'[4]

The basis of this characterisation of capitalist society was already laid in Marx's early and graphic descriptions of alienation. Performed not in order to satisfy a need but as a means of satisfying other needs, all work undertaken within capitalism is external,

alien, and 'shunned like the plague' wherever possible. Wor.
are left debased, exhausted, and denied, and the individual o.
'feels himself outside his work, and in his work feels outside
himself. He feels at home when he is not working, and when he is
working he does not feel at home.'[5] Alienated from the products
of their labour, their time, and their own selves, workers produce
and reproduce alienated relations both between themselves and
things and between each other. The relations of capitalist production are therefore reproduced in all social relations; circum-
scribing social reality, alienation comes to be perceived as the
necessary reality of daily life. In his later writings too, Marx
emphasised the estrangement or alienation intrinsic to capitalist
production. The commodity fetishism of *Capital* is a renewed consideration of the phenomenon in which relations between people
assume the form of relations between things. In the absence of any
real world of unalienated social experience, commodity relations
become mysterious and fantastic; labour is turned against the
worker and appears as an autonomous power, and because the
totality of these relations is presented as a natural order, the
worker loses all reason to challenge or understand the experience
of alienation.

The situationists argued that these alienated relations of
production are now disseminated throughout capitalist society.
Leisure, culture, art, information, entertainment, knowledge, the
most personal and radical of gestures, and every conceivable
aspect of life is reproduced as a commodity: packaged, and sold
back to the consumer. Even ways of life are marketed as lifestyles,
and careers, opinions, theories, and desires are consumed as surely
as bread and jam. Constantly creating new markets, the commodity relations of twentieth-century capitalism extend their grasp
to the very intimacy of people's everyday lives where nineteenth-
century capitalism built its geographical empires. And although
Marx had also recognised that commodity relations extend the
experience of alienation beyond the workplace, he retained a
sense of the worker being at home 'outside his work'. The spectre
that has haunted subsequent radical theorists is that this remaining realm of free and unalienated experience is increasingly
eroded by the encroachment of capitalist relations. And if
alienation really does extend to both work and leisure time, there
is a danger that it becomes completely meaningless, since there is
nothing with which to compare it and nothing in relation to which

it can be defined. The situationists argued that although the ubiquity of alienated relations does indeed make them increasingly difficult to contradict, it is always possible to identify some point of contrast or opposition to them. The desires, imaginings, and pleasures of the individual can never be completely eradicated: as a system which operates by transforming objects into commodities and people into their producers and consumers, capitalism cannot but sustain a sense of the reality it distorts. And this suggests that some contradiction between life as it is and life as it could be is preserved regardless of the spectacle's insistence on its own seamless inevitability.

Presenting the spectacle as 'the material reconstruction of the religious illusion',[6] Debord argued that the mediations of church and priest, the separation of body and soul, and the demands of sacrifice and deferred gratification which marked pre-capitalist society are now redeveloped to produce the same experiences of removal, alienation, and mystification. Seeking salvation and fulfilment in the spectacle of this world rather than the next, the producers and consumers of the spectacle are equally removed from their own lives and still live in a separated relation to themselves: 'The absolute denial of life, in the shape of a fallacious paradise, is no longer projected onto the heavens, but finds its place instead within material life itself.'[7] The spectacular world presents itself as a natural phenomenon, requiring no organisation, denying the existence of any economic foundation, and offering itself as 'an enormous positivity, out of reach and beyond dispute';[8] it is the 'moment at which the commodity completes its colonization of social life. It is not just that the relationship to commodities is now plain to see – commodities are now *all* there is to see; the world we see is the world of the commodity.'[9] And this vision of a united, complete, and natural social whole is a representation which compensates for the increasing fragmentation and alienation of daily life and belies the existence of all discontinuity and contradiction. The spectacle is the '*materialization* of ideology';[10] a society in which the particular perspective of the bourgeoisie is given a concrete form. It is a society asleep, in hibernation or a state of suspended animation, for which 'ideology is no longer a historical choice, but simply an assertion of the obvious'.[11]

This absolute realisation of commodity relations produces an entirely inverted world, in which everything 'that was directly lived has become mere representation',[12] a 'dull reflection'[13] of itself. Mystified by this removal, it is difficult to understand why the world appears to be so whole, natural, and unremarkable, yet is so extraordinarily difficult to really engage and feel at home in. 'The spectator feels at home nowhere, for the spectacle is everywhere',[14] and areas of life which were once untouched by the logic of the commodity form are now possible only within it. Free time is filled with provided forms of leisure and entertainment, and free choice is made from a pre-selected variety of goods, lifestyles, roles, and opinions. The content of life is swept aside by the commodity form in which it appears; all other means of judging, evaluating, and living in the world are emptied of their real meaning and reduced to the abstract standards of production and consumption. The spectacle is a society which continually declares: 'Everything that appears is good; whatever is good will appear.'[15] A world in which such circularity dominates all social experience is impoverished; only the commodity can exist, and as representations of the whole social world become increasingly tangible, the 'real consumer becomes a consumer of illusions. The commodity is this factually real illusion, and the spectacle is its general manifestation.'[16]

The contradiction which displaces the tautologous unity of capitalist society has long been identified in the tension between the forces and relations of production. In *The Communist Manifesto*, Marx and Engels observed that just as the end of feudal society was necessitated by the development of the forces of production beyond the social relations they supported, so the productive forces unleashed by capitalism project it into a crisis of its own.

> The productive forces at the disposal of society no longer tend to further the development of the conditions of bourgeois property; on the contrary, they have become too powerful for these conditions, by which they are fettered, and so soon as they overcome these fetters, they bring disorder into the whole of bourgeois society . . . . The conditions of bourgeois society are too narrow to comprise the wealth created by them.[17]

The consequent crises of over-production which mark bourgeois society can be temporarily assuaged, primarily by the cultivation of new markets, but their resolution can only be achieved with the abolition of the social and economic relations which lag behind the forces of production. The situationists agreed that the contradiction between the forces and relations of production is the essential antagonism of capitalist society, and were similarly at home with Marxist conceptions of history and class. The spectacle remains a class society, founded on a system of production which separates workers from one another, the products of their labour, and the commodities they consume. Regardless of the abundance of spectacular society, the essential poverty of everyday life left the situationists convinced that the proletariat is still reproduced by capitalist social relations as the class capable of realising and superseding the economic contradictions of capitalism. And the image of unity and seamless self-sufficiency which modern society cultivates is itself a product of the separations, divisions, and contradictions which riddle the spectacle. 'The unreal unity the spectacle proclaims masks the class division on which the real unity of the capitalist mode of production is based.'[18]

But the waters of western Marxism in which the SI played were those which considered the essential problem of modern capitalism to lie with its ability to contain, rather than produce, class conflict and economic crisis. To generations of Marxist theorists, bourgeois society had seemed increasingly able to deal with the economic contradictions implicit in it, and the situationists were not alone in their concern with the effects of increasing alienation on the ability of the proletariat to gain consciousness of its strength and significance. Crisis had always been averted, not least because the extension of the market necessary to the solution of crises of over-production was largely achieved by the extension of commodity relations into discourse, culture, and everyday life. For earlier theorists such as George Lukács and Antonio Gramsci, cultural and ideological institutions exerted an unprecedented stranglehold on working-class consciousness, propagating a world view in which capitalism appears as the only possible system of social and economic relations. And in the 1960s work of Herbert Marcuse, capitalism's cultural and ideological stabilisers were emphasised still more with claims that capitalist social relations have infected the very souls of those who live within them. For Marcuse, the working class had been bought off by a society which allowed no dissent from the single dimension of a dominant capitalist ideology, and in his work, the role of the proletariat was displaced by a new faith in the desires and imaginings of the unconscious mind and those social groups free to explore them.

Other theorists, like those involved in *Socialisme ou Barbarie*, a post-war movement whose membership included Cornelius

Castoriadis (who also wrote under the names of Paul Cardan and Pierre Chalieu), Claude Lefort, Pierre Canjuers, Jean-François Lyotard and, for a short time, Guy Debord, kept their faith in the proletariat and argued that the dissemination of alienated relations throughout every aspect of daily life merely paved the way for a radical and all-encompassing contestation. *Socialism ou Barbarie* defined the 'struggle of human beings against their alienation, and the ensuing conflict and split in all spheres, aspects, and moments of social life'[19] as the central locus of modern opposition. And it was not merely capitalist social organisation in which unprecedented levels of alienation were observed: the group defined Soviet society as bureaucratic or state capitalist and argued that bureaucratisation was the common feature of Soviet, eastern, and western European societies. This was a position which Debord carried into the SI, pausing only to distinguish between the diffuse spectacle of advanced capitalist society and its concentrated totalitarian form.

Both *Socialism ou Barbarie* and the SI redefined the proletariat in relation to the spectacular homogeneity of everyday life, reconstituting class society in terms of a division between those who give and those who take the orders, and identifying as proletarian all those who have no control over their own lives. 'The triumph of an economic system founded on separation leads to the *proletarianization* of the world,'[20] declared Debord, and rebellions against the powerlessness and mediocrity of ordinary life become the motor of a revolution which springs not from material poverty but from the absence of control. There is therefore no question of the proletariat having disappeared under the weight of consumerism; on the contrary, the extension of commodity relations to all aspects of daily life merely enlarges the revolutionary class.

Indeed, the situationists contemptuously dismissed claims that the proletariat had been eradicated. 'Where on earth can it be? Spirited away? Gone underground? Or has it been put in a museum?' laughed Vaneigem. 'We hear from some quarters that in the advanced industrial countries the proletariat no longer exists, that it has disappeared forever under an avalanche of sound systems, colour TVs, waterbeds, two-car garages and swimming pools.'[21] Pointing to a plethora of wildcat strikes, riots, and other manifestations of dissatisfaction, Vaneigem quoted a French worker in support of his case that even material abundance cannot compensate for the absence of passion and autonomy. 'Since 1936

I have been fighting for higher wages. My father before me fought for higher wages. I've got a TV, a fridge and a VW. If you ask me it's been a dog's life from start to finish.'[22] And although it appeared to the Debord of 1967 that the proletariat 'has utterly lost the ability to assert its own independence' and its illusions about itself, it had certainly not been eliminated:

> indeed it remains irreducibly present, under the intensified alienation of modern capitalism, in the shape of the vast mass of workers, who have lost all power over the use of their lives and who, once they realise this, must necessarily redefine themselves as the proletariat – as negation at work in the bosom of today's society.[23]

If alienation is both the means and the end of spectacular organisation, all those who struggle to assert the negation of their alienation perform the proletariat's revolutionary role.

This conception of the proletariat enabled the situationists to see a nascent class consciousness in all rebellion against the poverty of everyday experience. So, for example, 'rebellious tendencies among the young generate a protest that is still tentative and amorphous, yet already clearly embodies a rejection of the specialised sphere of the old politics, as well as of art and everyday life'.[24] Together with struggles against the hierarchy and bureaucracy of union organisation, this sort of rebellion signals 'a new spontaneous struggle emerging under the sign of *criminality*'.[25] Calling for a new Luddism, this time turned against the 'machinery of permitted consumption', Debord pointed to all refusals of alienated work, leisure, organisation, and consumption as the ground of a revolutionary onslaught on spectacular society.

Lukács' *History and Class Consciousness* greatly influenced *The Society of the Spectacle* with its view that capitalist development produces elements which both deflect and encourage the proletariat's recognition of its position. On the one hand, the total occupation of social life by the commodity reifies consciousness to an unprecedented extent: 'as the capitalist system continuously produces and reproduces itself economically on higher and higher levels, the structure of reification progressively sinks more deeply, more fatefully and more definitively into the consciousness of man'.[26] But on the other hand, 'the commodity can only be understood in its undistorted essence when it becomes the universal category of society as a whole',[27] and the commodity's dissemination to all areas of everyday life makes it increasingly visible. Older forms of domination, those of church and family, for example, are swept aside when the commodity comes to 'penetrate society in all its aspects and to remould it in its own image',[28] and the 'commodity character of the commodity, the abstract, quantitative mode of calculability shows itself here in its purest form'.[29] Debord likewise argued that although the dissemination of commodity relations throughout social experience might make consciousness of them more difficult, it also produces the starkest of choices and the unprecedented possibility of a radical break with the whole. As the disaffected and the small-time saboteurs gain consciousness of their alienation, they are faced with the choice of accepting the spectacular totality, or completely rejecting it: 'capitalism's ever-intensifying imposition of alienation at all levels makes it increasingly hard for workers to recognize and name their own impoverishment', but at the same time 'puts them in a position of having either to reject it in its totality or do nothing at all'.[30] Or, as a 1990s flyposter says to a kid sitting in the middle of a wasteland: 'Have you ever considered a career in total revolution?'

Such a perspective did not endear the situationists to traditional forms of political organisation. The playful libertarianism of their avant-garde roots made them see both the revolutionary party, always in danger of developing as an end in itself, and the theoretical presuppositions on which it is based as the irredeemable components of the old world of separated contemplation. Debord saw the failure of the early revolutionary movements and the development of Marxism as a scientific discipline encouraging an emphasis on economic contradiction as the mainspring of revolution which merely reinforces the passivity and sacrifice of capitalist social relations.

It became important patiently to study economic development, and once more to accept, with Hegelian tranquillity, the suffering it imposed – that suffering whose outcome was still a 'graveyard of good intentions.' All of a sudden it was discovered that, according to the 'science of revolutions', *consciousness now always came on the scene too soon*, and needed to be taught.[31]

For Debord, the party, from which this education traditionally comes, merely encourages the endless deferral of the revolutionary moment. Even when the contradictions are obvious and openly acknowledged, the long wait for conditions to ripen means that possibility of their revolutionary supersession can remain a distant, and spectacular, dream.

For the situationists, the prospect of either revolutionary organisation or theory representing the working class was quite unthinkable. Since such representation is precisely the ground of alienation against which the revolution is effected, 'the revolutionary organization must learn that it can no longer *combat alienation by means of alienated forms of struggle*'.[32] It cannot 'represent the revolutionary class', but must 'simply recognise itself as radically separated from *the world of separation*':[33]

> when the proletariat discovers that its own externalized power conspires in the continual reinforcement of capitalist society, no longer merely thanks to the alienation of its labor, but also thanks to the form taken on by unions, parties and institutions of State power that it had established in pursuit of its own self-emancipation, then it must also discover ... that it is indeed the class which is totally opposed to all reified externalizations and all specializations of power. It is the bearer of a *revolution that can leave nothing outside itself,* that demands the permanent domination of the past by the present and a universal critique of separation.[34]

Alienated social relations must be negated at every point of the revolutionary struggle if the profound impoverishment of everyday life is to be countered: 'The revolutionary organisation must necessarily constitute an integral critique of society – a critique, that is to say, which refuses to compromise with any form of separated power and which is directed globally against every aspect of alienated social life.'[35] And the only principles of political organisation capable of fulfilling these criteria are those of autonomous self-management on which the idea of the soviet, or workers' council, is based.

Although workers' councils do not overcome all the problems of separated organisations and hierarchies, such autonomous forms of organisation certainly raise the right questions and subject all forms of hierarchy and mediation to a rigorous critique. And the situationists were convinced that it is to the establishment of councils that the revolutionary organisation must work, without, however, producing a separated ideology of councilism itself.

Once embodied in the power of workers' councils – a power destined to supplant all other powers worldwide – the proletarian movement becomes its own product; this product is the producer himself, and in his own eyes the producer has himself as his goal. Only in this context can the spectacle's negation of life be negated in its turn.[36]

This had also been the position held by the young Lukács, who argued that the tight organisation and rigorous hierarchy of the Leninist party was merely the reproduction of the alienated relations produced by capitalism. Only the workers' council 'spells the political and economic defeat of reification',[37] since the increasing mechanisation and specialisation of capitalist production demands that the worker's activity 'becomes less and less active and more and more contemplative'.[38] Capitalism's 'image of a frozen reality that nevertheless is caught up in an unremitting, ghostly movement at once becomes meaningful when this reality is dissolved into the process of which man is the driving force.'[39] And those who produce and reproduce alienated social relations cannot be given consciousness of this meaning by some external power, but must actively realise it themselves. For both Lukács and the situationists, only workers' councils embodied the autonomous and direct forms of political participation by which this driving force might be realised. Capable of refusing all external mediation and resisting the spectacular separations of capitalist life, the situationists envisaged self-managed councils as both the means of social transformation and the basis of post-capitalist social organisation.

This hostility to all forms of separation led the situationists to adopt what might be characterised as a maximalist position, from which all experiences of alienation, representation and hierarchy were ascribed to capitalist social relations.[40] Alienation, no matter how natural or necessary it might turn out to be, must be contested as if it were the sole consequence of capitalist society: only from this extreme position is the reversal of perspective necessary to the critique of the spectacle possible, and any stance which fails to subject the totality of existing society to a rigorous critique is vulnerable to accommodation within it. In *History and Class Consciousness*, Lukács' own use of the term 'reification' was similarly broad. Reification, the reduction of the individual to the thing, appears in a society which satisfies 'all its needs in terms of commodity exchange',[41] and constitutes 'the immediate reality of every person living in capitalist society'.[42] Later criticising the term 'reification', Lukács pointed out that it confused those forms of alienation for which capitalist social relations are really responsible with those which form part of the natural separation of the human subject from the world. This position, he argued, had led to an analysis which on the one hand fostered the idea of some immutable human condition, and on the other demanded the impossible development of a consciousness capable of overcoming an alienation which was really the natural attribute of consciousness and not at all specific to capitalism. But the situationists' decision to hold capitalism responsible for all forms of alienation was a tactical response to the problem of criticising a society in which it is increasingly difficult to distinguish the natural from the socially constructed at any point. Everything must be contested in order to ensure that no remnants of the old world were carried over into the new, and if alienation is the defining characteristic of the social and discursive relations in which we live, then it is alienation in all its manifestations which must be contested. Although this was a stance which left the situationists vulnerable to charges of Utopianism for their invocations of a post-revolutionary world free of all mediation, specialisation, domination, and hierarchy, theirs was not an attempt to do away with the conflict between the individual and the world, but rather to interrogate every moment of their interaction.

This position was reinforced by the situationists' conception of the 'situation' itself. 'So far philosophers and artists have only interpreted situations', they declared, paraphrasing Marx and taking a swipe at Sartre: 'the point now is to transform them. Since man is the product of the situations he goes through, it is essential to create human situations. Since the individual is defined by his situation, he wants the power to create situations worthy of his desires.'[43] Great importance had been attached to the way in which one is situated in the world by Sartre and those philosophers, including Heidegger and Kierkegaard, who exerted some influence on existentialist philosophy. For Sartre, 'there is freedom only in a situation, and there is a *situation* only through freedom'.[44] The human subject which acts 'for itself' (as opposed to the object which exists 'in itself') is always already thrown into the world and is only able to choose and act in relation to it. The freedom of the existentialist subject is not the unlimited ability to choose anything, but the ability to act in and against the world in which it finds itself. 'There can be a free for-itself only as engaged in a resisting world. Outside of this engagement the notions of freedom, of determinism, of necessity lose all meaning.'[45] In Hegel's conception of the development of human self-consciousness, to which Marx, Lukács, Sartre, and the situationists were all indebted, social awareness and human freedom again develop out of the struggle against nature and the recognition of oneself in productive activity or labour on the world. In this dialectical conception of the world, the separation and antagonism between consciousness and the world, the subject and the object, is necessary to human development: it is out of this difference or friction that full self-consciousness emerges. And the purpose of situationist attacks on this separation was not to achieve a Utopian world of perfect stasis without the possibility of future change or development, but one in which the real adventures of historical life could be played out in a society which, 'having brought down all its enemies, will at last be able to surrender itself joyously to the true divisions and never-ending confrontations of historical life'.[46] So the attack on all forms of separation and mediation was really a challenge to the existing conceptions of difference and contradiction. The situationists were not determined to end all separation, but to live in a world which had emerged out of the radical critique of that which exists.

Although it is the sufferings and struggle of our labour on and against the world which have brought us to our present state of consciousness, human consciousness and its expression is merely fettered and arrested by the illegitimate perpetuation of alienated relations of production beyond the need to survive. 'The accumulation of production of ever-improving technological capabilities is proceeding even faster than nineteenth-century communism predicted. But we have remained at the stage of a superequipped prehistory.'[47] Freedom from this prehistory would liberate us from necessity and launch us into a new world of free choice and playful extravagance, and it is the supersession of the relations which preclude these freedoms which must motivate the contemporary revolutionary project. 'We need to work toward flooding the market – even if for the moment merely the intellectual market', argued the situationists, 'with a mass of desires whose realisation is not beyond the capacity of man's present means of action on the material world, but only beyond the capacity of the old social organisation.'[48] It is in the play born of desire that individuals should now be able to recognise themselves, progressing with a new and chosen set of relations no longer dictated by the ethos of labour and struggle but governed by the free and playful construction of situations, of which the revolutionary moment is the first and the best.

For the situationists, one of the central mechanisms by which the spectacle precludes the possibility of such a world is its cultivation of the myth that it is the only system of social organisation capable of providing the means of survival. Indeed, capitalist relations of production have always been justified on the grounds that they facilitate the satisfaction of basic needs, and if work performed in order to survive has been the stick of capitalist relations, the possibility of achieving freedom from this necessity has been its carrot, its heaven on earth. The prospect of increasing free time, leisure, and the opportunity to enjoy the fruits of one's labour is continually held out as the reward of increased productivity. And the situationists argued that although the economic and technological achievements of capitalism have made the prospect of this reward a real possibility, the alienated relations of production which were necessary to the abolition of material privation and the satisfaction of basic needs are now perpetuated without justification. Economic growth has 'given rise to an *abundance* thanks to which the basic problem of survival, though solved, is solved in such a way that it is not disposed of, but is rather forever cropping up again at a higher level'.[49] Alienated production was only necessary to a people desperate to survive; now that the forces of production unleashed by capitalism have rid us of this desperation, the social relations which once facilitated human development have become its brake and hindrance. Societies have been liberated from 'the natural pressures occasioned by their struggle for survival, but they must still be liberated from their liberators'.[50] New threats and enemies are continually introduced to combat that of material poverty: the perpetual terrors of nuclear war, epidemic, and environmental disaster reproduce an ideology of the urgent need to survive. The horizon of capitalist Utopia must constantly recede: 'The satisfaction of basic needs remains the best safeguard of alienation; it is best dissimulated by being justified on the grounds of undeniable necessities.'[51] At a time when survival could have become an imperative of the past, superseded by a life free from the demands of need, everyday life remains 'governed by the reign of scarcity' and organised 'within the limits of a scandalous poverty'.[52]

This poverty is enforced and reproduced through the production of commodities which pretend to offer satisfactions they continually deny. 'Consumable survival *must* increase, in fact, because it continues to enshrine deprivation.'[53] Even the most banal and unnecessary of commodities is presented as a means of survival – 'how can you live without X soap powder?' – or sometimes offered as a more obvious threat: 'you cannot live without a credit card', or 'you need to use cosmetics'. 'As poverty has been reduced in terms of mere material survival', wrote Vaneigem, 'it has become more profound in terms of our way of life.'[54] Integral to the rhetoric of advanced capitalist societies, the free realms of luxury, leisure, and consumption merely reproduce the alienated relations by which they were produced, introducing a new cycle of scarcity, privation, and the imperatives of survival. The spare time for which generations of workers struggled has been invaded by the very alienated relations from which it was supposed to have been a holiday: modern capitalism demands a 'surplus of "collaboration"',[55] and alienated consumption 'is added to alienated production as an inescapable duty of the masses'.[56] At such a stage of over-development and abundance, the workers who were once coerced into producing the goods they needed are now encouraged to consume the commodities they are told they need; the extension of commodity relations to all areas of social experience means that the worker is not even free from them outside the workplace. Leisure is defined in terms of commodified time, activities, and goods; free time is spent, and the realm outside work is increasingly the province of alienated relations.

> All of a sudden the workers in question discover that they are no longer invariably subject to the total contempt so clearly built into every aspect of the organisation and management of production; instead they find that every day, once work is over, they are treated like grown-ups, with a great show of solicitude and politeness, in their new role of consumers.[57]

No longer a mere adjunct to production, consumption becomes necessary to the circulation of commodities, the accumulation of capital, and the survival of the spectacular system.

But consumption merely reproduces the alienation and isolation experienced in production. Increasingly meaningless

nmodities are circulated and contemplated as external and
stile goods: intrinsically dissatisfying, they embody alienated
social relations and take their entire meaning from the spectacular
whole in which they arise. 'The whole life of those societies in
which modern conditions of production prevail presents itself as
an immense accumulation of spectacles.'[58] A staggering abundance of commodity choices is offered, and identification is
demanded not with a single commodity but the commodity system
itself: it is the spectacle as a whole which is advertised and desired.
The lights, the opportunities, the shops, the excitement: the
attraction of capitalist societies has always been their glamorous
dynamism, the surfeit of commodities and the ubiquity of choice
they offer. But in practice, anything can be chosen except the
realm in which choice is possible. One can choose to be, think, and
do anything, but as the roles, ideas, and lifestyles possible within
capitalist society are allowed to appear only to the extent that they
appear as commodities, the equivalence and homogeneity of commodities is inescapable in the most private aspects of life. The
shops always carry everything except the thing one really wants;
they are 'full of things', but one cannot buy all of them, still less all
the shops. The act of choosing between a variety of commodities,
whether they are roles or things, lifestyles or opinions is, by virtue
of its place in the alienated whole, fated to be an instance of 'false
choice offered by spectacular abundance';[59] an irrelevant and
meaningless choice between empty and equivalent commodities.

Every product represents the hope for 'a dramatic shortcut to
the long-awaited promised land of total consumption',[60] but the
fulfilment of this promise is possible only with the attainment of
the totality of commodities, a desire which excites the accumulation of commodities but which is ultimately insatiable. 'The
satisfaction that the commodity in its abundance can no longer
supply by virtue of its use value is now sought in the acknow-
ledgement of its value *qua commodity*.'[61] Commodities circulate as
ends in themselves; goods which are one day presented as unique
and ultimate products, the very best and the very latest goods, are
replaced and forgotten the next:

> what this means for the consumer is an outpouring of religious
> zeal in honour of the commodity's sovereign freedom. Waves of
> enthusiasm for particular products, fuelled and boosted by the
> communications media, are propagated with lightning speed. A

film sparks a fashion craze, or a magazine launches a chain of clubs that in turn spins off a line of products. The sheer fad item perfectly expresses the fact that, as the mass of commodities becomes more and more absurd, absurdity becomes a commodity in its own right.[62]

And the life of the consumer becomes increasingly absurd as well, able to find identity only in the act of pointless consumption. 'In this way reified man proclaims his intimacy with the commodity.'

Following in the footsteps of the old religious fetishism, with its transported convulsionaries and miraculous cures, the fetishism of the commodity also achieves its moment of acute fervor. The only *use* still in evidence here . . . is the basic use of submission.[63]

This intimate identification of the individual with the commodity is born out of the attempt to escape alienation: the search for some unity and meaning in the midst of increasing fragmentation and isolation. But the commodity's role in the reproduction of alienated relations makes this fulfilment impossible: the society of commodity abundance produces its own contradictions. It needs to cultivate new needs and awake new desires, but can never allow them to be fulfilled since its own imperatives for constant innovation and increased production and consumption are dependent on a continued struggle for satisfaction.

Unable to allow participation on terms other than its own, the spectacle propagates the image of participation and invites everyone to 'join in' with the happy whole whilst at the same time ensuring that this totality is illusory and unattainable: a strong, appealing, but empty image. In principle, one can have anything, do anything, be anything, and go anywhere, but one cannot choose or define the whole in which these abundant choices are made. Everything is offered, and everything has great appeal, but the something it is possible to choose is impoverished and mundane. The world is an exciting place, but the bit in which one lives might be as dull as ditch-water. As the representation of itself, life is complete and fulfilling; as it is actually possible to live it, it is fragmented and disappointing. It is only in the context of the advertised whole, the image of spectacular unity, that the commodity has meaning: just as the colourful stripes of knitwear on the shelves of a Benetton shop conceal the single colour of each item, so the consumption of all commodities entails an immediate loss of their glamour.

The sole real status attaching to a mediocre object of this kind is to have been placed, however briefly, at the very center of social life and hailed as the revelation of the goal of the production process. But even this spectacular prestige evaporates into vulgarity as soon as the object is taken home by a consumer – and hence by all other consumers too. At this point its essential poverty . . . stands revealed – too late. For by this time another product will have been assigned to supply the system with its justification, and will in turn be demanding its moment of acclaim.[64]

It is, of course, necessary that the promised land remain unattainable. Everyone knows that gas central heating will not really make them feel more at home; perfumes do not bring everlasting happiness, and holidays can't make one's dreams come true. But these grand desires are constantly advertised, and the realisation that gas central heating does not fulfil its promises does not make our desire to belong in the world disappear. Even though we are condemned to seek fulfilment amidst the fragments of alienated commodities and second-hand experiences, the constant innovations of commodity production merely encourage our search for satisfaction, our eager watch for the next best thing.

In the midst of these perpetual cycles of redevelopment, revolution is, of course, the one change precluded by the spectacle. Change occurs within the spectacle, but the spectacle is static: time frozen into its own commodification and constantly reproducing itself in cycles of return. Every new commodity presents itself as the last, the perfect, and the ultimate: consume this product, try this experience, be this person, and you will never want for more. But wanting more is an experience built into the alienated commodity: desires are only raised and never fulfilled by its privation. Yesterday's innovation is continually superseded, and the ultimate product has an ever-decreasing life span. The car to end all cars, the holiday of a lifetime, the perfect kitchen – the best, the biggest, the final achievement of production and design – all are passed over in favour of a new finality with an accelerated movement. 'Something that can assert its own unchanging excellence with uncontested arrogance changes nonetheless', and every 'new lie of the advertising industry implicitly acknowledges the one before.'[65] The commodity must simultaneously be the last and the latest; the end of history is declared and denied every day. And so the spectacle continually affirms that 'there was history, but "there is no longer any history"', a point made by Marx and developed by both Lukács and Debord.[66]

In *The Society of the Spectacle*, Debord agreed with Marx that capitalist relations of production have imposed a sense of linear time on a world whose pre-industrial time had been experienced as cyclical. 'The victory of the bourgeoisie was the victory of a *profoundly historical* time – the time corresponding to the economic form of production, which transformed society permanently, and from top to bottom.'[67] Lived in relation to the seasons, the hours of light and darkness, and the phases of the moon, the time of pre-industrial societies returned upon itself and embodied no sense of progress. But the accumulation of capital entails the constant development of all social relations: there is no cyclical return, but only the necessity of change. Capitalist production makes time historical, irreversible, and universal. Its history is no longer made up of a series of isolated events, but produced in the accumulation of capital and commodity production: 'the worker, at the base of society, is for the first time not materially estranged from history, for now the irreversible is generated from below'.[68] And, merely by 'demanding to *live* the historical time that it creates, the proletariat discovers the simple, unforgettable core of its revolutionary project; and every attempt to carry this project through . . . signals a possible point of departure for a new historical life'.[69]

The senses of time and history generated by capitalist production may be irreversible and progressive but, experienced purely in terms of commodified and spectacularised moments, they are necessarily lived at a distance: contemplated and observed without the possibility of real engagement. 'So the bourgeoisie unveiled irreversible historical time and imposed it on society only to deprive society of its *use*.'[70] And in this purely economic time, spectacular time manifests itself as a pseudo-cyclical form of 'augmented survival in which daily lived experience embodies no free choices and is subject, no longer to the natural order, but to a pseudo-nature constructed by means of alienated labour'.[71] Spectacular time builds 'on the natural vestiges of cyclical time, while at the same time using these as models on which to base new homologous variants'.[72] Week and weekend, the morning after the night before, the news and the soap, the annual holiday and the office party: all these provide new cycles which punctuate and veil the reality of linear time. 'Cyclical time was the time of a motion-less illusion authentically experienced; spectacular time is the time of a reality in transformation experienced as an illusion.'[73] The festivals and events which the cyclical time of pre-capitalist society required to mark its passage and return are recreated in the spectacle as pseudo-festivals, in which the only available roles are those of audience, consumer, or star. Carnivals and festivals are outlawed when they threaten to transgress these spectacular forms.

In the spectacle, time is advertised and consumed as free time, time out, time to drink tea, eat chocolate, invest, and retire. Measured quantitatively in units of production and consumption, it is spent, wasted, and saved. Sliced into saleable units, time is sold as 'moments portrayed, like all spectacular commodities, *at a distance* and desirable by definition'.[74] This is epitomised by the selling of '"fully equipped" blocks of time':[75] the all-inclusive shopping mall and the package holiday in which time 'sheds its qualitative, variable, flowing nature; it freezes into an exactly delimited, quantifiable continuum filled with quantifiable "things" [. . .] in short, it becomes space'.[76] Travel, made easier by tech-nological development and the imposition of the global market, is translated into tourism, 'the chance to go and see what has been made banal',[77] and the peculiar characteristics of places are lost in the dissemination of commodity equivalence. The mass planning of the 1960s produced a 'new architecture specifically for the poor',[78] and encouraged the development of a homogeneous space interspersed with 'temples of frenetic consumption',[79] shopping centres, leisure centres, new towns, and environments which continually declare: 'On this spot no one will ever do anything – and *no one ever has.*'[80] As the recent development of theme parks, reconstructed villages, architectural pastiche, and the heritage industry shows, both history and space become objects of contemplation: geographical areas are increasingly places to look at rather than to live in, and although it is possible to go anywhere, there is less and less reason to do so.

With qualitative difference emptied out of every aspect of the spectacular world, all possibilities of real engagement and partici-pation are removed. Even the most devastating criticism can assume the mundane superficiality of the commodity form and, translated into spectacle, the most transgressive of gestures loses its impact. Capitalism 'paints its own picture of itself and its enemies, imposes its own ideological categories on the world and its history'

while real 'historical changes, which show that this society can be
superseded, are reduced to the status of novelties, processed for
mere consumption'.[81] But the situationists were convinced that the
perpetual raising and dashing of hopes, desires, and histories on
which capitalism is dependent left it vulnerable to subversion on
every front. 'Capitalist civilisation has not yet been superseded
anywhere, but it continues to produce its own enemies everywhere.'[82] And to the immobile surfaces of the spectacular world
they responded with a dynamic conception of dialectical critique,
intended to expose the spectacle as a particular moment of the
historical time it denies, undermining its claims to universality and
revealing it as a partial construct masquerading as a real world.
Lukács' answer to the ubiquity of alienated relations had been to
argue that 'the developing tendencies of history constitute a
higher reality than the empirical "facts"',[83] and the situationists
also based their critique on the idea that the possibilities of transformed social relations bear a greater meaning than the
immediate realities of the spectacle in which they arise.

Debord presented dialectical critique as a way of thinking 'that
is not content simply to seek the meaning of what is but aspires to
understand the dissolution of everything that is – and in the
process to dissolve all separation'.[84] Situationist theory therefore
conjured two perspectives: that possible within existing social relations, and that made possible by their supersession. History,
change, participation, reality, and every meaning developed
within spectacular society must be reinterpreted in the light of a
perspective of the possible. The struggle against alienation
demands a total reversal of perspective, embodied in a theory
which again puts reality on its feet and posits a totality of historical
development beyond the existing, pseudo-totality of the spectacle.
But this reversal cannot be a contemplative turn made by theory
alone, and it is useless to ponder the theoretical possibility of social
contestation. The contestation of alienation is also a struggle
against the separations and specialisations of an intellectual programme, and if an effective critique can only be generated from
within spectacular relations, it must also be realised as a practical
contestation. 'A critical theory of the spectacle cannot be true
unless it joins forces with the practical movement of negation in
society.'[85] Neither can the spectacle be opposed by some pre-
existing, uncontaminated, or authentic reality. It does not present
a situation in which two worlds, the real and the spectacular,

conflict: even this 'separation is part and parcel of the unity of the world, of a global social praxis that has split up into reality on the one hand and image on the other'.[86]

> The spectacle cannot be set in abstract opposition to concrete social activity, for the dichotomy between reality and image will survive on either side of any such distinction. Thus the spectacle, though it turns reality on its head, is itself a product of real activity. [. . .] Each side therefore has its share of objective reality. And every concept, as it takes its place on one side or the other, has no foundation aside from its transformation into its opposite: reality erupts within the spectacle, and the spectacle is real.[87]

There are no free realms or pockets of social experience untouched by the spectacle in which terms such as 'authenticity', 'meaning', or 'reality' maintain their independent meaning uncontaminated by commodity relations. Everything is compromised by its appearance within the spectacle, and all the terms in which this can be expressed are themselves the products of spectacular society. Even the subject against which commodity relations are pitted 'can only arise out of society – that is, out of the struggle that society embodies'.[88] Likewise, 'the pseudo-need imposed by the reign of modern consumption' cannot be opposed to 'any authentic need or desire that is not itself equally determined by society and its history'.[89] The critique of the spectacle can only be an immanent critique: there are no absolute standards, authentic human beings, or transcendental truths on which it can be based.

The implications of this position were developed in the situationists' analysis of the Watts riots in Los Angeles in 1965. Dealing with a situation which has since reasserted itself in countless instances from Handsworth to Brixton, the situationists argued that the looting of the Watts district was 'the most direct realisation of the distorted principle, "To each according to his false needs" – needs determined and produced by the economic system that the very act of looting rejects.'

> But since the vaunting of abundance is taken at its face value and immediately seized upon instead of being eternally pursued in the rat race of alienated labour and increasing but unmet social needs, real desires begin to be expressed.[90]

Regardless of the actual booty, what the rioter really takes is the
spectacle literally. The spectacle which offers itself as a whole is
taken as such: the spell of the shop window is broken and the
objects are revealed for what they really are in relation to their
subjective appropriation – useful, beautiful, empty, or worthless as
the case may be. The real desire which begins to emerge is for the
power to choose, to assign value, to control what is offered and that
which is possible. During the 1990 Poll Tax riot in London, it was
the signs of conspicuous consumption that were attacked: the most
expensive shops, the brightest neon signs, and the most prestigious cars. Caught up in the fracas by an accident of traffic flow, a
vintage car was spared by the crowd. Was this the remnant of an
old respect which the emerging consciousness should overcome,
or the manifestation of a new system of values which distinguished
between one form of consumption and another? From a situationist perspective, there is no tribunal at which such questions
can be decided, and certainly no possibility of distinguishing between the 'good' values of the revolutionary consciousness and the
'bad' ones of spectacular reification in advance. It is only when the
real possibility of actively effecting a particular situation arises that
'real desires begin to be expressed'.

The situationists' entire theory was based on the assumption
that both the objective and subjective ingredients of a new society
are already present within the spectacle, so that all that is needed
is a reversal of the perspective in which spectacular society is lived.
They insisted that the construction of situations 'begins on the
ruins of the modern spectacle',[91] and their condemnations of
existing society left no room for calls for a return to nature or any
pre-capitalist age. The situationists envisaged a future in which the
creativity, imagination, technology, and knowledge developed
within capitalist society would allow us to abolish work, satisfy
desire, create situations, and overcome all the problems posed by
the perpetuation of outmoded social and economic relations. In
the practical contestation of the spectacle, the 'secret of negation's
potential' will be unveiled,[92] and all the efforts of the revolutionary organisation and its theory must be directed towards the
develop- ment of an active 'propaganda of desire' to arouse direct
consciousness of 'the appalling contrast between the possible constructions of life and its present poverty.'[93] The material conditions
for a world of playful engagement, uncommodified leisure and
unqualified pleasure had long been achieved. The spectacle was

conceived as a society poised on the brink of revolution, saved only by its ability to control those manifestations of the desires and dissatisfactions that would disturb it.

Paying no regard to the distrust with which the traditional organs of opposition treated absenteeism, unofficial strikes, 'mindless violence', shop lifting, graffitoed advertisements, and every attempt to take momentary control of ordinary life, the situationists were convinced that such daily acts of disruption and resistance to work, authority, and consumption showed that the spectacle was already and always being contested. The development of increasingly sophisticated devices with which the control and removal of real experience is effected is matched by the sophistication of their appropriation by the very subjectivity it intends to control. Pirate broadcasters crowd the airways, fax machines send works of art in office hours, desk-top publishers produce propaganda, and electricity meters run backwards all over the developed world. Just as everything which appears in opposition to the spectacle can be brought within it, so everything which appears within spectacular society can be reclaimed by the consciousness which seeks to subvert it.

The situationists were aware of the difficulties in their theoretical stance. Although they could claim that the desires to participate in history and construct the situations in which one lives are reproduced by spectacular relations as surely as they are denied, they could offer only the hope that the consciousness of these desires would develop to the point at which a wholesale onslaught on the social totality was possible. And for all the sophistication of their conception of immanent critique, the situationists did not avoid the problem of finding some point of opposition to spectacular society. No matter how accurate, a theory, as Debord acknowledged, is useless in itself; of *The Society of the Spectacle*, he wrote:

> Anyone who reads this book attentively will see that it gives no kind of assurances about the victory of the revolution, nor of the duration of its operations, nor of the rough roads it will have to travel, and still less about its capacity, sometimes rashly boasted of, to bring perfect happiness to everyone.[94]

But although the situationists protected themselves with arguments that those who help 'the epoch to discover what it can do' are 'no more sheltered from the defects of the present than innocent of the most baneful of that which may come to pass',[95] Debord was convinced that 'those who really want to shake an established society must formulate a theory which fundamentally explains this society'.[96] With characteristic self-assurance, Debord was convinced he had achieved this goal. 'I flatter myself', he wrote in 1979, 'to be a very rare contemporary example of someone who has written without being immediately contradicted by the event.' He continued: 'I have no doubt that the confirmation all my theses receive ought not to last right until the end of the century and even beyond. The reason for this is simple: I have understood the factors that constitute the spectacle.'[97]

This confidence marked all situationist writing. Convinced that their integration of cultural practice and political theory produced a unique and devastating formula for the critique of everyday life and the transformation of the social world, the SI treated the vast majority of contemporary analyses of consumer society with the contempt it was sure they deserved. The situationists were of course in a most unusual and fortuitous position: all earlier critiques of the everyday had been developed within academia, avant-garde artistic, literary, and political movements, or the minds of a few brave rebels, poets, and dreamers. Rarely had there been a collective attempt to overcome the fragmentations attributed by the situationists to spectacular relations and develop a unified critique of every aspect of daily life.

The 1960s were witness to a host of theoretisations dealing with the proliferation of forms of communication, information, and consumption. Many bemoaned the superficiality of modern life and decried the absence of real experience, and the situationists were not alone in their view that the development of capitalist relations required renewed analyses of their production and re-production. And although the question of alienation preoccupied many post-war intellectuals, observations of the ubiquity of alienated social relations produced unprecedented difficulties for social critique wherever they were made. Without the assurance of some realm free from the influence of commodity relations, the possibility of negating their hegemony is compromised and problematic. In *One-Dimensional Man*, Marcuse argued that while the structure of capitalism remained fundamentally undisturbed, new forms of domination and integration make alienation integral to consciousness itself. The apparent tolerance and variety of modern capitalism conceals its totalitarian tendency to eradicate any alternative dimension of thought or experience. Indeed, Marcuse claimed that 'the extent to which this civilisation transforms the object world into an extension of man's mind and body makes the very notion of alienation questionable'.[98]

Attempts to defend the subject against the encroachment of commodity relations were thrown into further disarray by the rise of structuralist and semiological theories which questioned the whole notion of subjective experience and encouraged a turn away from the humanism of the western Marxist tradition. These theoretical developments gradually undermined every aspect of the situationist project, which nevertheless pursued its attacks on the alienating effects of modern society with a flagrant disregard for the new concern with signs and structures. Structuralism was seen as the spectacle's expression of itself, a philosophy which proclaimed the end of history as surely as the world in which it arose, with its claim 'that a brief freeze in historical time is in fact a definitive stability'.[99] Structuralism, argued Debord, sees 'the eternal presence of a system that was never created and will never disappear';[100] it is a '*thought underwritten by the State*, a thought that conceives of the present conditions of spectacular "communication" as an absolute'. It is not structuralist theory itself 'that serves to prove the transhistorical validity of the society of the spectacle', but 'the society of the spectacle, imposing in its massive reality, that validates the chill dream of structuralism'.[101] From a situationist perspective, structuralist analyses of the codes and categories in which everyday life is framed and produced were far too willing to take the spectacle literally. The situationists were certainly concerned to understand the role of the signs, codes, images, and messages which constitute modern life, but they remained convinced that these were merely the consequences of an over-developed system of alienated production, requiring no new science of signs or structures. The spectacle, insisted Debord, is not 'a product of the technology of the mass dissemination of images',[102] nor a 'collection of images; rather, it is a social relationship between people that is mediated by images'.[103] The spectacular world which lends itself so well to structuralist and semiological analysis 'is both the outcome and the goal of the dominant mode of production'.

It is not something added to the real world – not a decorative element, so to speak. On the contrary, it is the very heart of society's real unreality. In all its specific manifestations – news or propaganda, advertising or the actual consumption of entertainment – spectacle epitomizes the prevailing model of social life. It is the omnipresent celebration of a choice already made in the sphere of production, and the consummate result of that choice.[104]

Although it is only with the later work of Baudrillard that the situationist project comes into open conflict with the consequences of the turn away from critical negation foreshadowed by the development of structuralist analyses, it is undoubtedly with Baudrillard's early writings, in which commodities begin to circulate without reference to meaning, utility, or value, that situationist theory resonates most clearly.

Debord and the young Baudrillard shared the view that consumption was occupying an increasingly central role in the lives of the inhabitants of advanced capitalist society, arguing that the circulation of commodities almost becomes an end in itself, quite regardless of the subjects who buy, sell, and produce them. Baudrillard's first book, *Le système des objets*, was close to many of the ideas of *The Society of the Spectacle* which narrowly pre-dated it. Charting the rise of the consumer society, Baudrillard argued that we live in an increasingly closed relation to commodities which assume an unprecedented plasticity, multi-purpose functionalism and superficiality. A new morality of consumption, circumscribed by leisure, advertising, and fun, replaces the work ethic of a society geared around production, and a society of rapid and pointless change comes to dominate lived experience: 'Everything is in motion, everything is changing, everything is being transformed and yet nothing changes. Such a society, thrown into technological progress, accomplishes all possible revolutions but these are revolutions upon itself.'[105]

Like Debord, Baudrillard argued that commodities have meaning only within the whole – the spectacle – in which they appear. 'Few objects today are offered *alone*, without a context of objects to speak for them. . . . Washing machine, refrigerator, dishwasher and so on have different meanings when grouped together than each one has alone, as a piece of equipment.'[106] Although at this stage Baudrillard retained the possibility of a critical relation to the consumer society, invoking forms of irrational violence and resistance to symbols of consumption such

as cars, neon signs, and shops, he also tended to argue that alienation had become complete and unsurpassable. Social relations
ascend 'from pure and simple abundance to complete conditioning of action and time and finally to the systematic organization of ambience, which is characteristic of the drugstores, the
shopping malls, or the modern airports in our futuristic cities'.[107]
'Multiple forms of refusal' might come together for a while, as they
did in 1968, but there could be no necessity or predictability about
their development. In his 1973 text *The Mirror of Production* and the
subsequent publications considered later in this book, Baudrillard
came to see social critique as an increasingly unforeseeable, dispersed, and purposeless reaction to a world in which commodities
are displaced by a system of signs. Replacing the Marxist critique
of political economy with a logic of sign value and fetishism,
Baudrillard increasingly argued that modern society is characterised not merely by an extension of commodity relations, but by
the conspicuous consumption of commodities as signs of social
status and personal identity.

By this point in the development of Baudrillard's work, the
process of spectacularisation and the removal of meaning identified by Debord is completed, with the absolute abstraction of the
commodity which signifies only itself. There can no longer be any
distinction between the real and the advertised thing, and thus no
experience of poverty, disappointment, or disillusion in the act of
consumption. All that is consumed is the sign of the object: a sign,
such as 'revolutionary new washing machine' which signifies only
itself and conceals or belies nothing else. Whereas Debord argued
that commodities circulate *almost* solely for the sake of abstract
buying and selling, Baudrillard gradually removed all sense of the
'almost' and claimed that commodities have become pure signs
which no longer even pretend to point to anything real. Two of the
phrases – 'no longer' and 'always already' – which pepper
Baudrillard's more recent texts express his position perfectly: it is
no longer possible to speak of the real, and reality is always already
become spectacle. Situationist theory always teeters on the brink of
this position, continually advancing towards the abyss of a society
made up of meaningless and inexorable signs, but always pulling
its arguments back to the *terra firma* of a real world experienced by
real people. For Debord, it is no longer easy to speak of the real,
and reality is always already vulnerable to spectacularisation. But
there is none of the inevitability of Baudrillard's bleak picture of

homogeneity and meaninglessness. The leap into hyperreality is never made, and the struggle to assert and resolve the contradiction between reality and its spectacular inversion in the moment of revolution remains the defining characteristic of situationist theory.

Chapter 2

'. . . a world of pleasures to win, and nothing to lose but boredom'

If modern society is a spectacle, modern individuals are spectators: observers seduced by the glamorous representations of their own lives, bound up in the mediations of images, signs, and commodities, and intolerably constrained by the necessity of living solely in relation to spectacular categories and alienated relations. In *The Society of the Spectacle*, Debord's primary concern was with the internal contradictions of spectacular society, and his speculations about the desires and imaginings which might negate it were confined to considerations of the opposition the spectacle actually produces itself. But in *The Revolution of Everyday Life*, Vaneigem had few qualms about making attractive, inspiring, and sometimes unsupported claims on behalf of the radical subjectivity he saw rising against the spectacle at every turn.

Vaneigem's radical subject negates the seductive glamour of the spectacle with demands for active participation; it responds to the mediations of spectacular life with forms of immediate communication and direct control; it challenges the spectacle's claim to circumscribe reality with actions and gestures which allow for forms of self-realisation in another, broader, chosen context. A creative, imaginative, and sensuous subjectivity, it takes the promises of the spectacle literally, willing the end of all separation, and refusing to perpetuate the sacrifices, deferrals, and endless layers which mark its relationship to the world. It wants to strip away the veils of commodified experience to gain the immediacy of a world directly lived, in which the potential revealed by technological and cultural experiment are unleashed, and the possibilities of a world free from work, need, and sacrifice can be explored. In short, the radical subject demands the right to construct the situations in which it lives.

The political demand to be in control of one's own life and environment, participating in the world with a frank immediacy free of all separation, hierarchy, and bureaucracy, is also the poetic and sensual desire to be really in the world, feeling its most intimate reality, which has been raised in long traditions of religious, artistic, and political expression. Generations of poets, prophets, and revolutionaries,[1] not to mention lovers, drug-takers, and all those who have somehow found the time to stand and stare, have craved the experience of complete integration: the moment of absolute excess, unity, communion, and utter completion; the glimpse of how it is to be truly found and profoundly lost at the same time. 'The eruption of lived pleasure', wrote Vaneigem, 'is such that in losing myself I find myself; forgetting that I exist, I realize myself.'[2] But those who have found this point at which they are also lost have often run away from it too, shocked by the realisation that oneness with the world entails the loss of the ability to think, experience, criticise, or reflect upon it. While the radical subject is ecstatic, it cannot express itself; as soon as it is separated again, it cannot remember how it felt at the time. Much situationist writing gives the impression that such painful paradoxes would disappear in the post-revolutionary world. Since the spectacle is said to take the principle of 'divide and rule' to its absolute extreme, its supersession must be the end of all separation, alienation, and every form of division; a harmonious destination at which all historical struggle is finally, orgasmically, reconciled. This was indeed the absolute with which the situationists contested spectacular relations. But they were quite clear that there is no static haven of pleasure on demand on the other side of even situationist barricades. And although the situationists were sure that new dynamisms and conflicts would arise to shatter the idea that the ludic world is a Utopian point of arrival, they still posed the experience of ecstatic integration as the absolute contradiction to spectacular mediocrity and exclusion.

Futurism, Dada, surrealism, and a host of other movements and experiments were also guided by the will to gain immediate experience of the world and transform the everyday into a reality desired and created by those who live in it. Their manifestos were always full of urgent longings for a changed world, and their productions were shot through with searches for more intensity and desire. Although the artist can create atmospheres and realise fantasies only in the most limited of contexts, the products of the imagination can serve as a propaganda of the possible, and it was in this sense that the situationists acknowledged their place in the tradition of avant-garde agitation to which movements like Dada belong. Critical of the separated role of the avant-garde, the situationists saw themselves superseding, rather than merely contributing to, its history. But they loved Dada's nihilism, respected surrealism's subversions, and sifted through them for pretty gems and useful tools as they had hunted through Hegel and Marx. Although each movement adopted completely different strategies of dissent, both Dada and surrealism agitated against the removal of art to a separated realm in which it is practised by a few specialists within well-defined perimeters. They abandoned work in favour of play, disrupted notions of originality, genius, and artistic form, and experimented with forms of expression disallowed within capitalist society. Saturated with the feeling that reality is elsewhere, and real life sacrificed on altars of bourgeois production and consumption, the movements' protagonists argued and played with the system of values which entrapped them in ways the situationists could not but admire.

By the time the Situationist International emerged in the late 1950s, the ideas and tactics of both Dada and surrealism had been challenged and rearranged by a number of the less well-known tendencies discussed in this chapter. But these central movements continued to inform the style and atmosphere of the SI, in whose hands the techniques of a century of avant-garde contestation were to be forged into the weapons of a political armoury with which not only the values, but the entire network of social relations could be challenged.

Both Dada and surrealism arose in response to the enormous political events of the early decades of the twentieth century, with the First World War and the workers' movements which culminated in the 1917 revolution forming their backdrop. Dada can neatly be characterised as nihilistic art practised at the beginning of the century. But it remains impossible to define the movement without treading on its toes, since it was determined to control its own meanings and definitions, establishing its own criterion of success, and bowing to none of the values and interests adopted by conventional artistic and political practice. Dada was a broad and disparate movement, without any form of organisation, programme, or cohesion. It crossed national boundaries, transgressed those between art, politics, and daily life, and expressed itself in a variety of media, including poetry, performance, painting, cinema, typography, montage, and idiosyncratic combinations of each.

Dada emerged during the First World War from a group of deserters, dissenters, and refugees who had gathered in Zurich. Convinced that 'there must be a few young people in Switzerland who, like me, were interested not only in enjoying their independence but also in giving proof of it',[3] Hugo Ball was among those who set up the dadaist Cabaret Voltaire in 1916. The Cabaret became the focus for an extraordinary attack on cultural, moral, intellectual, and political values. 'We had lost confidence in our "culture". Everything had to be demolished,' wrote Marcel Janco. 'At the Cabaret Voltaire we began by shocking the bourgeoisie, demolishing his idea of art, attacking common sense, public opinion, education, institutions, museums, good taste, in short, the whole prevailing order.'[4] And in the eyes of the young dadaists, the system of values and relations which had produced the war was mirrored in the fine sensibilities, impeccable good taste, and implacable confidence of the bourgeoisie. A generation was being massacred in the names of culture, honour, reason, and civilisation, and these were the values which dada, in turn, set out to destroy. The absurdity of the word 'dada' was itself a provocation. Referring to everything under the sun and nothing in particular, it was intended to infiltrate the ranks of established meanings and demand that they justified their own validity in a world turned upside-down by the war.

Dada's impact was such that it could not be ignored: the press, artistic and political authorities alike were forced to speak of it in tones reserved for conventional disciplines, movements, and values. It was a nonsense word in a world it considered insanely sensible; its very presence challenged the solidity and certainty of all meaning. But although Tristan Tzara, one of Dada's most forthright protagonists, declared that the movement existed 'without aim or design, without organisation', Dada also insisted that 'there is a great destructive, negative work to be done. To sweep, to clean', and rid the world of the 'bandits who have demolished and destroyed the centuries.'[5] In many of its manifestations, Dada displayed overt political commitments and expressed the hope that new possibilities of living would emerge from the wreckage it left in its wake. And although it declared itself anti-art and agitated against the notions of creativity, genius, individualism, and originality inherent in the prevalent conception of art, it was not against the making, saying, and showing of things in which art is engaged. What it did oppose was any restriction on the means by which things are made, the ends to which they are used and interpreted, and the extent to which they are separated from the rest of life. In the belief that cultural values were inexorably bound up with social, political, and moral rela- tions, Dada rode roughshod over the conventions of perfection and order, harmony and beauty, appropriate media and literary form. Art and literature were its point of departure for an onslaught on the whole.

For the surrealists too, the First World War was devastating beyond itself and required a critique of the entire social order. Aware that 'the society which had sent them so gaily to death was waiting for them on their return, if they managed to escape, with its laws, its morality, its religions',[6] the surrealists professed their commitment to social transformation and searched for a new and more authentic reality on which to base their criticisms of existing social relations. And whereas the dadaists had declared a complete disregard for their predecessors, the surrealists actively sought a tradition of poetic, erotic, and impassioned rebels in which to place themselves. Among their heroes was Rimbaud, with his vision of the poet becoming 'a *seer* by a long, prodigious, and rational *disordering* of *all the senses*', embracing all forms 'of love, of suffering, of madness'[7] and seeking a life of real adventure. Jarry's pataphysical science of imaginary solutions; de Sade, the 'freest spirit that has ever existed';[8] the sinister beauty of Baudelaire's flowers of evil; Fourier's impassioned social theory; and Lautréamont's wild plagiarisms and juxtapositions: all decorated the surrealists' world. But of those more immediate and living influences, Guillaume Apollinaire, Jacques Vaché, and Dada itself were perhaps the most important.

Apollinaire filled the young surrealists with the possibilities of new and experimental forms of poetic communication. Observing that the technological wonders of light bulbs, metro stations, and aeroplanes had stolen the poets' show, he used the term 'surreal' to capture the 'new spirit' of a poetry capable of discovering and expressing the horrors and marvels of contemporary experience. And if Apollinaire infused the group with poetic dreams, Vaché instilled a Dada-like spirit of satirical derision in André Breton, the man with whom the surrealist group is most closely associated. Breton had been a close friend of the young Vaché, whose out-

rageous behaviour and scorn for authority left him with a lasting
antipathy to convention and propriety. Vaché bequeathed few
momentos of his short life; objecting to being killed in the war ('I
shall die when I want to die and then I shall die with somebody
else'[9]), he lived with an extraordinary sense of absurd comedy
crowned by a fatal dose of opium, taken with a friend, at the age of
only twenty-three.

It was, however, Dada which exerted the greatest influence on
the surrealist group which emerged in Paris in 1924. But Dada was
not merely an early or immature version of surrealism. Its satirical
attacks on all forms of value, order, and convention had a powerful
and distinctive air recognisable in a variety of later cultural and
political agitations. A great deal of dadaist activity was devoted to
the subversive rearrangement of words and images; the newspaper
had assumed an unprecedented importance during the war, and
the new mass media presented itself as an easy target. Tzara
advised aspiring poets to cut a newspaper article into words and
make a poem by shaking them out of a bag at random,[10] revealing
the hidden possibilities of language, and undermining notions of
creativity and genius by providing a way for anyone to work with
words. The introduction of scissors and glue liberated words and
presented advertisements, newspaper articles, and poems as
arbitrary patterns. And words themselves were made to appear as
chance arrangements of sounds and signs in Dada's performances
of brutist poetry and simultaneous poems, in which texts in different languages were read at the same time. Such stagings produced
the shocking effect of language as mere rhythmical noise, forcing
Dada's audience to face the emptiness and chaos of the world they
believed so comfortable and secure. Phonetic poems like Ball's 'O
Gadji Beri Bimba' and Raoul Hausmann's 'f m s b w', played with
the aural and visual effect of syllables and typefaces, providing the
'great step by which total irrationality was introduced into
literature'[11] of which Dada was so proud.

But Dada's interruptions of language and meaning were not
literally effected without reason: 'in these phonetic poems we
totally renounce the language that journalism has abused and
corrupted,' explained Ball. 'We must return to the innermost
alchemy of the word, we must even give up writing secondhand;
that is, accepting words (to say nothing of sentences) that are not
newly invented for our own use.'[12] This desperate search for
autonomy from all forms of compromise with existing meanings

and forms of communication marked the whole dadaist project. When Aragon wrote of his belief, 'childish as it may seem, that to name the War, even in order to oppose it, was to publicise it',[13] he put his finger on Dada's central dilemma: how was it possible to stand free of the despised values and structures whilst at the same time remaining sufficiently engaged to make some difference to them?

For a few years, Dada successfully walked this tightrope between involvement and disengagement. Notions of genius, originality, and every convention surrounding the work of art were beautifully undermined not only by Tzara's cut-up poetry but a wealth of biting collage, photomontage, and chance collections of a deconstructed and fragmented world. Marcel Duchamp's 'ready-mades' excited the dadaist concern with the objects and experiences of everyday life, and likewise challenged the means by which art may be judged as 'original' or 'plagiaristic'. Displaying objects such as a hat rack and a snow shovel, whose choice, he wrote, 'was based on a reaction of *visual indifference* with a total absence of good or bad taste', Duchamp declared 'that these ready-mades became works of art as soon as he said they were'.[14] Most famous of these pieces was a urinal, turned on its back and signed 'R. Mutt'. When the urinal, which Duchamp solemnly named Fountain, was rejected by an exhibition committee in 1917 on the grounds that it was plagiaristic and 'a plain piece of plumbing', this was the response:

> Whether Mr Mutt with his own hands made the fountain or not has no importance. He CHOSE it. He took an ordinary article of life, placed it so that its usual significance disappeared under the new title and point of view – created a new thought for that object. As for plumbing, that is absurd. The only works of art America has given are her plumbing and her bridges.[15]

The 'ready-made' declared that since nothing is owned or original, nothing can be plagiarised. 'Since the tubes of paint used by the artist are manufactured and ready-made products', wrote Duchamp in a note of triumph, 'we must conclude that all the paintings in the world are *ready-mades aided*'.[16]

This attack on all traditional definitions and evaluations of art was relentlessly pursued. But if the dadaists were convinced that the symbols and values of existing culture were always already compromised, they were unsure of the status of the world revealed by their deconstructions. Their hostility to all codes and principles meant for some that Dada could not concern itself with the creation of new laws and values, and nonsense was layered on nonsense without end. For others, however, a pure and authentic reality could be discerned in the wreckages they caused: Hans Arp believed that their deconstructions of the existing social and cultural codes revealed a new and more natural set of laws, and many were 'alert to the call of another reason, another logic, which demanded a different experience and different symbols.'[17] Arp spoke of his desire to 'destroy the reasonable deceptions of man and recover the natural and unreasonable order', describing Dada as being 'for the senseless, which does not mean nonsense. Dada is senseless like nature.'[18] Conducting his experiments with random collages, poems, and wood reliefs not in defiance of codes and principles, but 'according to the law of chance', Arp maintained that this was a way of 'creating pure life'.[19]

For the most part, Dada's purposeful and meaningful rejection of purpose and meaning was intended as an outrageous provocation of all bourgeois values. In Zurich, Dada had shown 'the bourgeoisie the unreality of his world, the nullity of his endeavours',[20] but this hostility only found a direct political expression in Germany, where Spartakist agitation poised the country on the brink of revolution. In Berlin and Cologne, Dada's satirical attacks became a powerful political weapon: the name of one dadaist journal had such an impact that its title, which translates as 'every man his own football', entered the language 'as an expression of contempt for authority and humbug', and one of its protagonists recalled that they 'carried a supply of gummed labels saying "Hurra Dada!" for sticking on the walls of police station cells'.[21] Dada's techniques of photomontage and caricature flourished amidst the working-class movements from which its Zurich roots were removed, and the situationists were later to insist that Dada 'had a chance for realisation with the Spartakists, with the revolutionary practice of the German proletariat'. It was their failure, wrote Mustapha Khayati, which 'made the failure of Dada inevitable'.[22]

There were clearly limits to the effectiveness of a project based on the attack of cultural values: 'seekers of an experimental culture', wrote the situationists, 'cannot hope to realise it without the triumph of the revolutionary movement'.[23] And the German dadaists were certainly aware that the project's antipathy to any form of commitment and its engagement, albeit hostile and critical, with the values of bourgeois artistic practice, had led it to an impossible apoliticism. Grosz and Herzfelde were sure that Dada's 'only mistake was to have been seriously engaged at all with so-called art'.

> Dada was the breakthrough, taking place with bawling and scornful laughter; it came out of a narrow, overbearing, and overrated milieu, and floating in the air between the classes, knew no responsibility to the general public. We saw then the insane end products of the ruling order of society and burst into laughter. We had not yet seen the system behind this insanity.[24]

Dada was eventually unable successfully to confront or step outside of the culture it despised. Doomed to find a place within the existing system of values, all it could do was ensure that its reception was made as difficult as possible. In this respect it was extraordinarily successful.

Dada's strategy was to embrace the contradictions and hypocrisies into which it was forced. Its deliberate cultivation of confusion allowed it, for a while, to effect an internal critique – a deconstruction – of reason, language, and culture. 'DADA remains within the framework of European weaknesses,' conceded Tzara; 'it's still shit but from now on we want to shit in different colours so as to adorn the zoo of art with all the flags of all the consulates.'[25] 'What we need', he wrote in his 1918 manifesto, 'are strong, straightforward, precise works which will be forever misunderstood.'[26] 'I am writing a manifesto and there's nothing I want, and yet I'm saying certain things, and in principle I am against manifestos, as I am against principles.'[27] Continually pressurised to be something it was not – an artistic movement, a literary school, a political challenge – Dada embraced this falsification too: 'Lying is ecstasy – which lasts longer than a second – there is nothing that lasts longer.'[28] But it was not merely lying. Tzara's manifestos were tactics in a struggle against a particular set of values and meanings, and Dada's provocations were not effected for their own sake, but for the sake of something new and better.

'Liberty: DADA, DADA, DADA; the roar of contorted pains, the interweaving of contraries and of all contradictions, freaks and irrelevances: LIFE', concluded the 1918 manifesto.[29] The movement saw itself making a clean break with the values of the past, a great flood which would wash away the war and affirm the possibility of a fresh start. The nonsensical was adopted for sensible ends; the pointless and absurd did have a point. Dada was, in effect, an attempt to take the propaganda of war and capital literally, as though it was continually saying: 'you want us to behave irrationally, so we will'. Nevertheless, trading on shock tactics, ridicule, and indeterminacy in the cultural domain, the movement could not survive without some larger social movement to effect the destruction of which it dreamed, and Dada was gradually forced into a dilemma of suicide or silence. Richter spoke for all the dadaists when he wrote, 'We were all fated to live with the paradoxical necessity of entrusting ourselves to chance while at the same time remembering that we were conscious beings working towards conscious goals',[30] and, unable to say anything that would not bring it within the existing cultural values and structures it despised, Dada finally made the graceful and politically astute move of abolishing itself.[31]

Like every subsequent movement with the scope of Dada, surrealism was to 'try to do something new/after knowing that because of Dada nothing is new',[32] and the surrealist project was undertaken in full consciousness of the successes and failures of its predecessor. A number of surrealists had been engaged with Dada; some, like André Breton and Louis Aragon, encountered it when Tzara journeyed to Paris in 1920. But they soon became aware of the fleeting effects of its nihilistic provocations. Describing his own movement towards the search for meaning, Aragon wrote that under the Dada flag he had 'felt the great power that certain places, certain sights exercised over me, without discovering the principle of this enchantment',[33] happy to suppose 'that nothing is worth the trouble, that two and two do not necessarily make four, that art has no importance whatever, that it is rather nasty to be a literary man, that silence is golden'.[34] The surrealists were concerned that this Dadaist conclusion stifled all attempts at progressive and critical art, literature, and political practice, removing purpose and direction from the critique of culture and society.

In an effort to rebuild the critical project, surrealism adopted a new set of tactics. While its protagonists were equally hostile to the cultural and social values derided by Dada and as determined as their predecessors to retain their independence and delimit their own activities, they were also aware that tactics of shock, evasion, and provocation had a limited effect. Unlike Dada, the movement

developed a rigorous discipline designed to safeguard its revolutionary aims, although this meant that surrealism was dominated
by matters of internal discipline, exclusions, and Breton's contested leadership. And instead of struggling in vain to stay free
from the influence of despised cultural codes, the surrealists
assumed the role of an artistic and literary movement with the
intention of subverting convention from within.

Surrealism was an overt search for the unity and integration of
all experience, with all separation held to be the consequence of
an artificial estrangement, the isolated component of the true
unity of surreality.

> Everything leads us to believe that there exists a certain point in
> the spirit at which life and death, the real and the imaginary, the
> past and the future, the communicable and the incom-
> municable, the high and the low, cease to be perceived as
> contradictory. Now it is vain to search for any other motive in
> surrealist activity than the hope of discovering that point.[35]

This was both the hope for a future society in which the coin-
cidence of these dichotomies would be realised, and an immediate
search for such moments of supreme interaction, 'unimaginably
dazzling, between man and the world of things.'[36] The surrealists
were passionately attached to those events marked by the eruption
of the marvellous into ordinary experience: stunning and hap-
hazard moments in which the fantastic surprises a world of mundane causality. They invoked a realm of splendour and possibility,
searching for the means to express all that is unexpected, fresh,
awesome, and vertiginous. Breton wrote of 'the breath of the
possible' touching one in the street; Aragon spoke of 'those
moments when everything slips away from me, when immense
cracks appear in the palace of the world. I would', he declared,
'sacrifice my life for them.'[37]

Whereas the dadaists had used the arbitrary to ridicule all belief
in order, the surrealists invested chance with a meaning and
significance derived from their general appropriation of Freudian
theory. Dreams and the wanderings of the imagination were said
to bear a significance beyond the manifest incoherence of their
images; random meetings between the material world and a 'secret
appeal from within' in everyday life were privileged as moments of
'objective chance', the ground of surrealist investigations of the
marvellous, the inspiring, and the impassioned. Surrealist activity

was devoted to the investigation of those attitudes, activities, and environments most propitious to the eruption of desire and the experience of the surreal: a dreamt object found in the street; a dreamt street found in the world; an imagined world fused into the real. Developing these moments into a set of alternative principles on which cultural activity could be based, the surrealists abandoned the dadaist tendency to negate all principles. They began something of a propaganda exercise to reveal the infinite possibilities and endless pleasures trapped in experiences and desires unfulfilled and hidden by a social system dependent on the smooth functioning of a rationality limited to the accumulation of capital. In Freudian terms, this was a rejection of the reality principle in favour of the pleasure principle. But whereas Freud had argued that some repression of the drives to pleasure was essential for the maintenance of civilisation, the surrealists wanted the entire social world to be arranged in harmony with desires, pleasures, and imaginings.

Experiments with automatism in writing, painting, and everyday life were conducted in the belief that the absence of conscious control over one's thoughts and actions would give some freedom to explore new and forbidden ways of thought and articulation. Automatic writing, for example, was an attempt to capture the essence of the stream of consciousness in forms which would express it in as pure and unadulterated form as possible. Aware of Freud's use of free association as therapy, Breton and Soupault decided to 'blacken some paper' with such thought, an exercise which they treated with a 'praiseworthy disdain for what might result from a literary point of view'[38] just as Duchamp had declared his indifference to orthodox means of artistic evaluation. But they were interested in this writing for other reasons, particularly those associated with the radically new perceptions of reality they might allow, and the surrealists saw their techniques revealing a new world, in which surreality, the union of the real and the imagined, might find its true expression. Like the random collage, the automatic text reduced the significance and responsibility of the individual poet and stood as a transcription rather than a production, a discovery rather than an invention. And many other surrealist constructions were inspired by dreams and daydreams; some of them combined images and words to produce 'poem-objects', and others were 'found', like the dadaist 'ready-made'.

The found object was said to be 'enough to undo the beauty of everything beside it',[39] and the surrealists had a treasury of such objects and places in Paris, itself the 'most dreamed-of of their objects'.[40] Places such as the Tour St Jacques, the Porte Saint-Denis, the erotic serenity of Place Dauphine, and the bustling markets of Les Halles (now home to an entirely different set of glass and mirrored marvels), were revered and often visited as sites peculiarly receptive to the surrealist explorer. In the streets of Paris, breathtaking possibilities and marvels, signs of another reality, and glimpses of the strange and disconcerting were perceived through chinks in the normality of everyday reality. Aragon's *Paris Peasant* and Breton's *Nadja* are scattered with detailed descriptions of signs, cafés, arcades, and little corners of the city, and the surrealists strolled the streets with the same freedom they exercised in the automatic text: that gained by the absence of conscious control. Drifting according to whim and desire, they explored the city and watched it reveal the marvels of objective chance and surreality.

This playful spirit combined with a delight in chance to produce an intense interest in games and playing. A phrase of Lautréamont's – 'Poetry must be made by all. Not by one'[41] – was adopted with enthusiasm in support of collaborative experiments with automatism and creativity. For the surrealists, Lautréamont's own juxtaposed images in *Les Chants de Maldoror* had undone every convention of language and its connection with the world, and they sought practices which could pursue this extravagance to its limits. Poems, drawings, collages, and dialogues of questions and answers were constructed by a number of people, generally in the manner of the well-known game 'Consequences', in which sentences are added to sequences hidden by the folds of the paper on which they are written. To play at this was to make an 'exquisite corpse', a phrase taken from an initial experiment in the technique, in which 'the elements of discourse confront one another in as paradoxical a manner as possible and so that human communication, from the outset diverted in this way, takes the mind registering it through the greatest adventure'.[42] Phrases as wild as 'The rouged and powdered lobster scarcely illuminates various double kisses', and 'The anaemic little girl makes the wax-polished mannequins blush', were obtained in these playful experiments.

The surrealists wanted to give the marvellous a reality in the everyday, capturing pure thought and prolonging the passion of fleeting pleasures and momentary desires. *Paris Peasant*, Aragon's 'modern mythology' of the city, identified love as the great experience capable of destroying constraint and mundanity. 'In love . . . in all love there resides an outlaw principle, an irrepressible sense of delinquency, contempt for prohibitions and a taste for havoc,'[43] he wrote, and love became a surrealist symbol of and incentive to revolt. The marvellous quality of the city streets was mirrored in what Aragon called the 'surrealist glow in the eyes of all women',[44] and as Paris epitomised the surrealists' city, so the heroine of Breton's *Nadja* symbolised their women: objects of desire, figures of beauty, muses and inspirations, childlike and powerful, mystical and receptive. To love a woman was to love a sorceress, an enchantress, a glamorous person. It was to commune with the source of all inspiration and marvel, to discover, as Breton wrote, that beauty 'will be convulsive or will not be at all.'[45]

Surrealist eroticism extended into all aspects of daily life and artistic experience, but the sexism and heterosexism of some surrealist writing and art has since thrown a shadow over the exuberant longings it expressed. Indeed, the fact that the products of the surrealist imagination sometimes offered no challenge to prevailing social and cultural conventions casts doubt on the possibility of access to a realm of the imagination free of all social and cultural construction and challenges its very existence. Although the difficulty of transcribing secret and hidden desires into the language and culture of a society which represses its experience was never fully articulated, the surrealists were clearly aware of this first problem. The paradoxical 'rational disordering of the senses' with which they were working meant that they wanted to voyage into the unknown while at the same time returning to tell the tale, expressing their adventures in the terms of existing structures of language and meaning. This desire to straddle madness and sanity, chaos and poetry, formed a central tension of surrealist activity. The most extraordinary of their discoveries assumed a place within the institutionalised worlds of art and literature they wished to subvert, and the most extravagant of their reveries had to be expressed in the discourses of the society they despised. But, reluctant to lose sight of the provocative wonders of unconscious realm itself, the surrealists' recognition of these difficulties served only to encourage their political development. If the entire prevailing system of social and cultural relations forced even the most radical of gestures to convention and conformity, they reasoned, the entire system must be at fault.

Although the surrealists' problematic engagement with the French Communist Party (PCF) produced more difficulties than it solved, their basic alignment with the Party's revolutionary sentiments was itself quite clear. The surrealists were convinced that the achievement of an impassioned social experience in which authentic communication, the realisation of art, and the union of individual and world would characterise everyday experience was possible only with the end of capitalism and the dawn of a new, ludic, age. Nevertheless, this awareness did not prevent the surrealists from pursuing their experiments in the cultural domain; indeed, their insistence on the autonomy of their project and its importance to a successful social revolution was the main point of their disagreement with the PCF, who failed to see why the surrealists seemed to accept so much of the Marxist project while refusing to drop their activities in favour of political duties. Of course, the surrealists considered that their actions were political, arguing that their propaganda of desire was as necessary as the Party's own work and insisting that although surrealism might consider itself 'in the service of the revolution', it would remain free to determine the nature of that service. The poetry concealed by capitalism could not be put off until after the revolution, and prohibited desires should not have to wait for their fulfilment. 'I really fail to see – some narrow-minded revolutionaries notwithstanding', wrote Breton, 'why we should refrain from supporting the Revolution, provided we view the problems of love, dreams, madness, art, and religion from the same angle they do.'[46] The group insisted that there was no ambiguity in their position: 'all of us seek to shift power from the hands of the bourgeoisie to those of the proletariat. Meanwhile, it is none the less necessary that the experiments of the inner life continue and do so, of course, without external or even marxist control.'[47]

For the surrealists, the exploration and articulation of reveries and desires served to expose the poverty of a reality organised solely for the perpetuation of capitalism. Their revolutionary dreams were extravagant and undisciplined by any party standards: their work was full of a rhetoric of revolution which prioritised the spirit of revolt and the 'metaphysics of the provocateur'.[48] Robert Desnos described the surrealist group as being held together by 'something that resembled the fellowship of those who are going to blow up a city in a spirit of revolt',[49] and for Breton: 'It is revolt itself, and revolt alone, that is the creator of life.'[50] At his most provocative, Breton declared: 'Surrealism was not afraid to make for itself a tenet of total revolt, complete insubordination, of sabotage according to rule, and . . . it still expects nothing save from violence.'

The simplest surrealist act consists of dashing down into the street, pistol in hand, and firing blindly, as fast as you can pull the trigger, into the crowd. Anyone who, at least once in his life, has not dreamed of thus putting an end to this petty system of debasement and cretinisation in effect has a well-defined place in that crowd, with his belly at barrel-level.[51]

It was not surprising that the Party was as hostile to such 'infantile disorder' as the surrealists were to the Party's bureaucratic seriousness. The populist 'workerism' of the PCF was completely at odds with surrealism's insistence that play, pleasure, spontaneity, and the 'outlaw principle' were the real ground of human dignity, and Tzara's exuberant invocations of life and liberty in the 1918 manifesto had bequeathed a fondness for the autonomous passion of the 'soaring flight of black flags'[52] of the anarchist tradition.

Regardless of their prevarications with the PCF, the surrealists' belief that to 'condemn the subversive is to condemn everything that is not absolutely resigned'[53] led to their involvement in and support for a number of political causes. They were signatories to calls for resistance to the fascist demonstrations in Paris in the 1930s, and against Renault after the death of eight workers; Benjamin Péret fought in Spain and he, Sadoul, and Aragon faced imprisonment for their subversive publications. Breton enjoyed a celebrated friendship with Trotsky; and the surrealists supported Moroccan and Algerian struggles for independence. Indeed, it was the horrors of the Moroccan war which led Breton to declare: 'I believe it impossible for us to avoid most urgently posing the question of the social regime under which we live, I mean of the acceptance or the non-acceptance of this regime.'[54]

For some, however, surrealism was always bluffing an anger which Dada had really felt. 'They give us a lot of piffle about the revolution – first the revolution of the word, now the revolution in the street,' complained Henry Miller.[55] Dada was 'more entertaining. They had humour at least. The Surrealists are too conscious of what they are doing. It's fascinating to read about their intentions, but when are they going to pull it off?'[56] And although surrealism's engagement with literary and artistic practice was intended to be subversive, the movement always carried a serious weight which Dada's careless extravagances avoided. Nevertheless, the surrealists cultivated an atmosphere of libertarian experiment and purposeful desire which has continued to thrive, and although some forms of surrealism lapsed into occultism, uncritical eroticism, and repetitions of earlier literary and artistic projects, others never lost their romantic attachment to revolutionary change and the possibility of a transformed reality. After the collapse of the 'official' surrealist movement in the post-war years, a variety of little papers, groups, and dispersed individuals continued to keep what Jean Schuster has called the red thread running through the surrealist rope in fine colour.[57] And some of these were among the currents which convened the Situationist International in 1957.

Ten years earlier, a group of surrealists had formed the Revolutionary Surrealist Group in an effort to revive the political urgency of a surrealism which had lost its way in France and among those who, like Breton, had been most closely associated with the 'official' movement. Of the figures involved in this enterprise, Christian Dotremont, a Belgian surrealist, and Asger Jorn, a Danish painter, were later to have a great impact on the Situationist International. Belgian surrealism had always retained a distinctive character with people like Paul Nougé, Marcel Mariën, René Magritte, and Jane Graverol producing some of the most radical forms of experimental art and poetry. And, in a definitive move away from the French movement, the group Cobra, which took its name from the cities from which its protagonists hailed (Copenhagen, Brussels, and Amsterdam), established a more 'northern' network of revolutionary artists. Dotremont and Jorn were joined by Noiret, Constant, Corneille, and Appel, and the group pledged itself to a collective onslaught on the specialisation of art and the elucidation of its revolutionary role. The movement blossomed, encompassing poets, musicians, painters, and theorists. Some of its most interesting experiments involved architecture and the city environment, with Constant developing a synthesis of architectural and revolutionary concerns which was also to find its place in the SI. This was also a theme developed by the International Movement for an Imagist Bauhaus (IMIB), a group which fused Enrico Baj's Nuclear Art movement and the remnants of Cobra, which had disbanded in 1951. Jorn remained one of the key figures of this movement too, making contacts with an extraordinary variety of artists including the Italians Pinot-Gallizio

and Simondo, and in 1956, all these strands converged with the
First World Congress of Liberated Artists, a meeting held in the
Italian town of Alba, where Jorn, Pinot-Gallizio, and Simondo had
worked the previous summer. The congress paved the way for the
establishment of the Situationist International in 1957, at which
the IMIB, the legendary London Psychogeographical Society, and
the Lettrist International (LI) were finally brought together.

The bankruptcy of post-war surrealism, fatefully marked by the
1944 publication of Maurice Nadeau's *The History of Surrealism*, had
also been noticed by the lettrists, a group which played a vital role
in the immediate history of the SI. The lettrists took surrealism's
search for a creativity stripped of the layers of social convention
and meaning to a glorious extreme and, under the initial direction
of Isidore Isou, a Romanian living on the Parisian borders of
insight and insanity, the lettrists also tried to perfect the dadaist
break between words and meanings by freeing letters from words
themselves. As autonomous signs and hieroglyphs, letters could
provide the bricks of a new creative process, attracting new
references, meanings, and chosen significances. Isou privileged
creativity as the central purpose of human life, arguing that since
creation was no longer the prerogative of God, anyone could do it
and so become god (a position which encouraged his megalo-
mania, his passion for the construction of great systems of thought,
and his enduring will to tell the world of his amazing discoveries
about everything from music to mathematics). The lettrists indulged
in some Dada-like provocations; in 1950 they disrupted the Easter
Sunday mass in Notre Dame, and they attacked Charlie Chaplin's
enthusiastic reception in Paris in 1952. Disagreements over this
last scandal provided the excuse for some of the lettrists to break
with Isou and establish the Lettrist International; including
Debord, Gil Wolman, and Michèle Bernstein, this group produced
the bulletin *Potlatch* and developed a number of the positions
which were later to form the basis on which the Situationist International was established.

In the struggles and failures of the cultural movements of the
first half of the twentieth century, the nascent situationists saw the
possibility of a final assault on the distinction between art and
everyday life and all the means by which the construction of a
society enjoying the fruits of technological and cultural achievement is denied. They were critical of the avant-garde's failure to
develop its spirit of revolt into a coherent critique, and called for

both the realisation of artistic transformations and the suppression of art as a separated and specialised practice. But the rhetoric of their criticism was suffused with surrealist provocation, and the great destructive game of Dada was also taken into the situationist project as a desire to clear the ground for new forms of communication, participation, and subjective experience. For Debord, Dada's role 'was to have delivered a mortal blow to the traditional conception of culture'; as for surrealism, its assertion of 'the sovereignty of desire and surprise, proposing a new use of life, is much richer in constructive possibilities than is generally thought'.[58] Only by the suppression of art as a category in its own right could the realisation and integration of the artistic and poetic into everyday experience for which Dada and surrealism had longed be achieved.

> Just as in the first half of the nineteenth century revolutionary theory arose out of philosophy (out of critical reflection on philosophy, out of the crisis and death of philosophy), so now it is going to rise once again out of modern art – out of poetry – out of its supersession, out of what modern art has sought and *promised*, out of the clean sweep it has made and of all the values and rules of everyday behaviour.[59]

Long the cultural safety-valve of a society which 'must above all prevent a new setting out of revolutionary thought',[60] the avant-garde had become as specialised and alienated as any other aspect of spectacular culture. Even so, Debord was convinced that the achievements of its cultural critique remained necessary to the success of any social revolution: the revolutionary movement 'cannot establish authentic revolutionary conditions without resuming the efforts of the cultural avant-garde toward the critique of everyday life and its free construction'.[61]

The situationists wanted to transcend the distinction between revolutionary politics and cultural criticism once and for all, and although there were later arguments and a major split on the question of art, they certainly went further than their predecessors in the collapse of these distinctions. Their initial interest, carried over from the LI, was centred on the environment in which the situations of the everyday are lived. *Potlatch* carried a number of pieces on urbanism and the city which argued that architecture 'must reach the point of exciting passion'[62] and converged in calls for a unitary urbanism, a critical study of the city utilising all artistic and technical resources. Not merely a variety of city planning, unitary urbanism was intended to broaden architectural concerns to the whole atmosphere of space and the possibilities of living in it. This perspective was promoted by Constant, who stayed on in Alba after the 1956 congress to design a sort of mobile city for some gypsies camped on Pinot-Gallizio's land. The building was to be completely flexible, open to internal design and continual modification according to the particular atmospheres in which its inhabitants might choose to live.

This sort of unitary environment required the study and negation of the relationship between the material world and its subjective experience. Emotions, desires, and experiences of all sorts differ according to the architecture of a space and the arrangements of colours, sounds, textures, and lighting with which it is created. The situationists pointed to the forms of conditioning imposed by shopping malls, night clubs, adverts, and even police methods of interrogation as evidence of the existence of a plethora of techniques by which experiences, desires, attitudes, and behaviour are presently manipulated. The width of streets, the heights of buildings, the presence of trees, advertisements and lights, the circulation of traffic, the colours of front doors, and the shapes of windows: urban lives are shaped in the most subtle and neglected ways by these arrangements of space. The situations in which we live are created for us.

Yet neither the artist, for whom the deconstruction of the city is too large a task, nor the revolutionary, for whom it is too superstructural a concern, show any interest in the effects of environments on those who live within them. This was incomprehensible to those involved in both the LI and the SI. 'We are bored in the city', declared Ivan Chtcheglov in 1953: 'we really have to strain still to discover mysteries in the sidewalk billboards',[65] yet are discouraged from expressing this boredom by the city's insistence that it is the most exciting place to be. People are similarly dissuaded

from making any criticism of architecture with the simple argument that they need a roof over their heads, just as television is accepted on the grounds that they need information and entertainment. People are made to overlook the obvious fact that this information, this entertainment, and this kind of dwelling place are not made for them, but without them and against them.[64]

If the avant-garde had failed to deliver the transformation of everyday reality it promised, so had the city planners: 'Urbanism promises happiness. It should be judged accordingly.'[65] Again, it was in the weighing of the actual against the promised and the possible that the situationists sought the radical negation of the spectacle.

The situationists' desire to become psychogeographers, with an understanding of the 'precise laws and specific effects of the geographical environment, consciously organised or not, on the emotions and behaviour of individuals',[66] was intended to cultivate an awareness of the ways in which everyday life is presently conditioned and controlled, the ways in which this manipulation can be exposed and subverted, and the possibilities for chosen forms of constructed situations in the post-spectacular world. Only an awareness of the influences of the existing environment can encourage the critique of the present conditions of daily life, and yet it is precisely this concern with the environment in which we live which is ignored.

> The sudden change of ambiance in a street within the space of a few meters; the evident division of a city into zones of distinct psychic atmospheres; the path of least resistance which is automatically followed in aimless strolls (and which has no relation to the physical contour of the ground); the appealing or repelling character of certain places – all this seems to be neglected.[67]

Concealed by the functional drudgery of city life, such areas of psychogeographical research were seen as the ground of a new realm of experiment with the possibilities of everyday experience.

One of psychogeography's principle means was the *dérive*. Long a favourite practice of the dadaists, who organised a variety of expeditions, and the surrealists, for whom the geographical form of automatism was an instructive pleasure, the *dérive*, or drift, was defined by the situationists as the 'technique of locomotion without a goal',[68] in which 'one or more persons during a certain period drop their usual motives for movement and action, their relations, their work and leisure activities, and let themselves be drawn by the attractions of the terrain and the encounters they find there'.[69] The *dérive* acted as something of a model for the 'playful creation'[70] of all human relationships.

Unlike surrealist automatism, the *dérive* was not a matter of surrendering to the dictates of an unconscious mind or irrational force. Indeed, the situationists' criticisms of surrealism concluded that 'the unconscious imagination is poor, that automatic writing is monotonous, and that the whole genre of ostentatious surrealist "weirdness" has ceased to be very surprising'.[71] Nor was everything subordinated to the sovereignty of choice: to *dérive* was to notice the way in which certain areas, streets, or buildings resonate with states of mind, inclinations, and desires, and to seek out reasons for movement other than those for which an environment was designed. It was very much a matter of using an environment for one's own ends, seeking not only the marvellous beloved by surrealism but bringing an inverted perspective to bear on the entirety of the spectacular world. *Potlatch* carried a lovely example of this inversion of priorities in the form of a letter addressed to *The Times* protesting against the redevelopment of London's Chinese quarter. After a defence of the area itself, the letter ends:

> Anyway, it is inconvenient that this Chinese quarter of London should be destroyed before we have the opportunity to visit it and carry out certain psychogeographical experiments we are at present undertaking . . . if modernisation appears to you, as it does to us, to be historically necessary, we would counsel you to carry your enthusiasm into areas more urgently in need of it, that is to say, to your political and moral institutions.[72]

In spite of situationist differences with the surrealist project, the situationists' *dérive* was of course inspired by surrealist strolls. It was Breton who had described the street, 'with its disturbances and its glances', as 'my one true element. There I partook, as nowhere else', he wrote, 'of the wind of circumstance.'[73] Surrealism had invoked a world of floating encounters through which the hunter of marvels drifts according to whim and desire.

> The means were simple enough; merely buy a Sunday ticket at a suburban railway station and shunt for hours and hours on all the tracks of a landscape of dislocation, on a journey whose end is never fixed in advance.[74]

The surrealists had also called for the 'irrational embellishment' of Paris; in 1933, *Le Surréalisme au service de la révolution* carried

Breton's responses to the question of whether one should 'preserve, move, modify, change or suppress' a variety of Parisian landmarks. The towers of Notre Dame were to be replaced by 'an enormous glass cruet, one of the bottles filled with blood and the other with sperm'; the Palace of Justice was to be razed and the site 'covered by a magnificent graffiti to be seen from an airplane'; and the Opera transformed into 'a fountain of perfumes' with the staircase reconstructed 'from the bones of prehistoric animals'.[75] This exercise was inverted in *Potlatch* with lettrist demands for the rational embellishment of the city of Paris, in which the metro was to be opened at night, the prisons opened, museums abolished, and statues renamed. Four solutions to the existence of churches were suggested: while Debord wanted them totally destroyed, Wolman wanted to empty them of all religious significance, Fillon argued they should be kept as places in which to experience fear, and Bernstein, most imaginatively, wanted to let them fall into ruins.[76]

With a backward glance at surrealism, Debord declared: 'That which changes our ways of seeing the streets is more important than what changes our way of seeing painting.'[77] Avant-garde disruptions of artistic and literary values had spawned a variety of means of displacing the usual contexts, meanings, and purposes of images and signs, and the situationist extension of such subversions to the environment developed such dislocation into a technique with wide political application. Out of the tradition which took letters out of words, inverted Notre Dame, and put urinals in galleries, the situationists developed an armoury of confusing weapons intended constantly to provoke critical notice of the totality of lived experience and reverse the stultifying passivity of the spectacle. 'Life can never be too disorienting,' wrote Debord and Wolman, in support of which they described a friend's experience wandering 'through the Harz region of Germany while blindly following the directions of a map of London'.[78]

Such disorientation was not craved for its own sake. But as a means of showing the concealed potential of experimentation, pleasure, and play in everyday life, the situationists considered a little chaos to be a valuable means of exposing the way in which the experiences made possible by capitalist production could be appropriated within a new and enabling system of social relations. Both the experiments of the avant-garde and spectacular society itself reveal the possibilities for the construction of situations, the manipulation of environments, and the creation of atmospheres and ambiances. To be able to play with techniques of conditioning and experiment with a multitude of environments and atmospheres in a world in which the imperatives of work and survival have long since passed was the situationist dream. Theirs was not a low-tech or no-tech vision of the future, but a world in which technological achievement comes into its own. 'We have invented the architecture and the urbanism that cannot be realised without the revolution of everyday life – without the appropriation of conditioning by everyone, its endless enrichment, its fulfillment.'[79] Chtcheglov's remarkable 'Formulary for a New City' experimented with 'a thousand ways of modifying life'. 'The hacienda must be built,' he declared, a phrase which enjoys a continuing significance in contemporary culture.[80] 'Everyone will live in his own personal "cathedral", so to speak. There will be rooms more conducive to dreams than any drug, and houses where one cannot help but love. Others will be irresistibly alluring to travellers.'[81] Chtcheglov considered the possibilities of the mobile house, changeable city environments, and the establishment of such areas as a 'Bizarre Quarter', a 'Happy Quarter', a 'Sinister Quarter', and advocated the 'changing of landscapes from one hour to the next' which again would result in 'complete disorientation'.[82] His message, one which ultimately got him locked away, was essentially this: 'It has become essential to bring about a complete spiritual transformation by bringing to light forgotten desires and by creating entirely new ones. And by carrying out an *intensive propaganda* in favour of these desires.'[83]

With the establishment of the Situationist International at the 1957 unification conference in the small Italian town of Cosio d'Arroscia, the attempt to weld these disparate desires for the transformation of the everyday into a coherent revolutionary perspective started in earnest. 'First of all we think the world must be changed,' began one of the documents presented to the meeting. 'We want the most liberating change of the society and life in which we find ourselves confined. We know that this change is possible through appropriate actions.'[84] Arguing that revolutionary action was lagging behind 'the development of modern possibilities of production which call for a superior organization of the world',[85] the document developed Chtcheglov's demands for the multiplication of desires and the construction of situations by

those who live them: 'we have to multiply poetic subjects and
objects [. . .] and we have to organize games of these poetic objects
among these poetic subjects.' This, it continued, 'is our entire
program, which is essentially transitory. Our situations will be
ephemeral, without a future: passageways. The permanence of art
or anything else does not enter into our considerations.'[86]

The contingency of this position was indicative of the situationists' distrust of all foundations, essences, and absolutes. The
spectacle and its negation were seen to be engaged in a perpetual
articulation; the radical subject invoked by the situationists desires
the destruction of the mediations of the spectacle, but is drawn on
no rigorous conception of human nature and has no universal
foundation. The immediate communion of love, the free expression of creativity, and the realisation of dreams are never merely
denied by the spectacle; on the contrary, they are constantly
advertised and promoted, and the circulation of commodities
depends on their maintenance. Nevertheless, the situationists'
enthusiasm for life in the face of spectacular survival was often
posed in terms of a faith in the existence of deep-seated desires.
Vaneigem was convinced that creativity, love, and play 'are to life
what the needs for nourishment and shelter are to survival',[87]
constituting a fundamental 'other' to capitalist relations. For him,
the alienation of the spectacle is not complete: the passion to
create reveals the persistence of desires for self-realisation; love
reveals the will for real communication; and play reveals the desire
for free and chosen forms of participation in the world. And there
are moments, be they poetic or erotic, which seem to represent
some pure pole of authenticity which will always survive the
vacuous equivalence of commodity relations.

The Revolution of Everyday Life was based on the conviction that
people live 'separated from one another, separated from what they
are in others, and separated from themselves. The history of
humanity is the history of one basic separation which precipitates
and determines all the others: the social distinction between
masters and slaves.'[88] In capitalist societies, the 'struggle for the
whole man' is constituted as a class conflict, and only the end of
this fundamental separation between classes can facilitate the
transcendence of all other distinctions and divisions. But the situationists were not content merely to state the historical necessity of
the class struggle. In what is perhaps one of his most famous
statements, Vaneigem declared: 'People who talk about revolution

and class struggle without referring explicitly to everyday life, without understanding what is subversive about love and what is positive in the refusal of constraints, such people have a corpse in their mouth.'[89] This was not merely a dig at the revolutionary who beats his lover, or the party whose discipline is worse than that of the workplace. It was an appeal for all contestation to issue from the subjective experience of everyday life, a demand for the end of a specialised politics removed from the very realm in which rebellion and dissent have their origins. Individual subjectivity 'is rooted in the desire to realise oneself by transforming the world',[90] the will to construct daily life with 'the most thoroughgoing fusion of reason and passion'.[91] Embarrassed by subjective experiences, dreams, and desires, people tend to ignore and reject the inner realm in which are dealt 'the most deadly blows to morality, authority, language and our collective hypnotic sleep'.[92] Yet it is here, in the intimacy and spontaneity of one's own self, that there persists a 'lived immediacy threatened on all sides yet not yet alienated'.[93]

> Who can gauge the striking-power of an impassioned daydream, of pleasure taken in love, of a nascent desire, of a rush of sympathy? Everyone seeks spontaneously to extend such brief moments of real life; everyone wants basically to make something out of their everyday life.[94]

This desire, the will to really live and experience the world at its cutting edge, was said to be the motor-force of both the spectacle and its revolutionary negation. It sells fast cars as surely as it produces dissatisfaction; it is continually commodified and in turn wrenched free from spectacular relations in a perpetual struggle for its realisation.

For the situationist., neither the factory nor the canvas were privileged sites of this contestation between desire and the false promise of its fulfilment. It is everyday life which provides the ground for a revolutionary theory and practice intended to cut through all separations and specialisations. 'We still have to place everyday life at the center of everything . . . . Everyday life is the measure of all things: of the fulfillment or rather the nonfulfillment of human relations; of the use of lived time; of artistic experimentation; of revolutionary politics.'[95] This was a position shared by the sociologist Henri Lefebvre. Indeed, there is much debate about who influenced whom: Lefebvre was involved in the

same pre-situationist milieu, and although the situationists considered him an incorrigible specialist in social critique and
disassociated themselves from his work when he plagiarised their
'Theses on the Paris Commune',[96] many of their ideas converged
with those expressed in his *Critique de la vie quotidienne*, published
in three volumes between 1947 and 1981. In this analysis of the
alienation of the modern world, Lefebvre argued that everyday life
and the commodities, roles, and discourses which populate it form
the basis of all social experience and the true realm of political
contestation. Lefebvre's work had been introduced by Dotremont
to the Revolutionary Surrealist Group in the 1940s, where his calls
for an art that would transform the everyday ('Let everyday life
become a work of art! Let every technical means be employed for
the transformation of everyday life!'[97]) had an immediate effect.
For both the situationists and Lefebvre, everyday life is the very
realm over which we should have control, yet it is experienced as
mundane and dull in its ubiquity. On the escape from the fragmentation and mediocrity of our own experience, we run blindly
towards the promises of wholeness, fulfilment, and unity implicit
in the world of the abundant commodity. And it is in the hopelessness of this scramble that the disjunction between the possibilities
of life and the impoverished realities of survival are most keenly
felt; it is here that the revolution becomes a living and immediate
possibility.

The transformation of the everyday 'is not reserved for some
vague future but is placed immediately before us by the development of capitalism and its unbearable demands.'[98]

> One can thus conclude that if people censor the question of
> their own everyday life, it is both because they are aware of its
> unbearable misery and because sooner or later they sense –
> whether they admit it or not – that all the real possibilities, all
> the desires that have been frustrated by the functioning of social
> life, were focussed there, and not at all in the specialised
> activities or distractions. That is, awareness of the profound
> richness and energy abandoned in everyday life is inseparable
> from awareness of the poverty of the dominant organisation of
> this life.[99]

It is 'life itself, which is cruelly absent' from the everyday. 'People
are as deprived as possible of communication and self-realisation.
Deprived of the opportunity to personally make their own

history.'[100] And this deprivation manifests itself in the spec-tacularisation of every aspect of life which, fragmented into 'specialised activities and distractions' and continually shown to those who might otherwise be living it, is contemplated at one remove. A variety of roles as broad and tempting as the spectrum of material commodities is offered for a consumption that pre-cludes the possibility of any real and autonomous engagement: it is not possible to potter in the garden without becoming a gardener; putting up a few shelves is difficult without assuming the role of a 'do-it-yourselfer'; listening to the music of a particular band involves a host of extraneous categorisations; and travel is difficult without tourism. Experiences are offered in 'everything included packages' not confined to holidays but manifest in shopping centres, arts centres, theme parks, and leisure centres. An interest in one aspect of such packages is difficult to sustain: if you like X, you'll love Y. And such promises are flattering. We like to be told who we really are because our alienation makes us unable to decide for ourselves. Even the refusal of a pre-established set of commodified patterns leads us into the roles, equally pre-ordained and unthreatening, of the individualist, the eccentric, the disaffected, or the revolutionary.

Vaneigem pressed the point in *The Revolution of Everyday Life*: 'The stereotyped images of the star, the poor man, the communist, the murderer-for-love, the law-abiding citizen, the rebel, the bour-geois, will replace man, putting in his place a system of multicopy categories.'[101] The commodification of human choice places every experience within a predefined role and enforces identification with a spectacular and specific category from which an experience of the whole is impossible.

> Under what we have called 'the colonization of everyday life', the only possible changes are changes of fragmentary roles. In terms of more or less inflexible conventions, one is successively citizen, head of family, sexual partner, politician, specialist, professional, producer, consumer. Yet what boss doesn't him-self feel bossed? The proverb applies to everyone: you some-times get a fuck, but you always get fucked![102]

The fragmentation of roles within modern society is an immediate consequence of the increasing division of labour demanded by capitalist relations of production; Lukács had observed that the specialisation of skills 'leads to the destruction of every image of the whole',[103] and for the situationists, the specialist and the expert were roles indicative of the separation running throughout the spectacle. Yet for all the authority and respect apparently invested in the expert, each 'is alienated in being out of place with the others; he knows the whole of one fragment and knows no realisation'.[104]

In every field – the production of cars, the reproduction of knowledge, and the servicing of people – a wealth of detailed knowledge is held in the isolation of suspended animation from the totality of social experience. Every lifestyle demands a commitment which can only be transgressed at the point of stardom, when the expert in one field is judged fit to pronounce on any other. Politicians can slide into broadcasting and athletes into Parliament with an ease which reveals the emptiness of all spectacular roles. And it is in the celebrities presented by the spectacle that the full spectrum of human possibilities is offered for consumption. The stars of the public realm have adventures, romances, scandals, and careers on behalf of those who can only spectate: 'Forgetting life, one can identify with a range of images, from the brutish conqueror and brutish slave at one pole to the saint and pure hero at the other.'[105] In *The Society of the Spectacle*, Debord argued that the celebrity, 'the spectacular representation of a living human being',[106] 'the opposite of the individual',[107] epitomises the alienated identification demanded by the spectacle. Glamorous objects of contemplation admired from afar, stars are shown basking in the spectacular whole: able to buy all the things in the shop and the shop as well, celebrities are model citizens who compensate for their spectators' inability to experience the whole. They present the image of integrated individuals, 'the admirable people in which the system personifies itself' who are, nevertheless, 'well known for not being what they are'.[108] The superstars of the 1960s and 1970s have now been superseded by the short-lived banality of the nine-day wonder, a development which perhaps reinforces the situationist argument that the real people are as nothing in comparison to the equivalent slots they fill.

'Eventually', observed Vaneigem, 'identification with anything at all, like the need to consume anything at all, becomes more important than brand loyalty to a particular type of car, idol, or politician.'[109] As the search for some identity amidst the distance and unreality of modern life intensifies, it 'matters little whether people are good or bad, honest or criminal, left-wing or right-wing:

the *form* is irrelevant'.[110] The transformation of ways of life into spectacular roles means that it is impossible to live them out with any sense of pleasure or fulfilment; events and experiences are valid only in terms of the representations and meanings given within the spectacular whole. And the vague awareness that one is performing a predefined role which carries its own set of associations, messages, and images means that an unfortunate self-consciousness creeps into the most ordinary of gestures. Life becomes clichéd, and real emotions can only be expressed in borrowed languages. Vaneigem argued that even the tiniest of gestures – opening a door, holding a teacup, a facial expression – and the most private and individual actions – coming home, making tea, arguing with a lover – have always already been represented and shown to us within the spectacle.

> The mechanism of the alienating spectacle wields such force that private life reaches the point of being defined as that which is deprived of spectacle; the fact that one escapes roles and spectacular categories is experienced as an additional privation, as a malaise which power uses as a pretext to reduce everyday life to insignificant gestures.[111]

Packaged and sold back to us, little can be done with a sense of authenticity: every gesture belongs elsewhere and returns to us as a hostile, external, and alienated moment.

What is meant by the everyday in 'everyday language' is therefore the mundanity and the banality that is excluded from spectacular representation. Devoid of its glamorous representation, experience becomes almost embarrassing, something of which one feels ashamed; an event without a camera barely occurs, and a commodity is meaningless without its advertised image. Without representation, life might as well not happen at all. Football provides an excellent example of this removal of real experience and its return as a simulated version of itself. Suppressed as a game of wild and often violent abandon played in the streets of late nineteenth-century towns whose normal business was suspended for several days, football became increasingly specialised; removed to the stadium and then to the television, participation in the sport became confined to club membership, gambling on the result, intimate knowledge of players and leagues, and the acquisition of emblems of involvement: badges, hats, scarves, videos, programmes, and, in the age of 'football hooliganism', scars and

trophies won in street and terrace fighting. It is well known that
supporters always run as they leave matches; when not pursued by
police horses this is generally because what the followers of the
game really want to do is play it. And of course they do: there are
thousands of league clubs in Britain, the big teams still scout for
talent among the amateurs, and in spite of the ubiquity of 'no ball
games' signs, goal posts are still painted on city walls. But the 'real'
football is now the spectacle of football; the televised match
becomes better than 'being there', and all forms of participation
in the game are downgraded or outlawed. 'Football fans took to
the Alcester streets following England's win in the World Cup on
Sunday', reported a small Midlands paper in 1990. 'Six people
started an impromptu football game at the traffic lights in Station
Road, watched by more supporters. But their game came to a
premature end when local beat officers confiscated the ball and
the crowd went home.'[112]

Desires for pleasure, excitement, and adventure are raised and
dashed at every turn, subjected to the palliatives of consumption
and diverted into banal scandals and pseudo-events. A diet of
fabricated and exaggerated news about the fictional characters of
soap-opera lives is offered in response to demands for real life and
intensity themselves raised by promises of the next episode, and a
concern for public opinion through polls, surveys, and market
research grows in inverse proportion to the real effect the public
can have. Wars, elections, and disasters assume a spectacular unreality which makes them indistinguishable from their fictional
counterparts, and participation in the public realm becomes an
isolated spectator sport of its own. Developments in communication and information technology make free and immediate exchange more possible, while the impoverishment of their use merely
reinforces the alienated pseudo-participation allowed by the spectacle. Teletext and Oracle may allow viewers to vote by telephone
on everything from nuclear war to the next episode of a soap opera,
but the scenario in which a nation of people unable to take control
of their own lives reaches in one movement for the telephone in
order to determine the life of a fictional character conjures a
picture of absolute alienation, the appearance of participation,
control, and communication emptied of all meaning. 'The trick',
writes Vaneigem, 'is that the spectators of the cultural and ideological
vacuum are here enlisted as its organizers. The spectacle's inanity is
made up for by forcing its spectators . . . to participate in it.'[113]

Even activities which might threaten the very existence of the spectacle are brought within the confines of commodified ways of life and, for the situationists, the colonisation of even the most radical gestures constituted one of the spectacle's most subtle mechanisms of control. The communist and the rebel may be consumed as readily as every other role, with their spectacular appearance precluding the possibility of their real experience. One cannot be a real rebel, but one can assume and consume the image of rebellion, most obviously manifest in material commodities – badges, T-shirts, posters, haircuts – to the advantage of the system as a whole. Dissent is turned into a spectacle of its own, and rebels become spectators of their own rebellion, consuming the life in which they want to participate, and slotting into a seductive and glamorous role in which they can have no real effect: 'all individual reality, being directly dependent on social power and completely shaped by that power, has assumed a social character. Indeed, it is only inasmuch as individual reality *is not* that it is allowed to appear.'[114] Having bought all the right clothes and read all the right books, would-be rebels find themselves unwittingly supporting commodity relations. Consumers of struggle and voyeurs of distant revolution, they are presented with pre-ordained paths: there are parties to join, papers to sell, meetings to attend, and demonstrations in which to intervene. For the most sincere of activists, the image of the revolutionary, the union leader, or the party organiser bears a seductive power of its own which belittles the reality of their political engagement. Dissatisfaction, wrote Debord, 'itself becomes a commodity as soon as the economics of affluence finds a way of applying its production methods to this particular raw material'.[115] Even the heroin addict, the football hooligan, the graffiti artist, and the truant are offered as pre-defined options to the disaffected who, in their attempts to escape from alienation into an expression of individuality, become accommodated within roles as hostile and removed as those from which they are escaping. Anything which arises within the spectacle is subject to its equivalence, and even the most hostile action can be made to reproduce the alienation of the whole.

But the situationists were not weighed down by such reflections. 'On the other hand', Vaneigem pointed out, 'the spectacle is fast approaching a saturation point, the point immediately prior to the eruption of everyday reality.'[116] There is resistance to the ready-made role and, surrounded by a glamour they cannot possibly sustain, spectacular ways of life continually reveal their poverty. The 'structures of the spectacle are in crisis', he wrote, 'because so many balls have to be kept in the air at the same time. The spectacle has to be everywhere, so it becomes diluted and self-contradictory.'[117] Vaneigem argued that 'roles now operate on a level perilously close to their own negation: already the average failure is hard put to it to play his role properly, and some maladjusted people refuse their roles altogether'.[118] And among these refuseniks are 'those who develop a theory and practice of this refusal. From such maladjustment to spectacular society a new poetry of real experience and a reinvention of life are bound to spring.'[119] Writing in 1967, Vaneigem did not of course have long to wait before he saw this new poetry in action on the streets of Paris.

The events of 1968 are remembered for the irruption of play, festivity, spontaneity, and the imagination into the political realm; a conjunction of which the situationists and the entire history from which they emerged had dreamt for years. And in spite of desperate attempts to separate workers from students and leaders from followers, this was certainly a time in which the pre-ordained roles and multicopy categories of the spectacle were refused. 'The construction of situations will be the continual realisation of a big deliberately chosen game',[120] the LI had declared, identifying the 'systematic provocative dissemination of a host of proposals tending to turn the whole of life into an exciting game'[121] as one of the great tactics of subversion and the goal of all provocation. 'Never work!' declared the slogans of 1968, opposing all labour to the playful activity of the post-revolutionary world. And in 1934, when Breton had described the objects of early surrealist criticism, it was work again which was his greatest target.

> Intellectually, it was vulgar rationalism and chop logic that more than anything else caused our horror and our destructive impulse. Morally, it was all duties: religious, civic, and of the family. Socially, it was work. Did not Rimbaud say: 'Never will I work, O torrents of flame!'[122]

This antipathy to work had characterised much surrealist writing. 'There is no use living if one has to work,'[123] wrote Breton, and it was common currency that openness to the surreal 'presupposes availability and only the idle can be at the complete disposal of chance'.[124] The situationists' analysis of capitalist development made such rhetoric a real possibility; Lautréamont's dream of a poetry made by all became the hope for a poetic world constructed by all. 'Just as it makes utopias possible', wrote Vaneigem, so 'modern technological expertise also does away with the purely fairy tale nature of dreams. All my wishes can come true – from the moment that modern technology is put at their service.'[125]

Revolution was conceived as the first freely constructed game, a collective transformation of reality in which history is seized by all its participants. Play, pleasure, and participation were to be the hallmarks of a new form of social organisation appropriate to a world in which the imperatives of survival no longer legitimise relations of domination, alienation, or the separation between the individual and the world. The euphoric fluidity of the revolutionary moment, in which experiences gain a tangible immediacy which makes a few days seem like years, comes out of the free and experimental play unleashed by the total rejection of existing rules. 'Revolutionary moments are carnivals in which the individual life celebrates its unification with a regenerated society,'[126] declared Vaneigem, invoking the festivity of a world displaced by an immediate passion for the here and now: 'the first few days of an insurrection are a walk-over simply because nobody pays the slightest attention to the enemy's rules: because they invent a new game and because everyone takes part in its elaboration.'[127] The joy of freely assumed roles is rediscovered in the midst of the contestation of those previously prescribed, and out of the ruins of commodified lifestyles and definitions emerge new patterns of playfully chosen and flexible identities like those one fleetingly adopts when playing charades or childhood games of make-believe. And play is also the charm with which the revolution is protected from hierarchy and mediation.

> An efficiently hierarchized army can win a war, but not a revolution; an undisciplined mob can win neither. The problem then is how to organize, without creating a hierarchy; in other words, how to make sure that the leader of the game doesn't become just 'the Leader'. The only safeguard against authority and rigidity setting in is a playful attitude. Creativity plus a machine gun is an unstoppable combination.[128]

The situationists wanted to develop this provocative love of play into a way of life. For Vaneigem, 'only play can deconsecrate, open up the possibilities of total freedom . . . the freedom, for example, to turn Chartres Cathedral into a fun-fair, into a labyrinth, into a shooting-range, into a dream landscape'.[129] Games were no longer to be the activities of alienated leisure time; freed from this separation and with a 'radical negation of the element of competition',[130] playing in the ruins of the spectacle was to be the central activity of everyday life. Play was seen as the stuff of life where work had been the stuff of survival: 'Ludic attraction is the only possible basis for a non-alienated labour, i.e. productive work',[131] and the ethic of play, adventure, and a creative, participatory life was posed as the negation of the entire spectacular perspective. 'We must start to *play* right now if the future is not to become impossible. [. . .] The vital objectives of a struggle for the construction of everyday life are the sensitive key points of all hierarchical power.'[132]

This conception of play was not, of course, sitting in the free realm untainted by spectacular relationships that is the revolutionary waiting room. Play and the participation it allows also fuels the spectacular world where, diverted into commodified roles and lifestyles, it both squanders and raises the desire for the real life invoked by the situationists. Neither was play the only point of contradiction to the impoverished forms of expression and exchange they invoked. Vaneigem sought points of opposition to commodity exchange in every conceivable area of life, investigations which led him through detailed histories of festivity, gratuity, unrestrained love, and all expressions of individuality. 'We must rediscover the pleasure of giving,' he wrote. 'What beautiful potlaches the affluent society will see – whether it likes it or no – when the exuberance of the younger generation discovers the pure gift',[133] he declared, invoking the feudal contempt for exchange as a 'will to deny interchangeability' in which 'so much room was left for play, humanity, gratuitousness, that inhumanity, religion and solemnity came at times to appear as secondary to such preoccupations as war, love, friendship or hospitality.'[134] And even though the 'cramped style of the nobility was only a crude sketch of the grand style which will be invented by masters without slaves', it was a 'style of life nonetheless – a world away from the wretched forms of *mere* survival which ravage the individual's existence in our time.'[135] Like the surrealists, Vaneigem saw love offering 'the perfect model of communication: the orgasm, the total fusion of two separate beings. It is a glimpse of a transformed universe.'[136] Diverted into a host of clichéd, commodified, and sacrificial relationships, love is a long way from the point at which it would be possible to say: 'I know you don't love me because you love only yourself. I am just the same. So love me.'[137] But it conjures the longing for a world in which such honesty and authenticity might be possible, and is 'bound to overflow into the will to transform the whole of human activity, into the necessity of building a world where lovers feel themselves to be everywhere free.'[138] Vaneigem was convinced that '*all* pleasure embodies the search for total, unitary satisfaction, in every sphere',[139] arguing that the dream of the absolute, excess, realisation, and a world in which words like 'utterly' could find a meaning, spills out of every moment of pleasure, eroticism, sensuality, and emotion.

But even Vaneigem's exuberant defences of radical subjectivity did not depend on the essentialist conceptions of truth, reality, and desire he sometimes evoked. 'I realise that I have given the subjective will an easy time in this book', he wrote, 'but let no one reproach me for this without first considering the extent to which the objective conditions of the contemporary world advance the cause of subjectivity day after day. Everything starts from subjectivity, but nothing stays there.'[140] Vaneigem did speak of the desire to build a passionate life, the passion for play, love, and creativity but, contrary to the impression given by some of his own more passionate and creative passages, the desire to live is not some inherent characteristic squashed and repressed by capitalist social relations. Endorsing Debord's insistence that the '*subject* can only arise out of society – that is, out of the struggle that society embodies',[141] Vaneigem defined the subjective desire for life as a 'political decision', made by those who refuse a world in which the 'guarantee that we shall not die of starvation entails the risk of dying of boredom'.[142]

The desire to live is chosen in the knowledge that the end of scarcity, the needs of survival, and the necessity of work have been made possible by capitalism and are stemmed only by its perpetuation. None of the building blocks of situationist theory – the subject, history, class, desire – were conceived as objective and ahistorical characteristics waiting to be identified, discovered, and labelled within a theoretical construction. Not even the creativity and spontaneity which could transform the everyday were regarded as the pure expressions of desire unleashed. And although Vaneigem defined spontaneity as 'the true mode of being of individual creativity, creativity's initial, immaculate form, unpolluted at the source and as yet unthreatened by the mechanisms of co-optation',[143] he also pointed out that spontaneity 'can never spring from internalised restraints, even subconscious ones, nor can it survive the effects of alienating abstraction and spectacular co-optation: it is a conquest, not a given'.[144] The post-revolutionary world is one in which people will be free to make and realise themselves in the world as they wish; a world in which the struggle for survival in which we are now trapped will become the struggle for life. 'History is leading us to the crossroads where radical subjectivity is destined to encounter the possibility of chan- ging the world.'[145]

The radical subject endorsed by Vaneigem is not waiting in some haven for the day of its release: it is actually made possible by the development of capitalist forces of production and the con- testation of the relations in which they arise. It is a free con- sciousness which emerges in the course of its daily resistance to the spectacular relations in which it arises and will decide its own nature in the process of their final contestation. Its desires are advertised on the underground, given away with ten gallons of diesel, and promoted in the entire ideology of spectacular life. They are offered in the form of self-contained and 'unitary' pallia- tives, from which no overspill is possible but which, according to Vaneigem, nevertheless 'entail two risks for Power. In the first place they fail to satisfy, and in the second they tend to foster the will to build a real social unity.'[146] It was the possibility of exploiting this double danger which encouraged situationist explorations of how the spectacle's own diversionary tactics could in turn be diverted into revolutionary weapons.

'. . . a single choice: suicide or revolution'

The path to the magnificent future envisaged by the situationists was not, of course, without its dangers, and one of the distinguishing features of situationist theory was its recognition that all forms of criticism, dissent, and resistance occupy an internal relation to the system they oppose. No matter how impassioned or desiring, it is impossible for the subject to stand outside the spectacle and pronounce on it from a position of clean removal, and any attempt to develop a critical analysis of the totality of social and discursive relations must recognise that the meanings, tactics, and goals with which it works are always already implicated within the relations of power they resist. The situationists did not, however, accept that the means and ends of resistance are always already defined by these relations, a position characteristic of many of the post-68 philosophies considered in the next chapter. The most radical of gestures is indeed vulnerable to integration, and expressions of dissent are often deliberately fostered as political safety-valves. But the situationists were convinced that none of this precludes the possibility of evading, subverting, and interrupting the processes by which effective criticism is rendered harmless.

Situationist talk of the recuperation of dissent was intended to convey the subtlety and effectiveness by which criticism of the spectacle is enlisted in its support. It carried a stronger meaning than terms such as 'integration', 'co-option', or the 'repressive tolerance' identified by Marcuse,[1] for although each of these expressed the way in which dissenting voices can be rendered harmless by their absorption into the spectacle, the notion of recuperation suggested that they are actually subject to processes of inversion which give an entirely new and affirmative meaning to critical gestures. Represented in the spectacle, the vocabulary of revolutionary discourse is taken up and used to support the existing networks of power: the theory 'that was developed by the strength of the armed people now develops the strength of those who disarm the people'.[2] Change, self-management, and autonomy have become the prerogatives of the right; revolution, the realisation of dreams, and the possibilities of a transformed life are now the domain of the advertising industry.

Although the situationists were neither brave nor foolish enough to think they could avoid engagement with the recuperative powers of the spectacle, they were convinced that any critical project must endeavour to sidestep and expose the whole process by which criticism is turned against itself. This effort determined the entire style, the methods, and organisation of the movement. Sometimes it produced an atmosphere of rigorous self-criticism and demands for perfection which even the SI was ultimately unable to fulfil, and the situationists did not always escape the implications of many of their attacks on other currents of radical thought and activity. But their often playful and disarming assumptions of arrogant superiority enabled them to produce devastating criticisms of many of those ostensibly engaged in radical critique for their complicity with the relations they sought to undermine. Condemning the cultural integration of artists, the pseudo-radicalism of students, and the unions' role in the pacification and absorption of dissent, the situationists showed how each assumes a spectacular and supportive role. The demands of anarchists and Utopians were decried as incoherent and confused by their deferral of revolution to some future point of magical metamorphosis; the prototype parties of the revolutionary Left were seen as enabling the spectacle to parade its image of tolerant pluralism while at the same time reproducing the hierarchy, bureaucracy, and mediations of capitalist relations. Radical academics provided the appearance of revolutionary critique while similarly reproducing the specialisation of knowledge and the lucrative elitism of their own roles, and those still committed to cultural production were dismissed for their displays of naïve self-interest.

A society in which 'the individual's own gestures are no longer his own, but rather those of someone else who represents them to him'[3] is capable of moving every experience and expression into a representation of itself. Critical discourse is subject to the same qualities of fragmentation, stasis, equivalence, and vacuity which mark every commodified aspect of modern society: turned into spectacle, criticism becomes an object of contemplation itself. Its impact no greater than that of the romantic novel or the weather forecast, it serves only to strengthen the image of rebellion and dissent willingly cultivated by the spectacular whole. Without the slightest hint of suppression or intolerance, the spectacle ensures that the appearance of real dissent precludes its real appearance. It becomes a part of that which it criticised and, like any other result of alienated production and consumption, returns packaged to those who created it.

The situationists argued that it is as a consequence of these recuperative powers that 'the ruling society has proved capable of defending itself, on all levels of reality, much better than revolutionaries expected'.[4] It should never be forgotten, they warned, that '*the bourgeoisie is the only revolutionary class that ever won*',[5] and all revolutionary criticism must recognise the failures of the past and learn from the implications and effects of this failure. 'Words forged by revolutionary critique are like partisans' weapons: abandoned on the battlefield, they fall into the hands of the counterrevolution and like prisoners of war are subjected to forced labour.'[6] In this way, for example, the word '"revolutionary" has been neutralised to the point of being used in advertising to describe the slightest change in an ever-changing commodity production',[7] and a commodity like beer can be sold with the slogan 'The Red Revolution is Coming'.[8]

The development of this perspective owed much to the situationists' avant-garde heritage, from which they learned a great deal about the tactics of evading and exposing the system of relations in which they worked. The gradual introduction of the avant-garde into mainstream culture provided a perfect case study of the recuperation of radical discourse. Dada's anti-art and surrealism's subversions have both assumed the mantle of institutionalised art, with their works exhibited, consumed, and reproduced in contexts which relieve them of all critical content. Forty years after their adventures, the dadaists looked in dismay at the fate of their agitations. Huelsenbeck observed that the weapons forged by Dada have been turned into 'popular ploughshares with which to till the fertile soil of sensation-hungry galleries eager for business',[9] and Duchamp lamented that the urinal with which he had once challenged the bourgeoisie was now admired for its aesthetic beauty.[10] Not merely are the actual works of such movements transplanted into foreign soil, but the forms, techniques, and the magic they worked are also used to ends entirely different from those with which they were developed. 'Everywhere Surrealism appears in recuperated forms: commodities, works of art, publicity techniques, the language of power, a model of alienated imagination, objects of devotion, and cultural accessories.'[11] Even the surrealists' deliberate attempts to evade this process were fraught with difficulty. Philippe Soupault recorded a conversation in which the early surrealist group expressed its unease at the speed with which its work was absorbed into the French literary tradition:

> the conversation took a sudden turn, fear of pleasing. We were being welcomed from the very beginning as successors, heirs, by our elders. Gide, Valéry, the *Nouvelle Revue Française*, Jacques Riviére, etc. A career like any other. It was already understood. Shit! Would Rimb[aud] or Lautr[éamont]. . . them, eh? Suddenly, it became a kind of dialogue, like challenges exchanged . . . . Deceive . . . . B[reton] defined the work of destruction we were to undertake with whoever else wanted to, but between us a secret engagement . . . . People must still believe that we are poets.[12]

Whereas Dada was engaged in a project of direct contestation with the structures of culture and society, the surrealists chose the path of subversion and sabotage. Setting themselves up as the 'enemy within', they adopted the role of double agents, masquerading as a literary school while at the same time undermining literature itself. This was, however, a difficult game to play. Eager that they should still appear as poets, the surrealists' writing accorded with certain senses of harmony, aesthetic appeal, and many other conventional values, and the inevitable confusions of double agency made them unable to put up a wholehearted resistance to the prevailing system of social and economic relations.

Although it was the surrealists' awareness of these problems which encouraged their development of an overt political consciousness, the movement remained rooted in the cultural domain. And for the situationists, any project which

> fails to sustain a praxis of radically overthrowing the conditions of life . . . does not have the slightest chance of escaping being taken over by the negativity that reigns over the expression of

social relationships: it is recuperated like the image in a mirror, in inverse perspective.[13]

In this way, 'the most corrosive concepts are emptied of their content and put back into circulation in the service of maintaining alienation: dadaism in reverse. They become advertising slogans.'[14] Aware of the 'danger of surrealism', wrote Debord, the bourgeoisie 'has been able to dissolve it into ordinary aesthetic commerce' and would now 'like people to believe that surrealism was the most radical and disturbing movement possible'. Cultivating a nostalgia for the excesses of surrealism, any attempt to effect a new cultural transgression is automatically reduced 'to a surrealist déjà-vu, that is, to a defeat which according to it is definitive and can no longer be brought back into question by anyone'.[15]

The view that such recuperations are the inevitable and generally insignificant fate of any peripheral, avant-garde, or critical movement was hotly contested by the situationists, for whom recuperation was synonymous with the processes of commodification and spectacularisation on which the spectacle is dependent. Anything which resists the alienation, separation, and specialisation of the spectacle must be brought within the confines of commodity exchange; challenges to the commodity form must be made to assume the vacuity and equivalence necessary to the reproduction of commodity relations. The situationists argued that collapses of the marvellous into the mundane or the critical into the counterrevolution are never signs of natural destiny or apolitical degeneration. On the contrary, such shifts are effected in order to remove the explosive content from gestures and meanings which contest the capitalist order.

Turned into commodities, works of radical art and political criticism support the system of relations they despised. The products of movements like Dada and surrealism are later used to reproduce the forces that 'dominate present social life both officially and in fact: noncommunication, bluff, frantic desire for novelty as such, for the rapid turnover of arbitrary and uninteresting gadgets',[16] and the gestures and discourses which disrupted or opposed commodity relations are forced to operate within them. Unchanged in their content, the commodity form they assume robs them of any intrinsic value, and all attempts to develop an understanding of modern society as a totality of social, economic, and cultural relations are similarly deflected into isolated perspectives from which only partial knowledge is possible. Revolutionary critique is diverted into fragmentary oppositions which, 'like the teeth on cogwheels . . . mesh with each other and make the machine go round, the machine of the spectacle, the machine of power',[17] and the absence of real political debate is concealed by endless rounds of apparent argument and meaningless contradiction.

> In a caricature of antagonisms, power urges everyone to be for or against Brigitte Bardot, the *nouveau roman*, the 4-horse Citroen, spaghetti, mescal, miniskirts, the UN, the classics, nationalization, thermonuclear war and hitchhiking. Everyone is asked their opinion about every detail in order to prevent them from having one about the totality.[18]

Vaneigem's list is dated: in the early 1990s it might include Acid House, satellite TV, the blasphemy laws, Saddam Hussein, and Ecstasy. But it is not *that* dated, and the observation that its general categories of concern remain unchanged supports Vaneigem's suggestion that the value and significance of such issues comes a distant second to the social purpose they fulfil.

In their own efforts to spark a movement capable of resisting accommodation within spectacular relations, the situationists attempted to build a critique which would bow to none of the distinctions, fragmentary perspectives, or classifications recognised by the spectacle. Taking elements from a variety of often contradictory perspectives and treating theories, vocabularies, movements, and gestures as a huge toolbox from which anything useful might be selected, they tried to construct a revolutionary theory whose only claim to validity would lie in the possibility of its practical realisation. Theirs was to be a unitary critique which would transgress distinctions between theory and practice, a separation which it was argued 'provides the central basis for recuperation, for the petrification of revolutionary theory into ideology' and transforms 'real practical demands [. . .] into systems of ideas'.[19] What prevents the recuperation of situationist theory, declared the SI, is not its claim to universal validity, but 'the fact that all situationist ideas are nothing other than faithful developments of acts attempted constantly by thousands of people to try and prevent another day from being no more than twenty-four hours of wasted time'.[20] Only such an engagement allows a theory to retain some critical negativity in the midst of the spectacle's bland affirmations.

The situationists adopted some aspects of the forms of organisation developed by their avant-garde predecessors. Together with the internationalism and eclecticism of Dada, the internal discipline exercised by the surrealists was carried into the SI where it served the primary purpose of constituting a group in control of its own destiny, a movement impossible to define in terms other than its own. The SI resisted all attempts to institutionalise its theory as an ideological 'ism', and insisted that the group should have 'nothing in common with hierarchical power, no matter what form it may take. The SI is thus neither a political movement nor a sociology of political mystification [. . .] the SI holds to a permanent revolution of everyday life.'[21] Confident that their analyses were of lasting significance and would always reach those who sought to negate the totality of capitalism, the situationists also refused all exhortations to populism and mass appeal. 'Let us spit in passing', declared René Viénet, on those who 'have the nerve to claim that the workers are incapable of reading *Internationale Situationniste*, that its paper is too slick to be put in their lunchbags and that its price doesn't take into account their low standard of living.'[22] Cultural definition was spurned just as readily. 'We are artists only insofar as we are no longer artists: we come to realize art,'[23] they insisted, refusing to confine themselves to any specialised area of operation, and mixing theoretical development with a variety of scandals, partisan propaganda, and cultural interventions.

Defining themselves as the 'last of the professions', the situationists declared:

> The role of the Situationist, the amateur-expert, the anti-specialist, will remain a form of specialisation until the moment of economic and mental abundance when everyone will become an artist in a sense which artists have never before achieved – in the sense that everyone will construct his own life.[24]

In response to a questionnaire ('a form of pseudodialogue . . . to elicit people's happy acceptance of passivity under the crude guise of "participation"'[25]), the situationists claimed that what distinguished them from every other movement was their development, 'from a revolutionary perspective, of a new, coherent critique of the society as it is developing *now*', a project which obliged them to 'make a practice of breaking completely and definitively with all those who oblige us to do so' and initiate 'a new style of relations with our "partisans": we absolutely refuse disciples. We are interested only in participation at the highest level; and in setting autonomous people loose in the world.'[26] Describing themselves as a 'Conspiracy of Equals, a general staff that *does not want troops*',[27] the situationists argued that they were articulating an everyday resistance recognisable and familiar to those who experienced and exercised it but which otherwise received no expression. The SI clearly saw itself marching way ahead of other revolutionary groups and cultural movements. Nevertheless, it was not a vanguard in the Leninist sense. Although the situationists recognised that a social revolution could only proceed on the basis of a mass organisation, they did not pretend to be its nascent form.

> We don't claim to be developing a new revolutionary programme all by ourselves. We say that this programme in the process of formulation will one day practically contest the ruling reality, and that we will participate in that contestation.[28]

The central role of any propagandist movement was rather to open up 'the "Northwest Passage" toward a new revolution that must surge over that central terrain which until now has been sheltered from revolutionary upheavals: the conquest of everyday life. *We will only organise the detonation*', they declared; 'the free explosion must escape us and any other control forever.'[29]

Just as they wanted no followers and insisted that the revolutionary moment would sweep them away along with the rest of the old world, the situationists declared their hostility to leaders, celebrities, and all forms of hierarchical control. Since 'one of the classic weapons of the old world, perhaps the one most used against groups delving into the organisation of life, is to single out and isolate a few of their participants as "stars"',[30] Debord refused all the attentions usually lavished on Parisian intellectuals. Nevertheless, together with the impassioned confidence of his writing, the mantle of dogmatic leadership he seems to have assumed did little to free the situationists from the star system they wished to undermine. Debord remains surrounded by mysteries and intrigue encouraged by the murder of his publisher, Lebovici, in 1987, his refusal to show any of his films in France, legal wrangles over the translation and reproduction of situationist texts, and the general atmosphere of obscure conspiracy cultivated around the entire situationist milieu. Indeed, this air of secrecy increasingly became the means by which the situationists tried to satisfy their double need for both splendid isolation and impeccable participation in the spectacle. Debord's readings of Clausewitz and his fondness for war games and military metaphor encouraged the group's guerrilla mentality, and the situationists carried a kudos which ran counter to every condemnation of the spectacle. The group's extravagant claims for the social revolution and its own theories almost seemed to come from some mysterious inside source, as though the SI had a privileged access to the truths of spectacular society. But to a large extent, this atmosphere merely arose from the combination of intelligent analysis and a deliberate attempt to avoid accommodation within spectacular relations. 'It's not the monopoly of intelligence that we hold', wrote Vaneigem, 'but that of its use.'[31]

One of the more unfortunate results of this strategy was the weaving of a web of personal intrigues and hostilities which continues to entrap those engaged in many post, pro-, or neo-situationist tendencies. Refusing disciples, followers, and the slightest hint of divided loyalty, the situationists tolerated no fellow-travellers and reserved the most damning of their condemnations for the 'pro-situs', spectators whose passive admiration of the SI was said to leave them both resentful and 'dazzled by the success'[32] of the movement which would not admit them. Of some seventy people who passed through its ranks, sixty-six resigned or were expelled; in the journal, some 540 other people were jeered at for their complicity with the spectacle (although the large number of people insulted should be set against the 940 who were mentioned altogether).[33] Some later groups inherited the worst aspects of the situationists' desperation to be the most extreme and sophisticated of revolutionaries, realising tendencies to cynicism, personal recrimination, soul-searching, and a perverse moralism which condemns anything that does not promise to produce the revolutionary moment. Attempts to refuse any compromise have often led to an insidious holier-than-thou attitude which delights in the slightest personal slip or the first hint of selling out, buying in, doubt, or personal interest; a generation of radicals fell over themselves to establish their own autonomy, exorcising and denying their own spectacular seduction by situationist theory, and busily condemning one another as pseudo-revolutionaries and agents of the spectacle.

The collapse of the movement was followed by bitter recrimi-
nations and an extreme reaction against Vaneigem's poetic pleas
for the radical subject, with many subsequent interpretations and
developments of situationist ideas positioning themselves in either
Debordist or Vaneigemist camps. Some of Vaneigem's own later
work reinforced the view that his position tended towards a politics
of personal liberation, and the question of the extent to which
desires can be fulfilled within capitalist social relations had
surfaced throughout the group's existence. In the early 1960s,
bitter arguments led to the exclusion of eight German situationists
grouped around the journal *Spur*, and a group of Scandinavian
members disparagingly referred to as 'Nashists'. Besides an
unknown quantity of personal disputes, the central argument was
over the compatibility of individual artistic creation with the
situationist demand for a unified and uncompromising struggle.
Similar differences had surfaced in the expulsion of Alexander
Trocchi who, excluded from the SI in 1962, had established his
own Project Sigma, a network designed to 'alert, sustain, inform,
inspire, and make vividly conscious of itself all intelligence
everywhere'.[34] Debord's insistence that the SI should remain as
uncontaminated as possible by any involvement in the spectacle of
alienated production and consumption was matched by those,
including Heimrad Prem, Asger Jorn, and Jorgen Nash, who
argued that demands for the realisation and suppression of art in
everyday life could not preclude the continuation of struggles with
and against artistic practice. Nash and a number of those who left
the SI with him established the 'Situationist Bauhaus' in Sweden,
turning his farm into a centre for artistic experimentation from
which a journal, *Drakabygget*, was published and some scandals
were organised, most famously the decapitation of the mermaid in
Copenhagen harbour. Jacqueline de Jong, a Dutch situationist
also expelled in the same fracas, published the *Situationist Times*
from 1962 until 1967. Both projects returned to the situationists'
artistic roots and were dismissed by Debord who, according to a
persistent but unsubstantiated rumour, nevertheless continued to
finance the SI's activities with sales of Jorn's paintings. It was after
this split that the situationists developed a coherent critique of the
society of the spectacle and adopted a more recognisable political
stance. But artistic intervention continued to characterise the
practices of the movement, with a number of situationists

developing their own cultural adventures and avant-garde tactics continuing to inform the situationists' subversive response to the recuperative powers of the spectacle.

Although all those involved in the movement were dismayed by the variety of recuperative pitfalls which faced them, their observations on the subject were not intended as nostalgic laments for the days when the rhetoric of revolution had a significance beyond the advertising slogan. Arguing that such inversions are possible only because they face no rival, the situationists were willing to admit that developments in washing-machine technology can be described as revolutionary only 'because the possibilities of a central *desirable* change are no longer expressed anywhere'.[35] Only when it is abandoned on the battlefield is the vocabulary of liberation vulnerable to recuperation, and the situationists did not consider it inevitable that arms should be lost forever. 'After dadaism, and in spite of the fact that the dominant culture has been able to recuperate a sort of dadaist art, it is far from certain that artistic rebellion in the next generation will continue to be recuperable into consumable works.'[36] The absorption and fragmentation of Dada and surrealism had not prevented the tactics of these movements from informing the situationists' own revolutionary programme, and the situationists suggested that recuperations are not necessarily effected 'without risk for the system'.

> The endless caricaturing of the most deeply felt revolutionary desires can produce a backlash in the shape of a resurgence of feelings, purified in reaction to their universal prostitution. There is no such thing as lost allusions.[37]

Recuperation is a dangerous game. There is always a chance that the promise of revolution on a billboard will be taken literally in the streets: even adverts for 'flaming tasty' burgers on hoardings set alight by rioters assume a meaning lost in the routine of their usual appreciation. 'Even when it is co-opted and turned against itself, poetry always gets what it wants in the end,' wrote Vaneigem. 'The "Proletarians of all lands, unite" which produced the Stalinist State will one day realise the classless society.'[38]

But reappropriations must be made with some care. Although it is, of course, still possible to speak of revolution after the term has been used to sell a washing machine or bank account, it cannot be used in the belief that such recuperations have been without effect. Every aspect of the meanings and struggles recuperated by the spectacle must be reinjected with the subjectivity that has been emptied from them. Language must be reinvested with desire, theory with its realisation, and gestures with the spontaneous pleasure of their creation. For the situationists, the tactics and subversions of spectacular relations did not need inventing, but only a name. The subjectivity which produces, consumes, and is itself produced and consumed by the spectacle is already busy looting it as well. It does not passively consume and obediently produce as the spectacle ostensibly intends: it sabotages, steals, plays in the supermarkets, and sleeps on the production line. The spectacle feeds on this energy at the same time as it denies its dependence on the imagination and creativity which sustain it, but as soon as the subject realises that power 'creates nothing, it recuperates',[39] the spectacle's myth of its own self-sufficiency collapses. The situationists were convinced that the only legitimate tactics of revolutionary criticism are therefore those which heighten this awareness, raising the desire for forms of autonomous action, self-realisation, and subjective expression denied by commodity relations. In 'Basic Banalities', Vaneigem declared:

> the spontaneous acts we can see everywhere forming against power and its spectacle must be warned of all the obstacles in their path and must find a tactic taking into account the strength of the enemy and its means of recuperation. This tactic, which we are going to popularise, is *détournement*.[40]

The closest English translation of *détournement* lies somewhere between 'diversion' and 'subversion'. It is a turning around and a reclamation of lost meaning: a way of putting the stasis of the spectacle in motion. It is plagiaristic, because its materials are those which already appear within the spectacle, and subversive, since its tactics are those of the 'reversal of perspective',[41] a challenge to meaning aimed at the context in which it arises. The notion was first developed by the Belgian surrealist Marcel Mariën, who wrote alongside Debord and Bernstein in the 1950s journal *Les Lèvres Nues*, and described *détournement* as a sort of embezzlement of convention.[42] The subversions of comic strips which the lettrists claimed as their own were perfect examples of such appropriation: in the pages of *Internationale Situationniste*, true love stories were confused with bubbles of political propaganda, and soft porn pin-ups declared, 'I love to sleep with Asturian miners, they're real men',[43] or insisted that the 'emancipation of the workers will be the work of the workers themselves'.[44] These methods were essentially reworkings of those employed by the dadaists and surrealists, extended by the situationists to every area of social and discursive life. For Debord, a 'dadaist-type negation' must be a feature of 'any later constructive position as long as the social conditions that impose the repetition of rotten super-structures – conditions that have intellectually already been definitively condemned – have not been wiped out by force.'[45] The dadaist critique of language must become 'a permanent practice of the new revolutionary theory',[46] since it is 'impossible to get rid of a world without getting rid of the language that conceals and protects it, without laying bare its true nature'.[47] Convinced that the poetry and desire revealed by the *détournement* of the language of information, bureaucracy, and functional control was vital to the success of the revolutionary project, the situationists proposed a situationist dictionary as 'a sort of codebook enabling one to decipher information and rend the ideological veils that cover reality', and considered it 'essential that we forge our own language, the language of real life'.[48]

Set free by their *détournement*, commodified meanings reveal a totality of possible social and discursive relations which exceeds the spectacle's constraints. Poetic discourse presages a world in which language plays with meanings the spectacle cannot under-stand; although it can be bought and sold like any other commodity, the desires and freedoms of poetry can never be completely flattened. 'In spite of what the humorists think, words do not play,' wrote Debord. 'Nor do they make love, as Breton thought, except in dreams. Words *work*, on behalf of the dominant organisation of life. And yet . . . they embody forces that can upset the most careful calculations.'[49] The situationists were not inter-ested so much in poems themselves as the free relationships invoked by poetic expression, which 'wants to reorient the entire world and the entire future to its own ends'.[50] Whereas surrealism 'in the heyday of its assault against the oppressive order of culture and daily life could rightly define its arsenal as "poetry without poems if necessary", it is now a matter for the SI of a poetry *necessarily* without poems'.[51] As the poet gleans the world and juxtaposes every element in the making of a poem, so the revo-lutionary should use the entire 'literary and artistic heritage of humanity . . . for partisan propaganda purposes'.[52] Respect for the inspired works of the past should be transformed into a respect for the ways in which they can be plundered and subverted: 'Any elements, no matter where they are taken from, can serve in making new combinations.'[53] Debord's use of Marx, Hegel, and Lukács in *The Society of the Spectacle* offered the possibility of freely constructed theory in the same way that Lautréamont's plagiaristic reworkings in *Les Chants de Maldoror* presented that of a poetry made by all.

Demanding a complete reversal of the spectacular perspective, the situationists argued that the critical theory which struggles against alienation must itself 'be communicated in its own language – the language of contradiction, dialectical in form as well as in content'.[54] A dynamic and fluid theory must place the meanings and vocabularies of the spectacle in a perspective which negates it, a dialectical totality in which the subversive qualities of 'past critical judgements that have congealed into respectable truths' are restored.[55] *Détournement*, the 'antithesis of quotation', is the 'fluid language of anti-ideology. It occurs within a type of communication aware of its inability to enshrine any inherent and definitive certainty.'[56]

> Even the style of exposition of dialectical theory is a scandal and
> an abomination to the canons of the prevailing language, and
> to sensibilities molded by those canons, because it includes in
> its positive use of existing concepts a simultaneous recognition
> of their rediscovered fluidity, of their inevitable destruction.[57]

Attempts to invest the language of the spectacle with difference and interruption were central to the situationist project, and their subversive plagiarisms of the existing world were both playful and purposeful. The Hegelian 'inversion of the genitive', which might, for example, turn 'the poverty of theory' into 'the theory of poverty', or 'consciousness of desire' into the 'desire for consciousness', was characteristic of all situationist writing, and, putting *détournement* into immediate practice, Debord wrote: 'Ideas improve. The meaning of words has a part in the improvement. Plagiarism is necessary. Progress demands it.'[58] *Détournement* surfaced in the situationists' use of comic strips and Asger Jorn's irreverent repaintings of kitsch reproductions. The industrial paintings made by Pinot-Gallizio and exhibited in Milan in 1958 challenged all ideas of artistic value when they were sold by the metre, made into clothes, and used to line the walls of the 'anti-material cave' shown in Paris in 1959. Buildings were appropriated by graffiti; a plethora of texts, graphics, and images were incor- porated into Debord's films; the language of scientific discourse found its way into the SI's psychogeographical research; and *détournement* characterised the upsetting of relationships with people, cities, and ideas with games, *dérives*, and constructed situations. *Détournement* became the 'signature of the situationist movement, the sign of its presence and contestation in contemporary cultural reality',[59] and was ultimately the sense in which the situationists conceived the social revolution: a gigantic turning around of the existing social world.

This continuity between the means and ends of revolutionary practice presented the situationists with the task of developing a consciousness, forms of organisation, and tactics of struggle which anticipate the possibilities of life in the post-revolutionary world. Although they recognised that anything short of total contestation is doomed to the fragmentation, equivalence, and mediocrity of the commodity, this merely encouraged the situationist conviction that the means by which the revolutionary moment is achieved must be continuous with its aims, avoiding all compromise and collaboration with the old world and sacrificing nothing to the moment of total contestation. The world in which the creation of situations would become an everyday reality must be continually anticipated in attempts to realise it. With a lovely sense of completion, the situationists effectively argued that situations must be created which facilitate the creation of the revolutionary situation which in turn produces the world in which the creation of situations is possible.

Although the situationists were convinced that everything arising in spectacular society is subject to representation within its commodified and alienating relations, their insistence on the necessity of developing a unitary critique of the spectacle implied that pockets of post-revolutionary consciousness can somehow arise in the pre-revolutionary present. The paradox of this position, equally present in the situationists' councilist demands for alternative systems of workers' organisations, is really that the revolution demands a consciousness which only the revolution can produce. Any critique of the spectacle as a dehumanising force is in danger of falling into self-contradiction if it admits that it is possible to play and enjoy some autonomy and control over one's own life within capitalist society. Moreover, the forms of alternative organisation and practice in which this consciousness appears within and against capitalist society are invariably vulnerable either to repression or some reformist form of peaceful co-existence. These misgivings were raised in Jean Barrot's *What is Situationism*, which complained that 'the S.I. did not know whether it was a matter of living differently *from now on* or only of *heading that way*'.[60] When Vaneigem declared: 'I want to exchange nothing – not for a thing, not for the past, not for the future. I want to live intensely, for myself, grasping every pleasure',[61] he was not merely giving an account of how life should be, but declaring his intention to take it in the here and now as a means of achieving a world in which such supreme self-satisfaction would be realised. And for Barrot, this conflation of the means and the ends of revolutionary activity could only lead to one of two dead ends. 'Either one huddles in the crevices of bourgeois society, or one ceaselessly opposes it to a different life which is impotent because only the revolution can make it a reality.'[62]

Vaneigem's *Revolution of Everyday Life* was originally entitled *Traité de savoir-vivre à l'usage des jeunes générations*, and, as Barrot disparagingly commented, it is indeed a handbook or guide to 'violating the logic of the market and the wage system wherever one can get away with it.'[63] One of Vaneigem's later books continued this line of attack with calls for industrial sabotage as a first step to the development of councils and self-management,[64] and workplace rebellion of the 'go on, phone in sick' variety has since been advocated by groups such as Processed World, for whom tactics of confusion and theft serve both to enliven work and undermine the logic of labour.[65] But are such tactics means of coping with capitalism or destroying it? Were the situationists more concerned with finding ways for real life to survive within the spectacle, or with the contestation of the spectacle itself? At their worst, they seem to have believed that the degeneration of the spectacle is 'in the nature of things'[66] so that any revolutionary organisation needs only to help it on its way. Convinced that the spectacle had reached saturation point and could go no further, they saw it producing its own antagonists and presenting the choice between life and survival with unprecedented clarity. But they also recognised that although the spectacle may not be capable of integrating its members forever, the act of choosing life was by no means inevitable, and at the very least required the dissemination of a great deal of enthusiastic propaganda to raise expectations, desires, demands, and consciousness of the possibilities already present. And although their awareness of the spectacle's tendency to recuperate all criticism teetered on the brink of conspiracy theory, a recognition of the flexible ability of capitalism to survive every earlier assault still enabled the situationists to insist that all present activity should be judged on its ability to raise the revolutionary stakes.

Agitations akin to those promoted by the situationists proliferated during the 1960s and have continued to emerge in subsequent years. But although the situationists supported those 'perpetrators of new radical acts' like the British 'Spies for Peace' scandal,[67] few of the adventures with which they were contemporary met with their approval. The SI attacked all those it considered to be agitating for an enjoyable life in the here and now without developing a coherent revolutionary critique as hopeless reformists. The 'revolution for the hell of it' attitude of the American yippies, the counter-cultures of play power, happenings, be-ins, and drop-outs were all haughtily rejected on the grounds that they left themselves open to recuperation and the miserable totality of society untouched.

The situationists were particularly critical of the Dutch Provos, who were followed by the Kabouters in their practices of Dada-like provocations and subversions. The Provo movement appeared in 1965, dedicating itself to the provocation of Dutch society and the 'Dreary People of Amsterdam'. Roel van Duyn, author of a book on Kropotkin,[68] was among those whose activities earned an initially repressive response from the authorities and an extraordinary level of popular support for attempts to construct a 'counter-society', a notion made famous by the 'white plans' for free bicycles, streets, and housing. The Provos won 13,000 votes and one seat in the municipal elections in Amsterdam, and regarded themselves as the manifestation of a new, heterogeneous class: the Provotariat. 'Happenings', participatory events at which the Provos excelled, were described as attempts 'to seize at least the little part in things that you ought to have and that the authorities try to take away from you', and 'a demonstration of the power you would like to have – influence on events'.[69] The Provos were united by little – '"We agree to disagree", they said'[70] – beyond 'imagination, which they could neither express in their daily lives and work in the factory, nor in their jobs, nor at the university, nor in traditional politics and opposition movements.'[71] But although from a situationist point of view the Provos were confined to demonstrating rather than contesting the power that one 'would like to have', they did pursue their attacks to the very pillars of Dutch society, particularly the church, the royal family, the security forces and, symbolically, the Lieverdje statue in Amsterdam, subverted to epitomise the 'addicted consumer'.[72] Their unprecedented displays of irony and absurdity did, of course, meet with the customary opposition of the police, which the Provos countered with the foundation of the Society of Friends of the Police, a tactic also used by the members of Kommune 1, a Berlin group in which one of the *Spur* group of ex-situationists was involved. (Kommune 1 established a Save the Police Committee in 1967 which called for a 35-hour week to give the police 'spare time for reading, leisure activities with their wives and girlfriends and time for giving vent to their aggressions by making love, and also time for chats with elderly passers-by to whom they can explain democracy'.[73])

'By our acts of provocation', wrote the Provos, 'we force authority to tear off its mask.'[74] Like Dada, however, they soon 'realised that their actions lost their meaning after they had lost their originality',[75] and the Provos declared their own dissolution at a 1967 happening. Their provocative tactics nevertheless appeared sporadically until their re-emergence with the Kabouters in 1970. Developing the theme of the development of an alternative, or counter-society, the Kabouters dressed as gnomes, produced numerous papers, organised happenings, and declared the foundation of the Orange Free State. They produced alternative plans and imaginative reforms for every area of Dutch life, many of which prefigured the demands of the later green movement. Legal protection for squatters, a newspaper, and networks of free services and cheap shops were established with the help of a large sum of money which mysteriously found its way into the bank account held by the Kabouters' free radio station, Radio 2000, and the Orange Free State was formally proclaimed as an autonomous network of self-managed councils. 'The revolution is in a hurry,' declared its protagonists.

> So the new society will have to make the most of its knowledge of sabotage techniques to hasten the transition from an authoritarian and dirty society to an anti-authoritarian and clean one.

In fact, the existence of an autonomous, new community in the heart of the old order is the most effective sabotage. But whatever techniques the people's army of saboteurs may use, it will always remember that it cannot resemble the old world's armies in anything, anything, anything.[76]

Playfully standing in the 1970 election, the Kabouters were themselves completely thrown to find that they had won 11 per cent of the vote, five council seats in Amsterdam, and twelve others throughout the country.

For the situationists, the Kabouters' mixture of revolutionary propaganda and democratic participation revealed their essential faith that the system was fundamentally resistant to change and could be only be prodded, provoked, and cajoled into allowing some freedoms in the present. A Provo text, for example, had spoken of the 'inevitable political and military holocaust', and the situationists saw the movement as

> an aspect of the last reformism produced by modern capitalism: the reformism of everyday life . . . the Provo hierarchy think they can change everyday life by a few well-chosen improvements. What they fail to realise is that the banality of everyday life is not incidental, but *the central mechanism and product of modern capitalism.* To destroy it, nothing less is needed than all-out revolution. The Provos choose the fragmentary and end by accepting the totality.[77]

The situationists were convinced that Provo and Kabouter actions would merely decorate and enliven the system they despised; indeed, to this day Amsterdam bears the legacy of these improvements. But was the value of such tactics confined to the reinforcement of the tolerant image of the society which contained them? The problem raised by Vaneigem's hedonism emerges again: is there any point in revolutionaries trying to make life more bearable within the society they wish to destroy? If the fatalism of 'after the revolution' is to be avoided, there clearly is. But people's attempts to live in the here and now must also undermine the system which condemns them to survival, and it was on these grounds that the situationists did of course give full support to what was also their own moment of glory: the May events of 1968.

It is difficult to ascertain the extent of the situationists' influence on those who took to the streets during this extraordinary revolutionary moment. But whether one considers that the movement had a direct impact on the events or had merely voiced the experiences of those involved for long enough to make this appear to be the case, 1968 certainly came close to a vindication of the situationists' insistence that their ideas were 'in everyone's mind'.[78] In the vocabulary, the tactics, and the aims expressed in the events, situationist theory seemed to come into its own barely a decade after the movement's inception.

Although the events were by no means confined to the universities, the immediate sparks flew within the French student milieu. In November 1966, a group of radical students took advantage of their colleagues' apathy and got themselves elected to the Strasbourg section of the UNEF, the French Student Union. They collaborated with the situationists on the production of a pamphlet later translated as 'Of Student Poverty Considered in its Economic, Political, Psychological, Sexual, and Particularly Intellectual Aspects, and a Modest Proposal for its Remedy', a publication produced with union funds and described in a local newspaper as 'the first concrete manifestation of a revolt aiming quite openly at the destruction of society'.[79] 'Of Student Poverty' placed a devastating attack on the role of the student in the context of the best expositions of situationist theory. Designed to provoke an extreme response, the pamphlet declared that capitalism demands the 'mass production of students who are not educated and have been rendered incapable of thinking'.[80] Although the student is 'close to the production-point' of knowledge, it argued,

> access to the Sanctuary of Thought is forbidden, and he is obliged to discover 'modern culture' as an admiring spectator. Art is dead, but the student is necrophiliac [. . .] a conspicuous consumer, complete with induced irrational preference for Brand X (Camus, for example), and irrational prejudice against Brand Y (Sartre, perhaps).[81]

The pamphlet ridiculed the students' privileges and belittled the manifestations of rebellion expected of them by their elders. 'They must understand one thing', it declared: 'there are no "special" student interests in revolution. Revolution will be made by *all* the victims of encroaching repression and the tyranny of the market.'[82]

The launch of the pamphlet was marked by a number of disruptions, including the display of a comic strip, *The Return of the Durutti*

Column, and its provocative distribution at the university's official opening ceremony. The university authorities took the union to court for its illegal use of funds, and the judge's summation of the case is often cited as one of the most illuminating accounts of the pamphlet's contents. 'The accused', he stated, 'have never denied the charge of misusing the funds of the student union. Indeed', he continued, 'they openly admit to having made the union pay some £500 [*sic*] for the printing and distribution of 10,000 pamphlets, not to mention the cost of other literature inspired by the *Internationale Situationniste.*' Rejecting 'all morality and restraint, these cynics do not hesitate to commend theft, the destruction of scholarship, the abolition of work, total subversion, and a world-wide proletarian revolution with "unlicensed pleasure" as its only goal'.[83] The scandal gave some notoriety to the situationists, who nevertheless tried to distance themselves from the role of 'leaders' of the Strasbourg students imposed by the media, later claiming that they 'had to defend themselves from being *recuperated* as a "news item" or an intellectual fad . . . as anyone can well imagine, the pitiful *student milieu* is of no interest to us'.[84]

The media's response to the Strasbourg scandal was mixed: the Italian *Gazetta del Popolo,* evidently unable to 'well imagine' this last point, reported that 'the Situationist International, galvanised by the triumph of its adherents in Strasbourg, is preparing to launch a major offensive to take control of the student organisations'.[85] *Le Monde,* however, related the situationists' 'messianic confidence in the revolutionary capacity of the masses and in their aptitude for freedom'[86] with some amusement, and it is true that 'Of Student Poverty' expressed the situationists' boundless faith in the impending 'revolutionary celebration' with great enthusiasm, as its closing passages reveal:

> To transform the world and to change the structure of life are one and the same thing for the proletariat . . . . As its maximum programme it has the radical critique and free reconstruction of all the values and patterns of behaviour imposed by an alienated reality. The only creativity it can acknowledge is the creativity released in the making of history, the free invention of each moment and each event: Lautréamont's *poésie faite par tous* – the beginning of the revolutionary celebration. For the proletarian revolt is a festival or it is nothing; in revolution the road of excess leads once and for all to the palace of wisdom. A

palace which knows only one rationality: *the game.* The rules are
simple: to live instead of devising a lingering death, and to
indulge untrammelled desire.[87]

The popularity of the pamphlet – quickly reproduced and translated into more than ten languages – encouraged the unprecedented discussion of situationist analyses and the avant-garde
heritage which informed them, developments hastened by the
1967 publications of Vaneigem's *The Revolution of Everyday Life* and
Debord's *The Society of the Spectacle.* The student agitations begun at
Strasbourg continued throughout 1967: students at Lyon, Nantes,
and Nanterre were involved in disruptions and occupations
culminating in the formation of the situationist-inspired *enragés* in
January 1968 and the heterogeneous *mouvement du 22 mars* in
which Daniel Cohn-Bendit and Jean-François Lyotard were
involved.

These developments culminated in the dramatic events of May
and June 1968 which, regardless of their repeated characterisation
as a mere 'student revolt', constituted an extraordinary social,
political, and cultural crisis involving a sustained – and wildcat –
general strike and the practical critique of every aspect of capitalist
life in roughly the terms prefigured in a decade of situationist
texts. They were by no means confined to France, but formed part
of a wave of revolutionary action which spread across eastern and
western Europe, South-east Asia and the United States. Nevertheless, as it arose in France, the crisis appeared to many to have come
out of the proverbial blue. In 1967, for example, Henri Lefebvre
ridiculed the situationist insistence that revolution was just around
the corner. 'Do they really imagine', he wrote,

> that one fine day or one decisive evening people will look at
> each other and say, 'Enough! We're fed up with work and
> boredom! Let's put an end to them!' and that they will then
> proceed to the eternal Festival and the creation of situations?

Remembering the Paris Commune, Lefebvre conceded that
although such a situation 'happened once, at the dawn of 18
March 1871, this combination of circumstances will not occur
again'.[88] Six months later, of course, he was proved profoundly
wrong: those involved in the May events did indeed make
impossible demands irreducible to higher wages or the details of
workplace organisation. But if his statement bears a particular

irony, he was not alone in his view. Sherry Turkle spoke for many when she commented: 'In terms of traditional economic and political analysis, the events were *impensable*, "unthinkable"; they *should* not have happened.'[89]

A great deal did, of course, happen. After large student demonstrations in early May, the Latin Quarter of Paris was occupied by the police and the student protests spread in a matter of days to factories and workplaces of all kinds. In some cases, this extension was spontaneous; in others, the students who had effectively disbanded the universities realised that they were powerless without the reproduction of their actions throughout all areas of social life and asked the workers for support. A general strike, called for 13 May, brought the country to a standstill and was prolonged by a series of wildcat strikes and occupations which amounted to some three weeks of action by more than 10 million workers. For one participant,

> A whole new epoch has just come to an end: the epoch during which people couldn't say, with a semblance of verisimilitude, that 'it couldn't happen here'. Another epoch is starting: that in which people *know* that revolution is possible under the conditions of modern bureaucratic capitalism.[90]

The size and the extremism of the movement took everyone by surprise. Describing its protagonists as 'guerrillas', the *Observer* correspondent wrote:

> With bewildering speed, these political guerrillas have been hurtled into politics by an anonymous surge of student unrest. By taking to the streets, they have set themselves against every organised political force in France. Both Government and Opposition last week tried desperately to contain them. Both failed.[91]

Indeed, the strikes and occupations of 1968 were largely effected against the advice and orders of the Communist Party and the largest trade union, the CTG. Mainly through its paper *L'Humanité*, itself subject to strike action on 15 May, the Party condemned the revolt, warning urgently against 'provocateurs' and urging people to return to work or confine their demands to economic or organisational issues. Beyond this, it did all it could to institute bureaucratic control over the factory occupations, demonstrations, and the events themselves. Participants in the *mouvement du 22 mars* recognised that revolution 'is as much of a threat to the Communist Party as to the factory owners',[92] and pamphlets produced in the occupied factories show that the warnings and entreaties of the established organs of dissent went unheeded: an Air France leaflet declared, 'Like the students, we must take the control of our affairs into our own hands',[93] and a leaflet from the Rhône-Poulenc workers asserted:

> The action of the students has shown us that only rank and file action could compel the authorities to retreat . . . the students are challenging the whole purpose of bourgeois education. They want to take the fundamental decisions themselves. So should we.[94]

Gestures to previous revolutionary situations were made: in a tribute to the Kronstadt revolt, the crew of the liner *France* took control of the ship in Le Havre, and the barricades and the festival air recollected the Paris Commune. On 19 May, the *Observer* reported: 'This is revolution . . . a total onslaught on modern industrial society.'

> In a staggering end to a staggering week, the commanding heights of the French economy are falling to the workers. All over France a calm, obedient, irresistible wave of working-class power is engulfing factories, dockyards, mines, railway depots, bus garages, postal sorting offices. Trains, mails, air-flights are virtually at a standstill. Production lines in chemicals, steel, metalworking, textiles, shipbuilding and a score of industries have ground to a halt . . . . Many a baffled and impotent manager is being held prisoner in his own carpeted office.

The following Sunday found the paper in more reflective mood, describing the 'great upheaval through which France is passing' as 'above all a crisis of the State. And not simply of the French State but of the State as it has been conceived in the Western industrial world and its offshoots since the eighteenth century.'

It was the breadth of the dissent which was so remarkable. Art students demanded the realisation of art; music students called for 'wild and ephemeral music'; footballers kicked out managers with the slogan: 'football to the football players'; gravediggers occupied cemeteries; doctors, nurses, and the interns at a psychiatric hospital organised in solidarity with the inmates. The national radio and television networks were gripped by strike action that lasted well into July 1968 as a result of government restrictions on the reporting of the street battles of May. The Odéon theatre was occupied and, like the Sorbonne, which was evacuated by the police and taken over by the students on 13 May, served as a forum for an extraordinary variety of discussion and debate. Costumes were stolen and worn for street fighting and, in the university, 'Young workers who "wouldn't have been seen dead in that place" a month ago now walked in groups, at first rather self-consciously, later as if they owned the place, which of course they did'.[95] Incitements to disaffect permeated the armed forces, and when de Gaulle ordered troops to head for Paris, he had to appeal to those based in Germany. The mass demonstrations, some of which numbered more than a million people, were remarkable for their diversity; nothing, it was said, could contain the 'row upon row upon row of them, the flesh and blood of modern capitalist society, an unending mass, a power that could sweep *everything* before it, if it but decided to do so'.[96]

The situationists were among the few who were not taken by surprise by the strength and ubiquity of the uprising. In 1971, a correspondent for *Le Nouvel Observateur* wrote: 'When one reads or rereads the *Internationale Situationniste* issues it is quite striking to what degree and how often these *fanatics* have made judgements or put forward viewpoints that were later concretely verified.'[97] Later in the same year the paper stated that *The Society of the Spectacle* 'has led the discussion of the entire ultraleft since its publication in 1967. This work, which predicted May 1968, is considered by many to be the *Capital* of the new generation.'[98] For their part, the situationists modestly insisted, 'we had prophesied nothing. We had simply pointed out what was already present,'[99] and the movement delighted in its refusals of all attempts to characterise it as responsible, victorious, or prophetic. 'What thus came to the light of consciousness in the spring of 1968 was nothing other than what had been sleeping in the night of "spectacular society", whose spectacles showed nothing but an eternal positive façade.'[100] At the same time, however, they were quite happy to see the confirmation of their theses in the events themselves.

> The fact that the strike had . . . extended to activities which had always escaped subversion in the past radically affirmed two of the oldest assertions of the Situationist analysis: that the

increasing modernisation of capitalism brings with it the proletarianisation of an ever-increasing part of the population, and that as the world of commodities extends its power to all aspects of life, it produces everywhere an extension and deepening of the forces that negate it.[101]

The situationists, who had 'denounced and fought the "organisation of appearances" of the spectacular stage of commodity society, had for years very precisely foreseen the explosion and its consequences',[102] declared the SI, insisting that the events were an affirmation of its view that 'the proletariat had not been abolished; that capitalism was continuing to develop its own alienations; and that this antagonism existed over the entire surface of the planet, along with the social question posed for over a century'.[103]

The situationists' view of the events is largely contained in *The Enragés and the Situationists in the Occupation Movement – France, May–June 1968*, in which René Viénet wrote:

in the space of a week, millions of people had broken with the weight of alienating conditions, the routine of survival, ideological falsification and the inverted world of the spectacle . . . . The festival finally gave real holidays to people who had only known working days and leaves of absence. The hierarchical pyramid had melted like a lump of sugar in the May sun . . . . The streets belonged to those who were digging them up.[104]

'Everyday life', he continued, 'suddenly rediscovered, became the centre of all possible conquests. People who had lived their whole lives in offices declared that they could no longer live in the way they had before.'[105] This was a perspective shared by the British papers. An article in the *Observer* concluded: 'As petrol dries up, people rediscover their legs. Everybody turns hitch-hiker. The spring air is intoxicating. "*Salut camarade!*"',[106] and an earlier edition of the paper had identified the object of the revolutionary critique as

the society organised for efficiency at the expense of liberty, the system which 'offers the people consumer goods and calls them freedom.' It is the system which adapts education . . . to the mass production of docile technocrats. It is the party system posing as true democracy, repression masked as tolerance.[107]

'Capitalised time stopped', wrote Viénet, and without any 'trains, tubes, cars or work the strikers recaptured the time so sadly lost in factories, on motorways and in front of the t.v. People strolled, dreamed, learned how to live. Desires began to become, little by little, reality.'[108] Another eye-witness account reported that a 'tremendous surge of community and cohesion gripped those who had previously seen themselves as isolated and impotent puppets, dominated by institutions they could neither control nor understand',[109]

There was indeed a great deal of talk about desire, unity, participation, and the liberation of spontaneous creativity in 1968, and the events of 1968 are often described as 'surrealism in the streets'.[110] With neither a transport system nor the urgency to get anywhere, the *dérive* became an aspect of everyday life; without the usual saturation of mass media, people chatted as never before. Alain Jouffroy recalled the 'great joy that we experienced for the first time in the streets of Paris during May 1968, that joy in the eyes and on the lips of all those who for the first time were talking to each other'.[111] Paying tribute to Fourier's identification of the building of barricades as the quintessential example of passionate work, Viénet noticed that the general strike unleashed new forms of playful activity.

> Fourier had already remarked how it took workers several hours to put up a barricade that rioters could erect in a few minutes. The disappearance of forced labour necessarily coincided with the free flow of creativity in every sphere: slogans, language, behaviour, tactics, street-fighting techniques, agitation, songs and comic strips. Everyone was thus able to measure the amount of creative energy that had been crushed during the time of survival, the days condemned to output, shopping, television, and to passivity erected as a principle.[112]

This was indeed a critique of the totality of lived experience which challenged even the traditional expressions of dissent and organised political activity, and found its expression in the council communism beloved of the situationists. General assemblies allowed for a maximum of participation, and strike committees, occupation councils, and a host of tiny spontaneously formed organisations did all they could to avoid the mediations of representation, bureaucracy, and hierarchy. Viénet was convinced that a '*manifestly Councillist* attitude'[113] prevailed, and the *Observer* noted that this challenge to organisational methods was perhaps the most alarming aspect of the revolution. In mid-May, Neal Ascherson claimed that the 'revolutionaries dream of a republic of workers' councils, a self-governing society . . . in which the "new human being" will emerge',[114] and two weeks later, the paper reported that 'the embattled strikers' had

> raised the cry for a 'government of the people'. It was horribly clear that the spark of revolution, struck by the student extremists, had found tinder on the shop floor. Suddenly, revolution seemed everywhere in the air, feared or hoped for.[115]

Although the situationists and the *enragés* formed the 'Council for the Continuation of the Occupations' and put out some of the best propaganda of the events, the situationists were far too small to constitute a very influential grouping. But their tactical refusals of categorisation were pursued by the entire movement. The events appeared to be completely spontaneous, with forms of organisation and strategies developing according to particular circumstances and orchestrated by no one. The overwhelming feeling was that the identification of a set of demands, a leader, or a simple purpose, would weaken and fragment the movement, leaving it vulnerable to accommodation and recuperation within existing social structures. In 1968, the demands of both workers and students arose out of discontent with specific situations, but almost instantaneously found their expression in impossible demands made of the social whole. The revolutionary moment passed only when their expectations were reduced to those with which the system could cope, such as the reform of the universities, greater freedom of the press, higher wages, and more worker–management co-operation.

Most commentators agreed with the *Observer* that one of the most significant strengths of the revolutionary movement was that 'it cannot be clearly identified . . . . It is raw explosive power.'[116] But attempts were also made to identify the leaders, 'stars', and organisers of the events. 'If leaders didn't exist, then they had to be invented. The press itself went on to install the Spokesmen, the Representatives, the Leaders. Obscure bureaucrats, vigorous professors, outspoken militants, were transformed by the press into the Lenins, the Maos and the Ches of the Revolution.'[117] 'Students in Revolt – and two of the men responsible', declared the *Guardian* in an article on Marcuse and Cohn-Bendit.[118] Alain Geismar, a Maoist student leader, and Jacques Sauvageot, head of the UNEF, were also cast in the role of leaders of the movement and, in the British press, it was the Trotskyist Alain Krivine who was most frequently identified as being in charge. Viénet observed that these three became

> the *apparent leaders* of a leaderless movement. The press, radio, and television, in their search for leaders, found no-one besides them. They became the inseparable and photogenic stars of a spectacle hastily pasted over the revolutionary reality . . . . This trio of ideological charm of 819 varieties could obviously only say the acceptable – and therefore the deformed and recuperated – tolerated by such a means of transmission. While the real meaning of the void which had propelled them out of the void was purely *unacceptable.*[119]

In situationist terms, the identification of leaders was an attempt to deny the possibility that people are capable of organising themselves; a recuperative tactic returning structures of domination, specialisation, and mediation to the movement and turning 10 million strikers into passive spectators of events over which they had no control. The *News of the World* held the situationists responsible when it reported: 'Their general headquarters is secret but I think it is somewhere in London. They are not students, but are what is known as situationists; they travel everywhere and exploit the discontent of students.'[120]

Certainly both the slogans of the period and the means by which they were communicated – graffiti on the walls and often on treasured statues and works of art – had a situationist air about them. The slogans which appeared in May declared: 'Live without dead time!', 'Play without shackles!', 'They're buying your happiness. Steal it!', and 'I came in the cobblestones'. Later, some became more angry but no less surreal: 'Society is a man-eating flower', and 'Comrades, if everyone was doing this . . . ' were joined in the Sorbonne by 'I take my desires for reality because I believe in the reality of my desires' was sacrilegiously painted across a wall, along with 'What if someone burnt down the Sorbonne?', 'Art is dead! Don't consume its corpse', and 'Run for it! The old world is behind you'.[121] Arguments abound as to whether these were displays of situationist or surrealist influence; when the issue was raised with the surrealist Jean Schuster in 1987, his response to the suggestion that 'the situationists stole the surrealists' thunder in 1968' was pert: 'If you read their revue and

Raoul Vaneigem's writings attentively you'll see that there isn't a single new idea in them.'[122] But when had the situationists ever claimed originality? Theirs was a patchwork of materials stolen from everywhere, and if surrealism's contribution to the revolutionary moment was particularly strong, it was obviously particularly useful. In 1968, surrealism was subject to a *détournement* of its own, taken out of the galleries and acted in the streets. Perhaps the most famous and significant of the slogans read: 'Under the cobblestones, the beach', an expression which captured both the tactics of the revolutionaries, for whom the cobblestones provided the most obvious weapons against the police, and the symbolic meaning of this *détournement* of the streets. Another slogan read, 'The most beautiful sculpture is the sandstone cobble, the heavy square cobble, the cobble you throw at the police', and André Fermigier pointed out that Duchamp's '"ready-made" finally realised its revolutionary potential when it took the form of paving-stones which the students threw at the CRS [riot police]'.[123] For Michel Ragon, 'the city once again became a centre of games':

> the great permanent theatre of the Odéon, the poster studio of the ex-Ecole des Beaux-Arts, the bloody ballets of the CRS and students, the open-air demonstrations and meetings, the public poetry of wall slogans, the dramatic reports by Europe No. 1 and Radio Luxembourg, the entire nation in a state of tension, intensive participation and, in the highest sense of the word, poetry.[124]

Anonymous, cheap, and immediate, the use of graffiti in the May events epitomised the avant-garde dream of art realised in the practice of everyday life. A transformation of its environment, graffiti was as powerful a form of subversion and engagement as the larger *détournement* of the city it inspired and reported.

If the tactics of *détournement* were present in the events, elements of recuperation peppered their aftermath. Thousands of accounts and explanations of the successes and failures of 1968 appeared in the following two years, collections of posters and photographs were published, and legend has it that souvenir cobblestones were on sale within days of the rioting. The twentieth anniversary of the May events was greeted with a blaze of publicity and enthusiasm quite different from the rather muted reception given to the tenth, and something of a media extravaganza brought endless representations and reconsiderations of 1968 to the 1980s. In a 'pull-out colour supplement', the *New Statesman* declared: 'In 1988 the revolution *will* be televised' and predicted that the year would contain 'Something for everybody. Biff cartoons will have a field day; die-hard situationists will denounce recuperation on a grand scale; *Marxism Today* will produce T-shirts decorated with tanks and warning us against provocateurs.'[125] More books appeared, the 'stars' of the movement were engaged in a plethora of radio, television, and newspaper reports, and references to the events appeared in 1988 advertisements. Publicity from the National Westminster Bank made use of the visual similarity of '68' and '88' in posters and leaflets which rather ironically offered 'a range of services to help you handle your money, so that you can get on with your work while still enjoying student life', packaging them in a series of political images with lettering reminiscent of the ink blocking of an *ad hoc* printshop.

Such appropriations do not go unnoticed. But, more than twenty years on, they are again accepted as part of an inevitable cycle in which fashions and styles come and go with a mysterious autonomy on which historical events are one influence among many. From this perspective, anti-art is bound to be integrated into art, radical theory will always become institutionalised and respectable, and real experience cannot but pass into spectacle. There is room for regret, but not for analysis, and it is to the situationists' credit that they delved beneath this superficial acceptance in their attempts to develop a theory of recuperation.

But the situationists' analysis of the fate of the dissenting voice does tend to conjure visions of some Orwellian 'Ministry of Recuperation', giving the impression that all criticism is deliberately taken into the realm of commodity relations and disarmed by conscious decision. As Barrot argued, the 'counterrevolution does not take up revolutionary ideas because it is malign or manipulative, let alone short of ideas, but because revolutionary ideas deal with *real* problems with which the counterrevolution is confronted.'[126] But although the situationists' view of recuperation can be read rather too conspiratorially, the shift of ideas they described was merely intended to express the effects of commodity relations throughout all knowledge, culture, and political discourse. For sure, talk of recuperation presupposes a central split or separation at the heart of the social world; an alienation to which everything, from subjective experience to revolutionary theory, is vulnerable. But the situationists did not conceive this as a static division between the subject and the power structures which oppose it. Invoking a dialectical and shifting play between the two, they argued that it is the logic of the commodity, rather than the existence of a particular set of rulers or government, which maintains the capitalist system. And just as the notion of recuperation implies no definitive distinction between the rulers and the ruled, so it precludes the possibility that the spectacle is a totalitarian and all-encompassing whole. If this were the case, there would be no sense of a realm from which critique could be recuperated; no 'us' who create and 'them' who recuperate; no good and evil of subjectivity and power. By definition, commodity relations are based on the appropriation of *something* from the workers and consumers to whom all subjects of capitalism are reduced, and unless it is accepted that modern society is no longer determined by the circulation of commodities, the situationist spectacle can never completely circumscribe reality.

Nevertheless, the view that late capitalism has indeed cut loose from commodity production and consumption gained great currency in the intellectual aftermath of the 1968 events. That the events happened at all showed that rebellion was still possible in spite of the sophisticated exercises of power effected within capitalist society, valorising situationist claims that subjective forces could overturn the logic of the commodity with the free play of desires, pleasures, and created situations. On the other hand, the failure of the events seemed to indicate that in spite of the extraordinary uprising against it, capitalist society was resistant to revolutionary upheaval. And the system's ability to withstand the challenges of 1968 led many radical theorists to wonder if their intellectual energies had not been devoted to the criticism of structures and institutions peripheral to the real functioning of society.

Although the rhetoric of both situationist propaganda and the events themselves was that of a radical distinction between classes, the treachery of the unions and many of the party organisations which claimed to represent both workers and students contributed to the difficulties of a simple account of who was on which side and whether, indeed, there were two sides at all. To the situationists, of course, the behaviour of the organised Left came as no surprise: 'Humanity won't be happy until the last bureaucrat is hanged with the guts of the last capitalist',[127] declared one of their slogans, and

Debord was later to argue that it remains the spectacle's 'highest ambition' to 'turn secret agents into revolutionaries and revolutionaries into secret agents'.[128] But the confusion between the appearance and the reality of political commitment was compounded by the indeterminate nature of the forces they were trying to overthrow. Where was the true locus of the power which dominated and repressed? Was it in the government, the police, the official opposition, the factories, the media, moral restraint, cultural values, the system of education, the love affair, all, or none of these? And what was the nature of the force contesting power? A radical subjectivity, opposing all forms of mediation and organising itself into cells of direct democratic control? Or a more shadowy subversive force unable to realise the revolutionary dream and capable only of aimless interruption and nihilistic festivity? The activists had of course contributed to this doubt themselves, running free from participation in all the forms and structures of the old world, sidestepping categorisation, and resisting definition within the conventions of organisation, leadership, and identifiable demands. And although the revolutionaries' provocative tactics of imaginative subversion had allowed an unprecedented challenge to conventional political action, even these attempts to challenge the established order were thrown into doubt in the intellectual debates which followed the events.

The post-68 philosophies developed by Jean-François Lyotard, Félix Guattari, Gilles Deleuze, and Michel Foucault suggested that the failure of the events necessitated new accounts of how society is organised and subverted. They introduced radical frameworks which subjected traditional conceptions of capitalism and revolutionary criticism to an unprecedented challenge. The activists' rejection of all forms of representation and leadership found its intellectual expression in the poststructuralist distrust of the authority of theory, and demands for direct democracy and the insistence that everyone should have a say about the detail of their everyday lives were transcribed into a concern for the specificity of experience. That both the representatives of the state and those of the working class had tried to maintain their power by denying the cacophony of dissenting voices pointed to discourse and knowledge as the real sites of power, and the fact that the social relations implicit in everything from sex to the management of football teams had been contested threw up the possibility that power was exercised differently in every area of life and could not be explained in terms of a single contradiction in the economic functioning of society. Such observations problematised all notions of critical practice and, in some cases, made them seem quite impossible. But none of these philosophers set out to prove that this was so. Like the situationists, their starting point was the observation that the most radical of gestures could somehow be absorbed within the existing structures of power, and the effort to expose and subvert the real mechanisms underlying these structures continued to motivate their work.

These theoretisations were not merely developed in the aftermath of the May events, however, but in the wake of structuralism as well, a perspective which had already displaced the notions of subjectivity, history, meaning, and reality central to revolutionary theory. Structuralism developed out of a linguistic theory to suggest that all experience arises within pre-existing structures, reducing all meaning to an effect of language and removing any sense of correspondence between language and the world. In the work of de Saussure, language was theorised as a system of signs which take their meaning from relations with one another rather than a reference to the world. The subject who had previously used language to interpret and communicate with the world became a subject constructed by this system of signs, and the idea that the world itself could be represented by language was superseded by the realisation that it is actually produced by it.[129] Although structuralism excited a renewed political debate which allowed contemporary capitalist society to be analysed as a complexity of interdependent relations, many theorists were dissatisfied with its inability to account for human agency, change, and interruption. The ahistoricism of a system of pre-existing social and linguistic structures allowed for no understanding of how it arises, maintains itself, or comes to suffer challenges of the order of those mounted in 1968, and the poststructuralist philosophies of the 1970s tried introduce some notion of historical fluidity into the system of signs which order and produce the world.

In part, this instability was provided by the Nietzschean conception of the world as 'a monster of energy without beginning, without end . . . a play of forces and waves of forces.'[130] Nietzsche's influence can be read in the work of Foucault, for whom this dynamism is populated by endless networks of power and knowledge, and Lyotard, whose development of a philosophy of multiple and positive desires was shared by Deleuze and Guattari.

Championing a world of incessant flux and becoming which underscores but is nevertheless dominated by reason's insistence on the stability of being, Nietzsche saw an endless movement of becoming, difference, chance, and chaos washing against the categories of reason to pose a recurring threat to the structures of unity, being, and universal truth. And in their rejections of any Hegelian conception of historical progress in favour of some sort of permanent contestation between order and its subversion, the poststructuralist philosophers opened up the possibility of new and productive frameworks in which to consider political action. But they also began to lose any sense of purpose and meaning, and struggled with the dilemma of Nietzsche's own work, in which a refusal to identify any realm of true meaning and reality conflicts with the desire to privilege the underlying world of chaos, force, and flow. And although this tension, from which neither Dada nor surrealism had escaped, was eventually collapsed in the postmodern philosophy later espoused by Lyotard and Baudrillard, the 1970s work of Foucault, Lyotard, Deleuze, and Guattari was all caught on a bridge between declarations that reality is a chaotic whirl and the certainty that it cannot be identified at all.

The postmodernity into which Lyotard later drifted escaped this dilemma at the price of a political despondency and celebration of meaninglessness. From the postmodern perspective, the demands made in situationist theory and the May events themselves were quite impossible. The immediacy of pure representation, direct communication and democracy, and the end of all separation, mediation, and alienation, were completely misguided dreams which believed it possible to express the inexpressible: true desires, immediate experiences, spontaneous emotions, and the reality of pleasures and angers. In the postmodern context, it is in the very act of articulation that such realities slip away; even the most imaginative means of communication remains trapped within the network of social and discursive relations which is the true ground of the exercise of power. It may be true that the party is more constraining than the workers' council, or the theoretical text less immediate than graffiti on a wall, but these are merely quantitative differences which cannot contribute to the qualitative goal of social transformation. The mediations of discourse are inescapable, and it is in them that the power and domination against which the revolutionary struggles are really exercised. Such observations make situationist condemnations of recupera- tion seem pointless and naïve. Believing they were attempting to avoid accommodation within structures of spectacular repre- sentation, the situationists failed to realise that all representation, and not just the forms peculiar to capitalism, is spectacular and recuperative.

With the contradictions of production and consumption losing their determining role, the essential distinction between life and its representation dissolves, and representation becomes the only realm in which the reality of experience can be known. Any sense of hidden values and meanings must be abandoned: reality is merely that which appears in discourse, and it is no longer possible to speak of the underlying authenticities of the individual, the intrinsic value of the commodity, or the real meaning of the recuperated text. Recuperation and *détournement* cannot be conceived as the strategies of opposing forces, but the eternal passage between equivalent contexts, so that the revolutionary posters printed in 1968 were no more real or authentic than their 1988 advertisers' simulation; the simulation is not a recuperation, since the original was never outside the play of discursive networks in the first place. Indeed, from this perspective there is a sense in which the 1988 poster is more honest than its 1968 counterpart: at least it does not pretend to refer to anything other than another poster, whereas the original carried the implicit claim that it was a faithful representation of the real desires of the people. The brute force of real events lives only through the images and appearances it assumes in the discursive world and has no reality outside the sum of all that is said, sung, painted, and filmed of it. Among the postcards produced for the 1988 exhibition of the Situationist International at the ICA was one declaring, 'Humanity won't be happy until the last bureaucrat is hanged with the guts of the last capitalist.' A tragedy, or an amusing irrelevance? From the vantage point at which much post-68 theory eventually arrived, such developments are just a fact of life; expressions of the human condition against which any struggle is doomed to unhappy despair.

Chapter 4

'Victory will be for those who create disorder without loving it'

The May events have served as the common springboard for a great deal of subsequent intellectual enquiry. The line of imaginative dissent to which Dada, surrealism, the situationists, and the activists of 1968 belong continually reappears in the poststructuralist and desiring philosophies of the 1970s, and the postmodern world view to which they have led is itself laced with the remnants of this tradition. But it was the failure of the revolutionary movement which preoccupied this trajectory of post-68 philosophy, culminating in the postmodern insistence that criticism is impossible, subversion futile, and revolution a childish and reactionary dream. And as France returned to some sort of political normality, the possibility that the most basic and heartfelt presuppositions of revolutionary thought were fundamentally mistaken was raised over and again.

A cursory reading of poststructuralist thought leaves revolutionary theory without a leg to stand on. The situationist distinction between the real and the spectacle is rendered meaningless by the claim that there can be no real existence beyond that which appears in discourse, and the assertion that the desires and experiences of the subject are somehow more authentic than those represented in the spectacle collapses in the face of suggestions that subjectivity is itself produced by the networks of discourse in which we live. Notions of class, totality, and historical progress are completely undermined, and the idea that all social relations are somehow answerable to a single principle of economic functioning is rendered untenable. But although poststructuralism is in some senses a radical break with the situationist project, a host of continuities makes it impossible to oppose the two world views completely. The interests, vocabulary and style of the situationists reappear in Lyotard's railings against theory and Foucault's maverick intellectualism, and the desiring philosophies invoked by Deleuze and Guattari continue to offer words on the 'art of living'.[1] The breadth of situationist theory and its magpie tactics of appropriation and *détournement* find their expression in the deconstructive eclecticism of poststructuralist writing, which similarly has no scruples about taking ideas, examples, and forms of expression from anywhere. Many poststructuralist texts are mixtures of poetry and philosophy, fiction and journalism, distinctions between disciplines, styles, and media are removed, and rigorous argument sits alongside unfounded speculation and unanswerable polemic. Like the situationists, they observe that the world now seems to be a decentred and aimless collection of images and appearances, characterise consciousness as fragmented, dispersed, and constructed by the social relations in which it arises, and declare the apparent impossibility of future progress and historical foundation. Situationist vocabularies of play, pleasure, and subversion reappear, and the politics of the everyday, consumerism, the media, the avant-garde, the city, language, and desire are themes common to both. Moreover, many theorists writing in the wake of 1968 continued the situationist search for some irrecuperable perspective from which an increasingly complex and all-encompassing social system could be opposed.

But these similarities do not extend to their conclusions. The situationists took the fragmentations of modern consciousness and the free-floating aimlessness of modern society as qualities specific to the spectacle, arguing that capitalism is largely maintained by its ability to present itself as a chaotic society which has broken free from all sense of historical progress. The spectacle appears as a moment with neither beginning nor end, a world of appearances which has no underlying realities to conceal, a society which is purely and simply as it appears to be. Fragmentations, confusions, and uncertainties were seen as the peculiar consequence of a society organised on the principles of commodity production and consumption, a stance which merely encouraged the situationists' search for the real mechanisms underlying these appearances. And although the poststructuralist philosophers clearly set out to undermine capitalist social organisation, the trajectory of their search for its underlying mechanisms led them dangerously close to agreement with capitalism's own self-image.

Lyotard's own doubts about the legitimacy of revolutionary

politics prefigured the May events. He left *Socialisme ou Barbarie* in 1966 amidst worries about the validity of many of the philosophical presuppositions of Marxist theory. The group's emphasis on alienation and the necessity of developing a critical subjectivity had increasingly cut it adrift from the economic imperatives of its Marxist roots, and without this material base, revolutionary theory was revealed as a moral critique of capitalism based only on an act of faith in humanity and the impossible desire for a future society of harmony and good will. Lyotard had no wish to return to the patient economism of orthodox Marxism, and retained his affection for the analysis thanks to which 'we were . . . able to hope to modify the course of capitalism, perhaps to put an end to it, by placing the force of radical critique at the disposition of the struggle of the oppressed, and on their side'.[2] But what if the foundations of this critique were quite misplaced, implying an impossible faith in the progress and reconciliation of dialectical thought? What if 'there wasn't any Self at all to experience contradictorily the moments and thus to achieve knowledge and realisation of itself? What if history and thought did not need this synthesis; what if the paradoxes had to remain paradoxes'?[3]

Questions of this order carried enormous political implications, the most disturbing of which suggested that the position of the oppressed was actually reinforced by the theories of liberation intended to transform it. Later observing that revolutionary struggles and their instruments 'have been transformed into regulators of the system',[4] Lyotard wrote:

> It is absolutely obvious today, and has been for quite some time that . . . the reconstitution of traditional political organisations, even if they present themselves as ultra-leftist organisations is bound to fail, for these settle precisely into the order of the social surface, they are 'recovered'.[5]

Was it really possible that the tactics and struggles of revolutionary politics were serving to maintain the systems they sought to overturn, so that recuperation was a consequence of the revolutionaries' unwitting participation in the goals and presuppositions of the status quo? At first, Lyotard observed, such questions 'frightened me in themselves because of the formidable theoretical tasks they promised, and also because they seemed to condemn anyone who gave himself over to them to the abandonment of any militant practice for an indeterminate time'.[6] Soon, however, 'the danger of political regression of which the Marxists warned, had ceased to frighten me',[7] and Lyotard embarked on a deconstructive adventure which raised the possibility that the forces of social revolution and those of the establishment were really not so far apart.

As a member of the *mouvement du 22 mars*, Lyotard's engagement in the 1968 events confirmed his doubts about traditional conceptions of revolutionary politics. The spontaneous upsurge of a multitude of perspectives, interests, and desires suggested that the attempt to reduce every manifestation of dissent to a single project belied a dangerous tendency to totalitarianism, squashing and concealing the real variety of differences and subversive forces which contribute to the revolutionary moment. Lyotard developed this position to argue that totalising theory, of which Marxism is a perfect example, is itself an agent of oppression and domination. His 1979 report on *The Postmodern Condition* suggested that theories are little more than good stories which make illegitimate claims to truth and universal validity and, in the process, deny the validity of all events, voices, and experiences which do not conveniently fit their analyses. Theories can appeal only to larger meta-narratives such as the belief in progress towards the truth, the discovery of the real, or the emancipation of the oppressed: stories common to religious, scientific, and philosophical discourse, yet quite unsupportable except by an appeal to themselves. There is no law which says that the oppressed will be freed; there is no reason why alienation should come to an end. These are fictions, acts of faith, and expressions of desire concealed by scientific pretension and secreted in the rigour of theory. None of this would matter if theories acknowledged their fictional status. Instead, they insist on their ability to represent reality, providing an accurate reflection of the external world. For Lyotard, however, what they really reflect is their own assumption that such representation is possible. Theories are circular and self-referential; they tell particular stories about the world and can claim no universal validity.

Any theory answers its critics with the demand for replacement: one theory must always be countered by another, and better, totalisation which accounts for everything its rival explains, and more besides. But, for Lyotard, it was not a matter of challenging the content of the theory which occupies the throne of truth, but the very assumption that such a throne exists. This position led to a hostility to all attempts to criticise theory, since the act of criticism itself assumes that a theory must be perfected: 'we have already said and repeated that we don't give a damn for criticizing, since to criticize is to remain in the field of the thing criticized and in dogmatic or even paranoid relations of knowledge'.[8] Dialectical criticism, the act of negating and opposing a body of thought or system of social relations, poses contradictions not for the pleasure or disruptive effect of making a difference in the world, but as a means to their resolution: the synthesis of opposites into a new and single unity. It is a 'deeply rational' and 'reformist' activity which challenges nothing and is 'deeply consistent with the system' since it shares the presupposition that a better theory is both desirable and necessary. The critic 'remains in the sphere of the criticised, he belongs to it, he goes beyond one term of the position but doesn't alter the position of terms'. And it is also

> deeply hierarchical: where does his power over the criticised come from? he *knows* better? he is the teacher, the educator? he is therefore universality, the University, the State, the City, bending over childhood, nature, singularity, shadiness, to reclaim them? The confessor and God helping the sinner save his soul?

'This benign reformism', he concluded, 'is wholly compatible with the preservation of the authoritarian relationship.'[9]

Unhappy with the very idea of a totalising world view, Lyotard's deconstructions of revolutionary theory were not attempts to produce a better theory, a more coherent body of thought, or a more rational perspective. On the contrary, they were intended to reveal the extent to which certain hidden intensities, desires, and assumptions interrupt the apparent rigour of theory. We should 'fight the white terror of truth with and for the red cruelty of singularities',[10] declared Lyotard, finding new and non-dialectical ways to challenge the dominion of theory, interrupting its unity, and breaking the consensus it demands. Taking up the situationist vocabulary of an economy of desires, Lyotard argued that the flux and becoming of the Nietzschean world is a realm of real intensity and desire allowed to exist only in the theoretical frameworks which deny and conceal its essential dynamism. But intensities continually break through the codes of theoretical discourse, interrupting its claims to intellectual rigour and revealing the extent to which the world is shaped and dominated by its discursive order. Thus in 1968, Lyotard saw the subversive explosion of eroticism, creativity, and the spontaneity of the prevalent 'attitude of here-now'[11] as an attack on both the social and discursive codes of existing order and the unifying dialectic of revolutionary theory. He argued that this 'politics of desire' prefigured new forms of social critique subversive of capitalist and revolutionary values, both of which codify desire and refuse to let it speak in its own voice.

This idea that the same underlying forces, intensities, and desires produce both order and its subversion was also present in Foucault's own 'non-critique' of dialectical thought, which presents networks of power as the underlying mechanisms with which social and discursive organisation and its resistance are constructed. Foucault argued that in its treatment of particular issues, local conflicts, and specific events, dialectical thought evades the 'always open and hazardous reality of conflict',[12] denying divisions and differences any meaning other than that they assume in the context of the whole. 'Dialectic does not liberate differences; it guarantees, on the contrary, that they can always be recaptured',[13] he argued, suggesting that although the identification of differences and contradictions is intrinsic to dialectical thought, they are only important for the sake of their future resolution rather than their intrinsic and immediate significance. In its search for fundamental contradictions and radical oppositions at the heart of social organisation, dialectical thought expects the plethora of other differences and antagonisms to ally themselves with the two great camps necessary to revolutionary change: if the central opposition is that of class, differences between men and women, gays and straights, students and teachers, and so on, must be subsumed within a class analysis. Otherwise, society would be construed as a multiplicity of separate areas of local antagonisms, each operating its own autonomous power struggle without hope of growth or resolution.

This is precisely the characterisation of social relations with which Foucault worked. His postulation of a framework in which dialectical thought is no longer possible conjured a totality so all-encompassing that it must properly be seen as a web of fragments without necessity, or origin. Social relations can no longer be defined in terms of a cohesive whole, and the analysis of the totality must be superseded by the study of an enormously complex series of specific power relations which manifest themselves throughout the social body. Foucault engaged with the overriding question thrown up by the failure of the May events: where, how, and to what ends power is exercised. To him, the events showed that the areas in which power needed to be contested were not confined to the economy, but extended to all social institutions and, beyond this, to cultural assumptions, structures of knowledge, systems of ideas, and forms of communication. The exercise of power is less homogeneous than a theory of spectacular society suggests: power is not reducible to a single cause or origin, but operates differently in each of a plethora of areas of life and discourse freed from any determining principle. Relations of power arise at every conceivable moment: at work, in bed, in the classroom, and the prison, individuals are continually exercising and responding to the exercise of power. There is therefore no essential dualism between the 'haves and have-nots' of power; power does not issue from a single source or move in one direction, and cannot be opposed *en bloc* but only in the particular areas of social and discursive life in which it manifests itself. Power is 'quite different from and more complicated, dense and pervasive than a set of laws or a state apparatus',[14] and it is not possible to identify a single dualism between those who exercise power and those who resist it.

Neither is it possible to consider power merely in the negative terms of domination and oppression: it is a positive force at work in a world which it actually produces. This enabling role is made possible through its exercise as knowledge, which does not arise in some independent realm from which it is appropriated and used by mechanisms of power, but engages in a 'perpetual articulation' with power to produce the world to which we wrongly assume our discourses refer. Brought into the public realm of language and meaning, all aspects of life are constituted by the discourse in which they are known, so that even the most definite of foundations is constructed and produced. Reason, society, history, and all conceptions of reality receive their existence within the discourses which seem to represent them; meaningless and lifeless without their representation, we cannot say that they have a reality which is later subject to the manipulations and distortions of power. The sovereign subject presupposed throughout western philosophy is itself a product of discourses which emphasise the negative, repressive, and dominating aspects of power: it has long been assumed that power exerts a negative and forbidding force which constrains and prevents the free functioning of some real or natural subjectivity. Power does not merely dominate individuals, who 'circulate between its threads; they are always in a position of simultaneously undergoing and exercising power. They are not only its inert or consenting targets; they are also the element of its articulation.'[15] The subject actually arises out of the networks of power and knowledge in which it lives, and all our conceptions of subjectivity are themselves the products of the discontinuous development of power relations in a variety of areas of social life.

For both Foucault and Lyotard, there is no 'self' to achieve knowledge and realisation in the world, and no subjectivity capable of acting on the world in order to transform it. Neither is there a world 'out there' to be transformed: history is a series of discontinuous struggles in a plethora of areas of social life, and society is merely the general effect of these particulars. Everything arising within the networks of power and knowledge which constitute the social makes some contribution to it: voices of dissent and assent, acts of defiance and complicity, theories of revolution and stability are equally the products of the relations of power to which they bring apparently contradictory perspectives. Political opposition is integrated within the structures it thinks it is opposing because the forms, mediations, and discourses in which it operates constitute the very relations of power it imagines itself capable of negating. Struggles are never pitted against power; they demand it, whether this demand is expressed in terms of calls for liberation, higher wages, justice, or rights. And it is in the course of this struggle for power that the world comes into being. Demands for sexual liberation, for example, bring sex and sexuality into the discursive realm and the networks of relations of power and knowledge which actually produce them. The very idea of sex as a reality later subject to the repression of taboos and silences is itself a discursive construction. This is not to say, of course, that sexual activity did not exist before it was spoken of. But when one comes to delve beneath layer upon layer of representations of sexuality for the 'real thing', Foucault's point that sex is actually produced and reproduced in the huge range of discourses in which it is shown seems far from absurd.

The same difficulty haunts the search for the truth we imagine is concealed under layers of ideology. For Foucault, the trouble with 'analyses which prioritise ideology is that there is always presupposed a human subject on the lines of the model provided by classical philosophy, endowed with a consciousness which power is then thought to seize on'.[16] Truth, like the promise of pleasure or revolution, is discursively produced as well. Indeed, all the meanings and realities to which we refer, and those we use as foundations for our criticisms of existing social relations, are constructed in the process of their representation, to the extent that representation itself becomes a meaningless term. For if reality only exists in discourse, there is nothing to be represented, and nothing, beyond an endless series of other discursive constructions, to which our discourses refer. We live within networks of messages, signs, information, and knowledge which produce our experience of ourselves, society, and all that we consider real. And, as power produces its subjects, so it gives birth to antagonists and the forms of resistance with which it is irreducibly implicated. Resistance is always already constituted by the relations of power it opposes; its means and ends of struggle are defined by the nature of the particular exercise of power it opposes, and all resistance inevitably arises in an internal relation to its object.

For the revolutionary, the implications of this position are profound and disturbing. If power is really exercised in discourse, so that the chimerical realities of experience, subjectivity, and the social world are only ever produced and never represented, it is not possible to say or do anything which undermines power itself. By virtue of its very articulation, dissent is always already recuperated, and all antagonisms and contradictions merely occur within the inescapable networks of power which constitute reality, society, and individuality. The paradigms of alienation, domination, and repression on which the revolutionary project has always relied all presuppose some lack, absence, or constraint, in which power is conceived as a negative force which merely inhibits that which already exists. But Foucault's conception of power as a productive and enabling force challenged all notions of the negativity required by dialectical thought. There can be no perspective from which power can be opposed, since power produces all perspectives, including that of its own resistance.

But although resistance is produced by power and cannot be seen as the authentic expression of some prediscursive subjective desire, the Nietzschean idea that there is a perpetual contest between reason and the raw events it circumscribes provides a perspective from which new forms of resistance are possible. 'To say that one can never be "outside" power does not mean that one is trapped and condemned to defeat no matter what,'[17] and although forms of resistance derive their very 'means of struggle' from the power relations with which they engage, it remains true that the 'analysis of power-mechanisms has no built-in tendency to show power as being at once synonymous and always victorious'.[18] The immediate political task must be to establish 'the positions occupied and modes of actions used by each of the forces at work, the possibilities of resistance and counter-attack on either side'.[19] Like Lyotard, therefore, Foucault argued that the tendency to universalisation inherent in dialectical thought must be abandoned to allow for the development of forms of knowledge which minimise and interrupt prevailing codes of domination. He advocated forms of counter-discourse, in which localised and specific forms of knowledge are pitted against the totalising theories which would claim them. Championing the subjugated and particular knowledges of those on the receiving end of power, he gave a voice to the hidden and excluded experiences which are the ground of the resistance which these configurations of power produce. This project surfaced throughout Foucault's work. One of the neglected consequences of the 1968 events was the imprisonment of more than a hundred activists, many of whom were involved in the widespread prison riots in France during 1971, after which Foucault helped to establish the *Groupe d'Information sur les Prisons*, a network developed to enable prisoners to speak counter-discursively of their own experiences from 'the underside of power'. It was out of this experience that *Discipline and Punish*, one of Foucault's most powerful studies of the development of the histories of the exercise of power, emerged.[20]

As the situationists had hunted among the remnants of specialised theories and particular practices for components of a new and totalising world view, Foucault's own use of moments of totalising theories reflected his idea that theories should be treated as tool-kits, from which conceptualisations and frameworks useful to particular struggles can be taken. And, far from developing theories which legislate for the people, he argued that intellectuals should likewise concern themselves with specific issues and particular struggles without seeing them as means to the end of a universal framework or examples of a theoretical stance. In 1968, he wrote, the 'intellectual discovered that the masses no longer need him to gain knowledge':

they *know* perfectly well, without illusion; they know far better than he and they are certainly capable of expressing themselves. But there exists a system of power which blocks, prohibits, and invalidates this discourse . . . . Intellectuals are themselves agents of this system of power.[21]

Shunning the traditionally public life of the Parisian intellectual, and resisting the imperative to develop a clear theoretical or political stance, Foucault's unorthodox forms of detailed genea-logical enquiry and localised research problematised both his life and work. 'I think I have in fact been situated in most of the squares on the political checkerboard, one after another and sometimes simultaneously,' he wrote, listing the roles of 'anar-chist, leftist, ostentatious or disguised Marxist, nihilist, explicit or secret anti-Marxist, technocrat in the service of Gaullism, new liberal' as examples of the roles foisted upon him. 'None of these descriptions is important by itself,' he declared; but 'taken together, on the other hand, they mean something. And I must admit that I rather like what they mean.'[22]

This gleeful sidestepping of convention and categorisation reappears throughout poststructuralist writing as a vital form of resistance to the ordered codes of discourse. Transcribing the situationist *dérive* from the city street to the domain of theory, Lyotard used the aimless playfulness of locomotion without a goal to describe the sort of drifting thought with which dialectical criticism can be abandoned, disallowing the arrogance of the theorist who judges, reflects, and represents the world, and pro-viding the only honest form of intellectual practice.

> Where do you criticise from? Don't you see that criticising is still knowing, knowing better? That the critical relation still falls within the sphere of knowledge, of realisation and thus of the assumption of power? Critique must be drifted out of. Better still: *Drifting is in itself the end of all critique.*[23]

Lyotard's drifting thought upsets and interrupts the discourse which uncritically assumes that it can represent the real, and it was for this reason that he regarded the tactics of the cultural avant-garde more useful than those of conventional politics: '"avant-garde" research, etc., actually make up the only type of activity that is effective, this because it is functionally . . . located outside the system; and, by definition, its function is to deconstruct everything that belongs to order'.[24] Since dialectical criticism can never challenge the rules of the game in which it is engaged, a drifting sort of thought must be able to engage with a theory, moving across and exposing its hidden intensities without being dragged into the need to develop a better and more thorough version.

These ideas were energetically pursued by Deleuze and Guattari. Introducing a multiplicity of desires which traverse and threaten both the organisation of society and its opposition, Deleuze and Guattari abandoned all vestiges of progress and surrendered to a world populated only by an ever more anarchic chaos of desires. Psychoanalysis, dominated in the aftermath of the May events by Jacques Lacan, had been crucial to the articulation of the undercurrents of intensity so important to the development of ideas about the deconstruction of the subject, and Deleuze and Guattari pushed the Lacanian subject, a fundamentally decentred and fragmented construct inevitably alienated by its positioning in the symbolic realm of discursive structures and relations, to an unprecedented extreme.[25] Promoting a positive, affirmative conception of desire which abandoned all the dark, repressive, and negative connotations it had previously borne, Deleuze and Guattari shamelessly pitted Lacan's imaginary, or pre-symbolic, realm against the orders of discursive structures and normalising. Oedipal, relations. An endless flux of desires takes the conceptual place of Foucault's relations of power, displacing the subject as the fundamental building block of the world and bringing a whiff of impassioned materialism to the otherwise somewhat rarefied post-structuralist air.

Deleuze and Guattari's 'micro-politics of desire' miniaturised society, discourse, subjectivity, and the body into an anarchic series of desiring machines which both produce and undermine the identities on which traditional political philosophy has relied. The fluxes of energy which constitute the macropolitical world are channelled and ordered by particular configurations of social codes, and in every form of social organisation the processes by which desires are coded and colonised are continually subverted by their own internal movements of deterritorialisation. Codes are established and scrambled in an endless play of stability and destabilisation produced by the desires which traverse all social relations, and Deleuze and Guattari presented a world of continual play between order and its subversion, in which any form of organisation is inevitably subject to the interruption of its own components. This is, however, a process to which the development of capitalist society brings an unprecedented acceleration. While new territories are mapped and desires are colonised by giant webs of production and consumption, the spiralling proliferation of commodities simultaneously decodifies earlier forms of regulation and allows the radical egalitarianism of their free circulation to flourish. Thus

> the very conditions that make the State or the World war machine possible, in other words, constant capital (resources and equipment) and human variable capital, continually re-create unexpected possibilities for counterattack, unforeseen initiatives determining revolutionary, popular, minority, mutant machines.[26]

On one level, Deleuze and Guattari presented a sophisticated reworking of the idea that capitalism produces its own grave-diggers. It is a system which 'continually seeks to avoid reaching its limit while simultaneously tending toward that limit';[27] a system which, in spite of all its systems of repression and dissuasion, and the wisdom it gains from each previous onslaught, cannot resist the lines of flight it produces and remains haunted by the question 'where will the revolution come from, and in what form'?[28] But since both codes and their subversion are engaged in a perpetual contest, one of Deleuze and Guattari's central concerns was with the ways in which gravediggers produce their own social order as well. If desire is to be conceived as a positive force, attention must be paid to the ways in which all the people, emotions, and experiences previously conceived in negative terms of repression, alienation, and domination, are in some sense always in a positive collusion with both the desires and repressions which shape them. Questions of where the revolution comes from must be joined by those which reveal the means by which revolutions are betrayed, an interrogation which might suggest that remnants of counter-revolutionary desire are invested in even the most radical of gestures.

For Guattari, the immediate political consequences of this perspective were that revolutionary struggles must 'break away from the dominant models, and especially from that model of models, capital (which consists in reducing the multiplicities of desire to a single undifferentiated flux – of workers, consumers, etc.)', rejecting the 'black-and-white simplification of the class struggle' and accepting 'the plurality of desiring commitments as possible links between people in revolt and the revolution'.[29] Revolutionary struggles become 'molecular'; configurations of desires rather than solidarities between people or social groups. Impossible to locate 'on the dominant coordinates, they produce their own axes of reference, establish underground, transversal connections among themselves, and thus undermine older relationships to production, society, the family, the body, sex, the cosmos'.[30] Molecular struggles assert the multiplicity of those desires, social groups, interests, and forms of expression which have no place in existing society; they constitute a challenge to the entire system of codes made by all those whose experiences are excluded by it. In the 1970s Guattari wrote:

> For the last decade, 'battle lines' widely different from those which previously characterised the traditional workers' movement have not ceased to multiply (immigrant workers, skilled workers unhappy with the kinds of work imposed on them, the unemployed, over-exploited women, ecologists, nationalists, mental patients, homosexuals, the elderly, the young etc.) . . . will their objectives become just another 'demand' acceptable to the system? Or will vectors of molecular revolution begin to proliferate behind them?[31]

This search for forms of political organisation and social struggle which would allow the proliferation of autonomous struggles runs throughout Foucault's philosophy of power and the desiring politics advocated by Lyotard, Deleuze, and Guattari. In 1973, Deleuze declared that 'the problem for revolutionaries today is to unite within the purpose of the particular struggle without falling into the despotic and bureaucratic organisations of the party or state apparatus',[32] a trap to which he opposed the freedom of a 'deterritorialised' thought of the sort developed by Nietzsche, whose discourse is 'above all nomadic; its statements can be conceived as the products of a mobile war machine and not the utterances of a rational administrative machinery, whose philosophers would be bureaucrats of pure reason'.[33] Nietzsche, wrote Deleuze, 'made thought into a machine of war – a battering ram – into a nomadic force'.[34]

Conceived by Deleuze and Guattari in terms of a refusal of the Oedipal family unit and, by extension, the hierarchies of state and discourse, this idea of the nomadic subversion of well-mapped territories of thought, code, and convention has always been characteristic of artistic and revolutionary currents in which the situationists were placed. The dadaist Francis Picabia had declared, 'One must be a nomad, pass through ideas as one passes through countries and cities,'[35] and the dadaist disregard for the boundaries of discourse, media, morality, cultural property, and intellectual originality reappears in surrealist transgressions of cultural convention and many later moments in which desires are pitted against the orders of state and society. The nomad bears a disruptive power and raises the spectre of individuals, social groups, and forms of action which derive their strength from their very elusiveness. The outlaw, the mad, and the disenfranchised; the unemployed, the dispossessed, and all those whose desires and behaviour are refused by the conventions of the established order, begin to constitute an unidentifiable 'class', threatening not because of the place it assumes within in capitalist society, but by virtue of its refusal of any place. This development of groups unable and unwilling to play the game of conventional protest and criticism has found an overt expression in the British free festival movement, where the idea of the nomad has been taken literally. The 'peace convoy' of the early 1980s has developed into a band of travellers whose demands for the right to congregate on ancient sites and common land have excited extraordinary levels of police repression. The travellers' contempt for property rights, their autonomous forms of organisation and exchange, and their imaginative refusals of work, acceptable social identities, moral and legislative codes, constitute a threat which is magnified by their refusal of all tidy and conventional forms of social criticism. Like Deleuze's nomads, they challenge the very existence of the codes through which events and desires are channelled and formed.

It is this ability to sidestep categorisation and remain a force unidentifiable within the existing structures of knowledge and power that gives the nomadic strategy its strength. And it is not merely in the lives of those who actually take to the roads that this evasive power is displayed. The defiance of identity was also cultivated to great effect by the Angry Brigade, an unorthodox terrorist group which engaged in a series of bombings in Britain during the late 1960s and early 1970s. Influenced by the tactics and propaganda of the situationists, the Angry Brigade made unequivocal demands for the immediate realisation of the radical, desiring subject within and against capitalist society. They promoted a sense of anonymity and ubiquity which earned them an inflated notoriety and sidestepped all attempts at easy definition, and although the majority of the attacks for which they claimed responsibility only involved the destruction of property, this was a strategy which also ended with long prison sentences. Their targets were symbolic and usually had some specific relevance: the Minister of Employment, Robert Carr, had his house bombed during strikes and demonstrations against the Industrial Relations Bill; Bryant's home was bombed during the builders' strike in 1971; and the Miss World contest was attacked in 1970. Many of the Brigade's communiqués were published in national newspapers, and all explained the reasons behind the group's actions and advocated the destruction of the mechanisms of control.

'To believe that OUR struggle could be restricted to the channels provided to us by the pigs, WAS THE GREATEST CON. And we started hitting them',[36] stated one proclamation, and a communiqué coinciding with the bombing of the Biba boutique in Chelsea read:

> 'If you're not busy being born you're busy buying' . . .
> The future is ours.
> Life is so boring there is nothing to do except spend all our wages on the latest skirt or shirt.
> Brothers and Sisters, what are your real desires?
> Sit in the drugstore, look distant, empty, bored, drinking some tasteless coffee? Or perhaps BLOW IT UP OR BURN IT DOWN.[37]

Against all external controls and structures, the Brigade put its faith in the spontaneity of the 'autonomous working class' and propagandised in favour of immediate action and the realisation of desires. Its ability to use the media and the efficiency of its attacks ensured it a serious reception. An editorial in the *Evening Standard* spoke of the 'red badge of revolution creeping across Britain', and declared: 'These guerrillas are the violent activists of a revolution comprising workers, students, teachers, trade unionists, homosexuals, unemployed and women striving for liberation. They are all angry.'[38] For its own part, the Brigade cultivated an image of a large, diffuse, and unidentifiable collection of dissenters: 'The AB is the man or woman sitting next to you. They have guns in their pockets and anger in their minds.'[39]

Now we are too many to know each other.

Yet we recognise all those charged with crimes against property as our brothers and sisters. The Stoke-Newington 6, the political prisoners in Northern Ireland are all prisoners of the class war. We are not in a position to say whether any one person is or isn't a member of the Brigade. All we say is: the Brigade is everywhere . . .

Let ten men and women meet who are resolved on the lightning of violence rather than the long agony of survival; from this moment despair ends and tactics begin. [40]

This last statement, taken from *The Revolution of Everyday Life*, was provocative in the extreme. The idea of a ubiquitous but unidentifiable threat was effective in that it allowed anyone to consider themselves 'members' and gave the impression to the authorities that the capture of a few individuals would do little to undermine the Brigade: 'THEY COULD NOT JAIL US FOR WE DID NOT EXIST',[41] they boasted. Reminiscent of the situationist insistence that 'our ideas are in everyone's minds', the Angry Brigade's tactics were cleverly designed to avoid the spectacularisation and hierarchy characteristic of more orthodox terrorist activities.

Although the Angry Brigade's greatest strength lay in the elusive air they cultivated, the identification of sites of power and resistance problematised by poststructuralist philosophies was further confused by other forms of terrorism. In Italy, the activity of the Red Brigades put the possibility of a clear distinction between the established order and its detractors into unprecedented disarray. Indeed, the Red Brigades have since become the reference point for debates developed by both Debord and Baudrillard on the whole issue of who it is that exercises power. The situationists' hostility to terrorist activity ('From the strategical perspective of social struggles it must first of all be said that one should never *play with terrorism*'[42]) was later developed by Gianfranco Sanguinetti, an Italian situationist much admired by Debord, with whom he wrote much of *The Veritable Split in the International* in 1972. Sanguinetti had caused a major scandal in Italy when he published his *True Report on the Last Chance to Save Capitalism in Italy* under the pseudonym Censor. When this text appeared in 1975, it was first circulated among government ministers and then figures of the literary establishment; this tactic convinced everybody that the text was the work of a government official since, as the newspaper *L'Europeo* commented, 'the things he knew were too important and too precise' to be the work of an outsider.[43] The revelation that it was the work of a young situationist caused a major scandal. Criticising the institutionalised Italian Communist Party as an agent of hierarchical control, the text also alleged that the Italian secret services were behind the huge Piazza Fontana bombing in 1969 for which several anarchists had been imprisoned (and one killed in the course of police enquiries). It is now widely accepted that state intelligence organisations and a variety of right-wing groups have infiltrated some left-wing and libertarian terrorist outfits, established others, and carried out a number of activities later blamed on anarchists and the Left.

Sanguinetti's 1978 text, *On Terrorism and the State*, developed these ideas to argue that the wave of Red Brigade activity in Italy was itself manipulated by the secret services. Pointing to the ease with which existing terrorist cells could be infiltrated or initiated by the secret services who would then be able to recruit genuine activists, Sanguinetti indicated the efficacy of such tactics for the entrenchment of the state. The spectacle of terrorism provides a socially cohesive common enemy, legitimises needs for vigilance, security, and new forms of police repression, and encourages the opinion that even the faultiest of democracies is superior to the reign of terror. And although the Brigades had first emerged out of the widespread industrial unrest of the early 1970s, they became increasingly dogmatic, hierarchical, and separated from these roots. From this perspective, the Red Brigades, or at least those activities carried out in their name, acted as a brake on the ongoing 'strategy of refusal'[44] which had characterised Italian political and industrial life since the 1950s. State violence of an extraordinary degree was indeed unleashed by the wave of terrorist activity in Italy during the period which culminated in the kidnapping and murder of Aldo Moro in 1978, and the awareness that some, if not all, of the terrorist activity was being deliberately propagated merely contributed to the sense of disorder and paranoia on the Left and the widespread panic in Italian society as a whole. The 1975 *Legge Reale* legalised the shoot-to-kill policy adopted towards terrorist suspects and resulted in the deaths of 150 people between May 1975 and December 1976; according to one commentator, there were some 3,500 'political prisoners' in Italy in 1980,[45] and the wave of terrorism produced a crackdown on all dissenting forces.

But the authorities were also reacting to a rather more ambiguous wave of protest which culminated in the huge demonstrations and widespread university and factory occupations in Rome and Milan in March 1977. The diffuse autonomists who gathered in the 'Movement of '77' enjoyed the active support of Deleuze, Guattari, and a number of other intellectuals appalled at the Italian state's repressive behaviour, epitomised by the imprisonment of sociology professor Toni Negri, tried as a 'leader' of the terrorists on the grounds that his published criticisms of the Red Brigades were a cover for his involvement. And in many respects, the politics of evasion and deterritorialisation implicit in the philosophies of desire found an immediate realisation and renewed developments in the Italian events of the late 1970s. The autonomists abandoned orthodox political and terrorist activity in favour of the tactics of 'cultural transformation, mass creativity, and refusal of work',[46] and although they displayed some affectionate admiration for the Brigades, they nevertheless refused the centralism of the terrorist cells in favour of a desiring politics and the guerrilla warfare of groups like those dubbed the Metropolitan Indians. It was the media which gave these rebels their name, largely because the only identifiable features of their paradoxical statements and disruptive actions were that they painted their faces and subverted city life. The Metropolitan Indians, wrote one sympathiser, 'habitually break into shops and appropriate useless goods . . . . They also frequently appear at the most elegant movie theatres in groups of about thirty people, naturally after visiting the most expensive restaurants where they obviously did not pay.'[47] 'Autonomous price setting' and the other 'guerrilla' tactics in which the Indians indulged posed a threat to all the conventions of social practice.

> Whoever paints his face taking the marks as an arbitrary characterisation of a future people; whoever appropriates in an exhaustive way all possible terms and treats language as a science of imaginary solutions; whoever refuses to explain himself and, despite this omission, doesn't stop robbing, nor in fact engages in any collective practice – such a person is the agent of subversions which have great significance.[48]

The Metropolitan Indians were secret agents playing in disguise, defining themselves as nomads and refusing to set identifiable goals. Their *détournements* of language, the commodity, and the city placed them in a firm relation to Dada, surrealism, and the whole tradition of satirical violence which the situationists had brought into the political realm. 'We hypothesise, then, the coming of an era which replaces the bearers of truth (divided unions, political groups with their identifying signs and their banners) with intelligence and shrewdness,' they wrote. 'This era will be based on the social possibilities of falsehood, on the technological possibilities resulting from the destruction of rules, on the free exchange of products, simulation, the game, the nonsense argument, the dream, music.'[49]

In Italy, the imaginative and subversive use of technology envisaged by situationist calls for an economy of desires was epitomised by the use of free radio stations. Radio Alice ran from February 1976 to March 1977, and was later described as a 'symbol of this period, of that unforgettable year of experimentation and accumulation of intellectual, organisation, political, and creative energies'.[50] In 1968, Radio Luxembourg had played a vital role in its running commentaries of the riots in Paris, and in Italy, Radio Alice used 'taped "subversive" cultural infills combining music, poetry and comment that were used as sandwiching between phone-in programmes . . . the radio station was used to inform insurgents of police manoeuvres'.[51] Free radio came to epitomise 'the design, the dream of the artistic avant-garde – to bridge the separation between artistic communication and revolutionary transformation or subversive practice'.[52] In the immediacy of the pirate broadcast, the autonomists saw the possibility of an irrecuperable form of communication. 'Alice looks around, plays, jumps, wastes time in the midst of papers illuminated by the sun, runs ahead, settles down elsewhere.'[53] A broadcast arises and disappears in one movement, so that 'desire is given a voice',[54] and the awareness that 'everything functions in the order of discourse'[55] no longer poses a regretful problem but opens the doors to a wider and subversive conception of this 'everything'. For Guattari, Radio Alice and the Movement of '77 showed that the 'economic, political and moral order of the twentieth century is breaking up everywhere, and the people in power hardly know which way to turn'.

The enemy is intangible – you hear a twig snap beside you, and you find your son, your wife, even your own desire is betraying your mission as guardian of the established order. The police got rid of Radio Alice . . . but its work of revolutionary de-territorialisation still goes on unabated, even affecting the nerves of the opposition.[56]

Radio Alice's optimistic appropriation and *détournement* of media confirmed the situationist insistence that new possibilities for the assertion of the imagination, spontaneity, and desires of subjectivity continually arise. 'The practice of happiness is subversive when it becomes collective,' declared Radio Alice. 'To conspire means to breathe together.'[57] The potential for subversion, sabotage, and *détournement* grows and changes with the means by which power is exercised and consolidated: as forms of communication and the dissemination of knowledge, culture, and information assume a greater sophistication and significance to the maintenance of the established capitalist order, so, in principle, at least, the possibilities of their appropriation increase.

Détournement does, nevertheless, depend on the possibility of some strategic sense of its purpose and an analysis of the nature of the social relations it contests. The exposure and appropriation of the exercise of power requires an understanding of where and how power functions: workplace sabotage and industrial action presuppose the importance of the economy; pirate radio and avant-garde action that of culture and media. The situationists' conviction that commodity relations can assert themselves anywhere led to an open-ended search for these loci of power and, for the SI, they were manifest in language, sexuality, art, the city, the factory, the university, and every aspect of individual, social, and discursive life. But these were always conceived as areas of commodification, producing and reproducing the alienated relations on which the economic system is based. It was the situationists' identification of an antagonism at the heart of society – a central principle of dualism, separation, mediation, or alienation – which enabled them to posit an unproblematised unified social experience as the goal of revolutionary practice.

The separation between the classes, power and pleasure, or the spectacle and the real on which the situationists relied was not conceived as a static division. Although it might be possible to distinguish between the progressive forces of contestation and the spectacle's forces of commodification at any given time, the battle-lines are by no means permanent. The recuperated can be reclaimed, and the subverted can be recuperated; that which bears the appearance of contestation might support the status quo, and the appearance of conformity may well conceal the reality of subversion. Nevertheless, in the Italy of the 1970s, the web of contradiction and ambiguity surrounding the roles of the Red Brigades and the Italian authorities was indicative of the growing difficulties of distinguishing between reality and its simulation: the questions of who is fighting whom, and which 'side' is served by any given action, becomes open-ended in a situation in which capitalist society loses the simplicity of its economic structure. Struggles over legitimacy and meaning begin to take place in the realms of the mass media and the popular imagination as well as in the courts and on the streets; the black and white distinctions between the haves and the have-nots of power collapse as domination is increasingly exercised in a multiplicity of areas of social and discursive life. The situationists' own identification of a multiplicity of relations of power itself begins to undermine the existence of a central contradiction at the heart of capitalist society.

The Italian events were refusals of a system of domination which could no longer be simply identified or cleanly opposed; a perspective from which the dream of unity and the resolution of contradictions were themselves denials of difference and dissent. For the Italians, as for Foucault, the development of social relations in which the exercise of power is increasingly dispersed and covert necessitated new forms of resistance and dissent which could no longer operate on the assumption that society was organised solely around the reproduction of commodity relations. Paul Virilio insisted that the praxis of the Movement of '77 'cannot be understood through an identity principle founded on categories of commodity',[58] and another observed: 'we stand before the paradox of a domination which is exercised without any government, a controlling of the system without a governing of the system'.[59] Guattari also insisted that 'capitalism does not aim at a systematic and generalised repression of the workers, women, youth, minorities'.[60] Far more flexible and varied than the scenario of simple domination suggests, the development of capitalism requires its endless response to the multiplicity of demands made upon it. 'Under these conditions, a semi-tolerated, semi-encouraged, and co-opted protest could well be an intrinsic part of the system.'[61] Guattari nevertheless defended those forms of protest which recognise this flexibility and threaten 'the essential relationships on which this system is based (the respect for work, for hierarchy, for State power, for the religion of consumption ...)'.[62] And although his calls for an awareness of the recuperative and co-optive powers of modern capitalism were qualified by an insistence that it is 'impossible to trace a clear and definitive boundary between the recuperable marginals and other types of marginals', Guattari's recognition that the 'frontiers actually remain blurred and unstable'[63] did not stop him hoping that the new networks of resistance made possible by the fine-tuned flexibility of contemporary social relations would converge in unforeseen forms of revolutionary struggle. There was still a sense that the struggles of particular desires and intensities might one day coalesce in a revolutionary movement.

But the reluctance to impose meanings on events, desires, and the raw immediacy of experience produced a hostility to all attempts to see desire and contestation as anything other than ends in themselves, with the consequence that the sole purpose of political agitation was merely to unleash desires, particularities, and intensities without entrapping them in some other purpose or project. And while the politics of desire which emerged in the Italian events made contestation a permanent feature of life, this very permanence carried the danger that all sense of reason and purpose is removed from political struggle. For Toni Negri, only the eternal return of forces of disorder could constitute the revolutionary milieu.

> There is only one way that I can read the history of capital – as the history of a continuity of operations of self-re-establishment that capital and its State have to set in motion in order to counter the continuous breakdown process, the permanent provocation-towards-separation that the real movement brings about.[64]

The situationist conviction that even the most sophisticated forms of capitalism produce their own subversions was translated into a vocabulary of simple reaction and permanent contestation: if the politics of desire allowed for new and exuberant forms of revolt, the moment of revolution became endlessly deferred.

The hopelessness of this permanent provocation left the radical politics of desire vulnerable to a theoretical crisis of its own. The wild and dissolute forces it invoked were seen to embody new foundations and essences to which the orders of capitalist relations could be opposed, rekindling the danger of a new essentialism in which resistance and contestation become the mere effects of a system already incapable of containing itself. And eventually, just as the situationist development of economic contradiction had been undermined by poststructuralist support for a multiplicity of sites of power, desire, and pure intensity, these invocations of flowing differences and instabilities were themselves undermined by claims that they too merely sustained the attempt to establish contradictions and prediscursive meanings. Baudrillard's later work is one of the main sites of this final critique, although the passage to the full-blown postmodernism for which he is best known took him through a line of thought parallel to post-structuralism which also allowed him to defend some underlying point of reference from which capitalist society might be under-mined.

After his initial critiques of the consumer society, Baudrillard soon abandoned the Marxist perspective of his early works to argue that modern society was no longer vulnerable to a critique based solely on the production and consumption of commodities. In a system of overproduction and accelerated circulation, objects begin to function as pure signs, the components of a hyperreal world in which all sense of real value and meaning is lost. Reality exists only in its reproduced and represented forms; it is 'always already' a simulation of its non-existent self, and it is no longer possible to catch a glimpse of original realities behind the veils of copies and appearance. By itself, the observation that we are surrounded by copies does not dispense with the real; it can even encourage the search for a 'real' real beyond the 'apparent' real, as it had for the situationists. But Baudrillard wanted to show the impossibility of the existence of such an underlying reality, insisting that the real that is apparently represented has itself disappeared in the midst of accelerating processes of simulation and reproduction, requiring us to speak of the copy without the original; appearance without a corresponding reality. The signs and images with which we are surrounded merely sustain our belief that something is being represented. But signs circumscribe the world. They represent no other, or better, or more real reality to which we can appeal: things are simply as they appear to be.

This position ultimately led Baudrillard to a complete rejection of any possibility of criticism, negativity, or political contestation: the hyperreal world is seamless and complete, allowing no contradiction or challenge to emerge. Yet even in the later works in which this position is taken to an extreme, some sense of antagonistic strategy emerges, and in *The Mirror of Production* and a number of other essays written in the 1970s, this discontinuity was given a relatively solid foundation in the notion of symbolic exchange. Baudrillard presented symbolic exchange as the ground of disruption and resistance, arguing that in the acts of giving, sacrifice, waste, and destruction, there is a form of exchange which completely ignores the imperative to value assumed by both capitalist relations and Marxist theory. This was a position which owed something to George Bataille and Marcel Mauss, both of whom had invoked notions of gift and sacrifice, with Bataille giving the sun as an example of an entity which gives light and warmth to the world without asking for anything in return, and Mauss remembering that sacrifice plays an important part in even such a unilateral giving. Baudrillard's conception of this sacrificial 'solar economy' invoked a primitive and pre-capitalist form of exchange which judges objects and experiences solely in terms of their symbolic value: the value assigned by those who give and receive them. It also resonated with Vaneigem's argument that the gift represents a realm of uncommodified activity which presaged post-capitalist forms of exchange, and the LI's journal *Potlatch* had taken its name from American Indian systems of exchange.

For Baudrillard, symbolic exchange opened up new possibilities of resistance to an ethic of productivism embraced by both revolutionary theory and capitalist society. Marxism, he argued, merely wants to achieve better relations of production and happier workers able to consume more useful and authentic goods. Its claims are purely quantitative, demanding not a revolution against political economy, but a transformation which nevertheless remains within the realm of labour, production, and consumption. Marxist theory reflects capitalism but does not challenge its values and foundations; it is the 'mirror of production' which inverts existing relations but offers them no fundamental challenge. But blatant waste, gratuitous consumption, extravagant gifts, and orgies of destruction offend everything sacred to the ethic of production and its mirror. The insistence that everything – objects, experiences, and people alike – has a value, whether it is that imputed by exchange or use, is central to both political economy and its critique; neither can tolerate its transgression. But symbolic values count for nothing; they generate no wealth and indicate no use, and it is precisely in this symbolic realm that the possibilities of a subversive ridicule of political economy emerge. It was possible for neither Left nor Right to understand why the Metropolitan Indians stole worthless goods, just as mindless violence and meaningless graffiti are gestures incomprehensible to the world of use and exchange. Free gifts can have a shocking and disorienting effect: in a post office queue, a man hands round a punnet of strawberries; waiting in a bank, a woman takes it into her head solemnly to distribute the leaflets on display. Both terrify the customers. Everyone takes the leaflets, but very few strawberries are eaten.

For Baudrillard, symbolic exchange was a point of essential opposition to a system of social relations which privileges value, meaning, and worth. Anything which refuses these attributes is subversive of a society which insists that meaning is invested in the multitude of signs, images, commodities, and messages which surround us. It follows that any real subversion or interruption of the values of existing social relations must itself proclaim its lack of value and worth; its refusal to engage with the very processes by which meaning is produced. Baudrillard clearly intended this refusal of meaning to be a refusal of orthodox meaning: an insistence that validity and worth must be self-generated and autonomously calculated, just as Dada's defiant attitude to all attempts to define it was an insistence that it would determine its own meaning rather than an absolute rejection of meaning *per se.* But Baudrillard's position soon collapsed into a complete nihilism with the claim that it is meaning itself which is the guilty party of social relations to which only the complete absence of meaning can be truly opposed. From this perspective, the dadaist who had sought disorder and absurdity as a means of exposing the horrors of the First World War was merely playing at nihilism, using the absence of meaning as a tactic in the struggle for better meanings and real value. Increasingly equating subversion with meaninglessness, Baudrillard finally argued that any form of activity which participates in the production of meanings, values, social relations, or revolutionary perspectives was doomed by its very participation to the dead end of reformism.

Like many of his contemporaries, the Baudrillard of the 1970s was convinced that the great fault of Marxism was that it reduced pleasure, spontaneity, and all the energies which make the revolution to mere components of a grand revolutionary plan. The really powerful events are those which cannot be transcribed into purposeful frameworks, those which are essentially meaningless, and refuse to be represented.

> The real revolutionary media during May were the walls and their speech, the silk-screen posters and the hand-painted notices, the street where speech began and was exchanged – everything that was an *immediate* inscription, given and returned, spoken and answered, mobile in the same space and time, reciprocal and antagonistic. [. . .] Institutionalized by reproduction, reduced to a spectacle, this speech is expiring.[65]

Pursuing situationist demands for forms of expression which sidestep the recuperation of representation within the spectacle, Baudrillard's nostalgia for some authentic immediacy and real communication later carried him to an extreme at which he was able to declare that May 1968 was 'a kind of pure object or event', completely irreducible to the representations and simulations of discourse. 'May '68 is an event which it has been impossible to rationalize or exploit, from which nothing has been concluded. It remains indecipherable. It was the forerunner of nothing.'[66] But Baudrillard's search for the irrecuperable had not yet reached the point at which authentic representation was inconceivable, and, in *The Mirror of Production*, he developed these claims for the immediacy of pure communication in a bitter attack on the stifling effects of Marxist theory. Invoking the spirit of Dada and surrealism, he wrote:

> The cursed poet, non-official art, and utopian writings in general, by giving a current and immediate content to man's liberation, should be the very speech of communism, its direct prophecy. They are only its bad conscience precisely because in them something of man is *immediately* realized, because they object without pity to the 'political' dimension of the revolution, which is merely the dimension of its final postponement.[67]

With claims reminiscent of Debord's attack on the collapse of the Marxist tradition into a 'graveyard of good intentions', Baudrillard argued that Marxist theory operates as a brake on the symbolic value and radical immediacy of revolutionary forces.

In the name of an always renewed future – future of history, future of the dictatorship of the proletariat, future of capitalism and future of socialism – it demands more and more the sacrifice of the immediate and permanent revolution. Ascetic in relation to its own revolution, communism in effect profoundly suffers from not 'taking its desires as reality'.[68]

For the 'idealists of the dialectic', he continued, 'the revolution must be distilled in history; it must come on time; it must ripen in the sun of contradictions.'

> That it could be there immediately is unthinkable and *insufferable*. Poetry and the utopian revolt have this radical presentness in common, this denegation of finalities; it is this actualisation of desire no longer relegated to a future liberation, but demanded here, immediately, even in its death throes, in the extreme situation of life and death. Such is happiness; such is revolution. It has nothing to do with the political ledger book of the Revolution.[69]

This privileging of the immediate spirit of revolt over the bureaucratic fatalism of revolution would have been at home in any situationist text: 'Those who have not yet begun to live, but are saving themselves for a better epoch', Debord had written, 'expect nothing less than a permanent paradise.'[70] But the extent of Baudrillard's departure from the entire dialectical tradition is clear in his attack on the entire vocabulary of separation, contradiction, and alienation. 'Instead of deluding men with a phantasm of their lost identity, of their future anatomy, this notion itself must be abolished,'[71] he declared, setting himself against all analyses which portray 'man as dispossessed, as alienated and relates him to a total man, a total Other who is Reason and who is for the future'.[72]

> What an absurdity it is to pretend that men are 'other', to try to convince them that their deepest desire is to become 'themselves' again! Each man is totally there at each instant. Society also is totally there at each instant.[73]

Marxist theory is incapable of grasping the pure intensity of revolt, 'or even the movement of society except *as an intricate ornament of the revolution*, as a reality on the way toward maturation'.[74] Reduced to an endless deferral and totalitarian dreams of a final resolution, it cannot accept that 'utopia is here in all the energies that are raised against political economy'.[75] It is in the very nature of these energies that all attempts to mould them into a revolutionary project or store them for some future moment of contestation are rejected: the strength of this 'utopian violence' is that it 'does not accumulate; it is lost'.[76] The desire for revolution is also the desire for an autonomy, singularity, and pure intensity which renders it impossible. The energies of revolt and the legislating project of revolution are irrevocably pitted against each other.

This respect for true moments of pure existence, immediacy, and unchannelled desire is the same energy which excited Lyotard's defence of forms of knowledge which would respect the pure event, Foucault's faith in the possibility of counter-discursive rescues of lost and subjugated knowledges, Deleuze's nomadic forays into the territories of codes, and Guattari's molecular desires. Each of these positions betrayed some nostalgia for an authentic, natural realm, no matter how irrevocably lost or impossible to articulate, which is only later betrayed by codes and representations. The recognition that discourse forges and shapes the world of which it speaks had certainly brought an unprecedented confusion to notions of reality and subjectivity, but it had not yet necessitated the abandonment of all senses of some prediscursive existence. And although each of these perspectives faced the problem, particularly strong in Foucault's work, that it is impossible for subjugated desires, events, and knowledges to come into their own without themselves assuming a dominant role in the network of power relations which had curtailed them, the philosophies of the post-68 period still carried the possibility of a politics which would allow them to flourish.

Lyotard's complaint against theory was really a distrust of all meaning and conceptualisation: it is the very act of naming, the incorporation of a moment or experience into the world of symbolic representation, that violates and corrupts its special singularity. Dialectical criticism and theoretical discourse might be guiltier than most, but any attempt to bring an event out of the real world into the world of signs imposes structures and codes on its immediacy, robs it of its vitality and gives it a meaning which it did not previously bear. Deleuze's work was also marked by pleas for a return to

> those states of experience that, at a certain point, must not be translated into representations or fantasies, must not be trans-

mitted by legal, contractual, or institutional codes, must not be exchanged or bartered away, but, on the contrary, must be seen as a dynamic flux.[77]

Any attempt to articulate experience is bound to entrap and curtail the essential fluidity, which is 'what underlies all codes, what escapes all codes, and it is what the codes themselves seek to translate, convert, and mint anew'.[78] And although Foucault intended to deny the possibility of some sense of reality prior to its discursive existence, his work is also marked by traces of some wild and untamed natural world on which discourse imposes itself. Foucault devoted himself to showing that we have 'employed a wide range of categories – truth, man, culture, writing, etc. – to dispel the shock of daily occurrences, to dissolve the event',[79] presenting this immediacy as the reality which his strategies of counter-discourse sought to reclaim. At times he even argued that it was still possible to speak of 'the body and its pleasures' as the ground of real experiences later subjected to domination and control.[80]

So although the overt message of the poststructuralist and desiring philosophies of the 1970s was that the search for the beach under the cobblestones made famous by a piece of 1968 graffito is hopeless, there was still a sense in which some memory of the beach persists. Arguing that the real is always that which escapes representation, so that more cobblestones are always found under the first layer, and truth, authenticity, and reality are the ever-receding horizons of our search, their attempts to undermine all appeals to prediscursive meanings continued to produce new sets of foundations. To be sure, these were posed as free-flowing bases, placed in an immanent and dynamic relation to the codes and powers they resisted. But it is clear that longings to preserve and protect at least a glimpse of the beach in moments untouched by language, the structures of knowledge, or the articulation of discourse shone through overt poststructuralist declarations that the immediacy of real experience is an impossibility, something that all discourse tries to convey but can never reach. It was the tension between these positions, which had also marked Nietzsche's identification of two orders of reality, which finally led both Lyotard and Baudrillard to a complete rejection of the latent naturalism which marked the work of Deleuze, Guattari, Foucault, and their own early writings.

In a discussion of the *mouvement du 22 mars*, Lyotard wrote that the activists with whom he had been involved had developed a critique of bureaucratic capitalism which had encompassed not only 'the State apparatus against society, not only of the party (revolutionary) in the face of the masses, not only of productive work in opposition to free creativity, but the whole of alienated life in the place of – what?'[81] In the movement's search for 'the other of the system of mediations, the other of all possible recuperation',[82] it found itself referring to 'an image (to a representation?) of non-representative life, of the spontaneous, natural, immediate, savage, "non-referential"'.[83] By the mid-1970s, Lyotard had unequivocally rejected this paradoxical nostalgia for the pure event, the real experience, the wild and untamed naturalism of immediate life and liberated desire. Increasingly unhappy with any faith in the return of the repressed, he eventually attacked even the memory of a lost immediacy and all remnants of hope in the possible re-emergence of a distant authenticity. In his 1979 *Economie Libidinale,* Lyotard emphatically insisted that there is no natural self or world to be lost or rediscovered:

> there is no external reference, even were it immanent, from where the separation of that which belongs to capital (or political economy) and that which belongs to subversion (or libidinal economy) can always be properly made; where desire would be cleanly legible, where its *proper economy* would not be scrambled.[84]

Convinced that the proposal of any 'other' to capitalism, be it symbolic exchange or the negativity of desire, is fraught with insuperable difficulties, Lyotard argued that the assertion of some real desire or authentic subjectivity places us on the slippery slope to totalitarianism. Any search for contradictions assumes the possibility of their resolution; the identification of gaps and separations in the social order assumes that it represses, alienates, and falsely represents a reality which will one day return. Like Baudrillard, Lyotard argued that a dangerous and illusory dream of wholeness and completion is postulated by any theory based on alienation, which cannot but carry some conception of the true creativity, spontaneity, and autonomy of the human subject.

Against situationist theory, Lyotard's later work insists that the distinction between the spectacle and the real is finally collapsed. There is no possibility of finding the real object behind the commodity, and real meaning is inseparable from its spectacular representation. True creativity cannot be distinguished from the representation it receives in capitalist society, and authentic desires cannot be extricated from their commodified reality. But while there is no sense in which desire can be placed in opposition or contradiction to any system of domination, Lyotard was far from abandoning all notions of desire. With Deleuze and Guattari, he argued that there is some sense in which even the most exploitative and alienating forms of production are invested with the desires of those apparently passively subjected to them.

In a vicious attack on the patronising sentimentality of the revolutionary movement, Lyotard insisted that the language of suffering, pity, and redemption betrays a misplaced nostalgia for a golden age of free creativity which never existed. He showed the continuity between the revolutionary project and its religious equivalent, and argued that revolutionary politics inevitably portrays the working class as helpless victims who can do nothing to help themselves. Rejecting all notions of lack, want, and negativity, Lyotard's positive conception of desire allowed him to argue that people's desires are never stolen away or distorted, but produced and reinvested in the mechanisms of their own domination. People were not dragged screaming to the factory, he argued: at some level, they must have wanted to go; in some sense, they had enjoyed the privations and labours of capitalist life. This was a position made possible by Lyotard's provocative engagements with both Marxism, on which *Economie Libidinale* is in part a devastating commentary, and Lacanian psychoanalysis, which itself presupposed some sense of absence or negativity, albeit one impossible to conceptualise. But it was most immediately derived from his insistence that there is no essential difference or discontinuity between the economy of desires which had previously been set up as the 'other', the negation, of political economy, and the social and discursive relations of capitalism. In the endless generation of commodities, capitalism fulfils the desire for a multiplication of sites of pure intensity which had once served the revolutionary project.

With these renewed claims that there is a continuity between capitalist relations and even the most radical point of opposition to them, Lyotard finally abandoned the search for any 'other' to capitalism. There is complicity at every point, and nothing, not even a purely negative and non-existent point, nor the memory of a lost referent, can be spoken against it without becoming a contributory factor. At last, there is 'no need for declarations, manifestos, organisations, provocations'. Nor, he continued, in knowing anticipation of the situationist who glimpses one last hope, is there 'even any need for *exemplary actions*'.[85]

But even with the final collapse of their purpose and validity, subversion and interruption continue to emerge. Lyotard may have removed the purpose, but the processes persist. Anticipating Baudrillard's later claims that the meaninglessness of commodity exchange can be sabotaged by a nihilistic strategy which outstrips even the most frantic moments of capitalist relations, Lyotard declared that 'the dissolution of forms and individuals in the so-called "consumer society" should be affirmed'.[86] If the continuity of capitalism and its opposition is finally inescapable, the attempt to criticise it on grounds of mediation, alienation, domination, and separation merely sustains the rules already presupposed by the orders of capitalism. By joining in the race for better theories, more logical social relations, more immediate forms of expression and more authentic lives, revolutionaries only perpetuate the grand social myth of a final resolution and perfect unification; a myth which fixes our sights on an ever-receding horizon and prevents us from turning our attention to the immediacy of life in the here and now.

The possibilities for political and cultural contestation would appear to be bleak. If even the most radical gesture is doomed to reproduce the emptiness and vacuity of commodity relations, all sense of opposition and dissent becomes untenable and, as Lyotard insists, the only strategy it is possible to adopt is one which encourages and affirms the 'dissolution of forms and individuals'. But if opposition to capitalism is no longer an issue, this is only because Lyotard, like Deleuze and Guattari, sees it heading for its own inexorable destruction. And the loss of meaning inevitably achieved by capitalist social relations can itself be encouraged, accelerated, and appropriated in such a way that the limits of irrationality and vacuity to which capitalism continually tends are transgressed in a destructive excess of themselves. In the emergence of punk in the late 1970s, for example, lay the possibility of a threatening political response to the vacant superficiality of contemporary society. Contemptuous of earlier attempts to develop forms of association and activity in some sense better, more worthwhile, or more meaningful than capitalism, punk replied with a renewed emptiness and lack of meaning which turned the tables on all those who busily insisted that capitalism must be opposed by something better than itself. An attack on the established values and institutions of music, culture, and society, punk provided a vehicle for the growing disaffection of the post-sixties generation. It attacked royalty, the culture industry, and the political authorities, shocking the bourgeoisie and antagonising the establishment. But it also came to operate as a social safety-valve: once used to ripped jeans, safety pins, and mohican haircuts, the public became almost thankful that the rebellion was not more intrusive. Indeed, punk was accommodated so swiftly that the possibility was raised that it was in some sense already recuperated before it had even begun.

Two of punk's leading protagonists, Jamie Reid, a graphic artist, and Malcolm McLaren, manager of the Sex Pistols, were well-versed in situationist ideas. Reid's *Suburban Press*, six issues of which appeared in 1970, had 'a shit-stirring format, with thorough research into local politics and council corruption, mixed with my graphics and some Situationist texts'.[87]

> My job, graphically, was to simplify a lot of the political jargon, particularly that used by the Situationists. Far from being an obscure group in the mid 1960s, by the time of the Paris riots in 1968 they had captured headlines around the world and the imagination of a generation.[88]

Much of punk continued the tradition in which the situationists had worked. Operating musically as art that could be made by anyone, punk re-established the dadaist critique of culture and broke down the distinctions between art and life. Its graphics, for which Reid was largely responsible, cut up newspapers, safety-pinned clothes, rewrote comics, and parodied official notices. A Belgian holiday brochure was appropriated for the sleeve of *Holidays in the Sun*, on which its cartoon characters no longer said 'It's just a short excursion to see wonderful historic cities', but 'A cheap holiday in other people's misery'.

Although some of these *détournements* were either meaningless or reactionary, many of Reid's attacks on the culture of new towns, supermarkets, and superstars were ingenious. Authentic-looking stickers read: 'Buy now while stocks last'; 'This store will soon be closing owing to the pending collapse of monopoly capitalism and the world-wide exhaustion of raw materials'; and 'This store welcomes shoplifters'. 'Lies', was stuck onto newspapers; 'Save petrol, burn cars' onto vehicles; and, during the miners' strike, 'Switch on something for the miners' replaced 'Save It'. An apparently official invitation to move to a new town declared: 'A New Town like the Old Town – but NEW!'

> New Towns are being built, in the middle of the countryside, away from strikes, tenants' committees, claimants' unions, occupations, shoplifters, vandals, smog, dirt and noise. Away from all distractions, so you can get on with the job.[89]

Conscious of the problem of recuperation, Reid made many of his graphics refer to specific incidents or themes to prevent them from becoming 'decor for trendy Lefties' bedrooms'.[90] Punk was also a *détournement* of the culture industry and an attack on the notions of originality, genius, and talent. Undermining the music industry's monopolistic overproduction of 'superstars', punk generated the confidence that anyone could make music in the same way that Dada had insisted that everyone could be a poet or an artist. Informed by the situationist critique of the star system, punk spawned a generation of little bands, small studios, and independent record companies, as well as some very big corporations.

The most incisive critique of the punk milieu and its dissipation of dissent was *The End of Music*, a pamphlet circulated in 1978. It described punk as 'a bowdlerised realisation of Lautréamont's maxim "Poetry made by all"',[91] arguing that the movement carried 'no desire to negate music [. . .] merely to make it free, but leaving intact the antagonistic structure which turns audience against performer, creator against consumer and vice versa in a relationship of near reciprocal alienation'.[92] McLaren's shop 'Sex' sold the trappings of rebellion; some of the customers it attracted were formed into the Sex Pistols and a tide of nihilistic refusal of the spectacle was initiated. *The End of Music* suggested that McLaren had helped to recuperate the situationist critique which, 'after being suitably doctored', was used

> as a force able to keep pop and music kicking as pacification agent of the young proletariat both in terms of channelling energy into hierarchical aspiration, fake liberation from drudgery and the goal of a higher level of wage slavery with all its alluring but alienated sexual appeal.[93]

T-shirts bearing slogans like 'Be reasonable, demand the impossible', now meant 'buy some of my kinky gear . . . and help make me a rich man'.[94] So, just as Dada anti-art hangs in the galleries and surrealist dreams sell cars, the situationists joined every other failed critique and abandoned their weapons on the battlefield where their slogans were captured for T-shirts.

But *The End of Music*'s claims that punk was a recuperation of situationist theory are not definitive. It is certainly true that some of those who made their names and fortunes from the movement were quite aware that situationist-style agitation could be marketed to great effect. McLaren's acquaintence with the 'pro-situ' group King Mob had made him aware of situationist readings of recuperation and dissent, and on one level he probably did cynically cash in on working-class rebellion without a care for the effects of its commodification. But there is also a sense in which McLaren's tactics can be read as a rather more astute response. Aware that punk would in any case be recuperated, his own anticipation of its commodification did at least ensure that punk had some control over its own recuperation. By the time the dissatisfaction it expressed had grown into a marketable force, it had already been marketed. And if punk did recuperate anything, it was not situationist theory, but the possibility of effective dissent, a danger which, as *The End of Music* points out, punk shares with the spectacle of revolution presented in reggae and any other rebel music.

It is certainly interesting to note that so many of the good and great developed their all-too-easily transferable skills in the situationist milieu. Of those involved in the emergence of punk, media star Tony Wilson opened Manchester's 'Hacienda' in 1982 as a 'disco, videotheque, and venue' which aimed to 'restore a sense of place: "the Hacienda must be built"'.[95] Malcolm McLaren continues to make stars, and Richard Branson is now a knight. But punk's do-it-yourself ethic also produced a host of self-published fanzines and autonomous organisations, and the observation that fortunes were so easily made cannot belittle the sincerity, anger, and achievements of those involved in punk and its later manifestations. Punk provided a much-needed shot in the arm for the anarchist movement, with Class War's 'Stop the City' and 'Bash the Rich' campaigns providing some light entertainment and heavy policing during the 1980s and squats, the travellers, and a hundred and one imaginative and provocative phenomena developing out of the punk milieu.

There are clearly senses in which punk can be seen as an example of the affirmation of the nihilistic equivalence of capitalist social relations which Lyotard and Baudrillard had begun to advocate in the mid-1970s. It certainly did take the loss of intrinsic value to its own extreme and turn it back on itself. But if there was a theoretical resonance anywhere, it was with the situationists' insistence that the spectacle can be subverted by being taken literally. And although this may appear to be the same exhortion as that made by Lyotard and Baudrillard, the situationist insistence that such *détournements* of existing values are tactics in a larger strategy distances the two positions. For the situationists, nihilism was not to be applauded in itself, but as a moment in the contestation of the spectacle, a tactical response to a particular configuration of spectacular relations which could not be invoked as an end in itself. To respond to the reification of commodity relations with the declaration, 'Yes, I'm an ugly and worthless thing too', is to make merely one of a thousand subversive replies to the spread of commodity relations. Meaninglessness and lack of purpose are useful only to the extent that they operate with some other end in sight: chaos and absurdity are tactics appropriate to particular moments rather than steadfast rules of engagement. The post-68 interrogation of every point of exteriority or contradiction previously posed to capitalism was phrased in terms of another order of 'others': pre-social networks of power, the pre-discursive flux of desires, pre-capitalist systems of symbolic exchange. And the danger of this passion to search ever deeper for the basis of social organisation is that it spawns a paradoxically dogmatic insistence on the realm of the real it uncovers. Thus Baudrillard's invocation of symbolic exchange appeared as an immobile point of exteriority to capitalist social relations and forced him into a position from which any recuperation of this last realm would finally destroy all hope of presenting an 'other' to capitalism.

Nevertheless, the philosophies developed after 1968 alert us to the very real dangers of imposing meanings, structures, and teleologies on events, desires, and experiences which must speak for themselves. The critic who 'knows best', the theorist who seeks an ever-improved theory, and the intellectual who represents the true interests of those who cannot speak for themselves are utterly discredited by its insistence that there is no single perspective which can hold the world still enough to understand it. And yet this stance is not completely absent from poststructuralist thought. It is Lyotard who insists that there can be no more manifestos; Baudrillard who declares that there can be no repre- sentation without spectacle. Certainly this is an argument rather too easily made, and an effect which the writers considered here have done much to avoid: Foucault was not alone in insisting that his work too should be treated as a tool-kit which some people might find useful for particular purposes. In Italy, for example, this was certainly the sense in which the Movement of '77 ap- proached the work of the philosophers of desire. As one account of the Italian events explains, the 'end of politics' postulated by the poststructuralists was 'immediately translated into the Movement's language, that is, into concrete struggle', where it facilitated a search for 'new *political* areas of struggle, new territories for the massification of the struggle'.[96] And although the old dangers of deferment and dogmatism immediately assert themselves with the development of new connections and solidarities between the multiplicity of desires, interests, and social positions antagonistic to one another and the capitalist relations in which they arise, the warnings and provocations made by poststructuralist and desiring philosophies by no means invalidate purposeful political action.

The situationists were not at all reluctant to identify purposes and reasons to sift through and subvert the complexities of modern life. And for all the dangers implicit in the project to transform the totality of social and discursive relations, they were convinced that every gesture in the world tends towards such grand designs. Ultimately, the intensities and singularities which poststructuralism wanted to preserve cannot be conceived in iso- lation from some wider purpose; deconstructions are impossible without some intention, some search for meaning, improvement, truth, and reality. The absence of purpose and meaning cannot be championed as an end in itself: there is always some reason for any act of construction, deconstruction, or simple destruction.

In the late 1980s, however, a movement emerged which might seem to fit the poststructuralist bill. Orange Alternative brought a kind of Dada provocation to Poland; with tactics reminiscent of those adopted by the Dutch Provos and Kommune 1, it made no attempt to produce a coherent set of demands and introduced a maverick element into the political currents which have since transformed Polish society. Avoiding the 'star system of the official (Solidarity) opposition',[97] Orange Alternative, its heirs and allies will undoubtedly find themselves as out of step with the new regime as the old, but its satirical refusals of purpose and coherence were certainly provocative at the time. Orange Alternative celebrated International Children's Day in 1987 with an event in which 'dozens of participants dressed as gnomes or smurfs with red hats danced in the streets and distributed sweets'.[98] Poland's Official Day of the Police and Security Service, 7 October, was marked by an enthusiastic march in Wroclaw to 'thank' the police, in which they were showered with flowers, and embraced by the participants who were later arrested. The streets 'were flooded with Santa Clauses' at Christmas 1987, leading to the arrest of both bogus and 'real' Santa Clauses and a 2,000-strong demonstration calling for the 'release of Santa'. (King Mob had pulled a similar trick when a pseudo-Santa distributed 'presents' in Selfridges. 'Soon afterwards the shoppers were witness to the edifying spectacle of policemen arresting Father Christmas and snatching back toys from small children.'[99]) These subversions of the everyday extended to distributions of free toilet paper, sanitary towels, and an appeal to everyone to 'Vote Twice!' in the 1987 Referendum on social policy. There also were rumours of plans for a European happening in which people in every country dressed up as policemen.

Orange Alternative flourished 'by outwitting and embarrassing the authorities who maintain a system which relies on a single version of the truth for its survival and who are used to a more direct form of protest',[100] and it suffered with the increasing sophistication of police responses to its provocations. But its real strength was clearly its refusal to assume the mantle of an identifiable political or cultural force. When one of its protagonists was asked, 'Do you set up happenings in order to expose the totalitarianism of the system under which we live?', he replied, 'I do them because I do them, but one does things because of, or for something'. Another victory for the situationist perspective? Well maybe not. For he continued: 'Well, yes, when I was preparing for the gnome happening, I assumed that we would have a good time with sweets and streamers'.[101]

Chapter 5

'Flee, but while fleeing, pick up a weapon'

For all its problems, the playful breaking of codes and subversion of signs facilitated by much poststructuralist philosophy has had a powerful political effect. This has, however, been dissipated in more recent years by the incorporation of all poststructuralism into the heady hyperbole of the postmodern world view. And one consequence of this development is that postmodernism's abandonment of any critical perspective is still conducted with the language, tactics, and style of the entire tradition considered in this book. The postmodern condition is like Dada without the war or surrealism without the revolution; postmodern philosophers are the sold-out situationists who wander without purpose, observing recuperations with a mild and dispassionate interest and enjoying the superficial glitter of a spectacular life. Naïvely offering an uncritical home to the notion of the spectacle, postmodern discourse is filled with chatterings about a concept it never imagines was once saturated with revolutionary intent.

The situationists had always been aware that the term 'spectacle' could easily be robbed of its critical force, recuperated as a descriptive concept and appropriated to serve the ends of spectacular society itself. 'Without a doubt', Debord had declared in *The Society of the Spectacle*, 'the critical concept of the spectacle is susceptible of being turned into just another empty formula of sociologico-political rhetoric designed to explain and denounce everything in the abstract – so serving to buttress the spectacular system itself.'[1] This has indeed been the fate of the situationist critique of the spectacle which, twenty years after its initial development, now appears in a spectacular form of its own: a context which precludes all critical appraisal and is content to describe and celebrate the ahistorical world of image, sign, and appearance.

In the midst of these affirmations, Debord spoke out again in 1988. His *Comments on The Society of the Spectacle* charted the recent development of the spectacle, reintroducing the possibility of its criticism to the postmodern world and asserting the continuing validity of situationist theory. Since the 1967 publication of *The Society of the Spectacle*, he wrote, and following the failure of the events of 1968, 'the spectacle has continued to gather strength'. Indeed, in 'all that has happened in the last twenty years', Debord argued, 'the most important change lies in the very continuity of the spectacle'.[2] It has 'learnt new defensive techniques, as powers under attack always do',[3] and is now stronger as a result of its success 'in raising a whole generation moulded to its laws'.[4] Only two explicit changes have occurred. The first, observed by Debord in his 1974 *Preface to the Fourth Italian Edition of The Society of the Spectacle*, and reiterated in the *Comments*, is that a new and cynical honesty has entered the spectacle's representation of itself.

The society of the spectacle had begun everywhere in coercion, deceit, and blood, but it promised a happy path. It believed itself to be loved. Now it no longer says: 'What appears is good, what is good appears.' It simply says: 'It is so.' It admits frankly that it is no longer essentially reformable, though change be its very nature in order to transmute for the worst every particular thing. It has lost all its general illusions about itself.[5]

The spectacle no longer pretends its world is happy, unified, and capable of fulfilling every desire. 'Going from success to success, until 1968 modern society was convinced it was loved. It has since had to abandon these dreams; it prefers to be feared. It knows full well that "its innocent air has gone forever".'[6] And the end of this illusion is accompanied by the increasing homogencity of the modern world. Debord's early distinction between the concentrated and diffuse forms of spectacular organisation is abandoned in favour of a single category: the integrated spectacle, to which cold war differences between bureaucratic totalitarianism and capitalist pluralism are increasingly insignificant. 'When the spectacle was concentrated, the greater part of surrounding society escaped it; when diffuse, a small part; today, nothing. The spectacle has spread itself to the point where it now permeates all reality.'[7] Without any sense of difference or opposition in the world, 'this reality no longer confronts the integrated spectacle as something alien.'[8]

This would appear to mark a significant departure from the revolutionary optimism of *The Society of the Spectacle.* 'Beyond a legacy of old books and old buildings', writes Debord, 'there remains nothing, in culture or in nature, which has not been transformed, and polluted, according to the means and interests of modern industry.'[9] Possessing 'all the means necessary to falsify the whole of production and perception', the spectacle 'is the absolute master of memories just as it is the unfettered master of plans which will shape the most distant future'.[10] Its discourse 'isolates all it shows from its context, its past, its intentions and its consequences. It is thus completely illogical. Since no one may contradict it, it has the right to contradict itself, to correct its own past.'[11] These Orwellian references – books and buildings being the only vestiges of the old world to encroach on the Winston of *1984* as he stumbles through falsified histories and manufactured revolution – bode ill for the revolutionary project. The essential opposition between the real and the spectacle would seem to be lost forever, drowned in a flow of images which 'carries everything before it' and leaves the spectator with neither the time nor the space to think, reflect, remember, or judge.

Convinced that the spectacle is no longer the hidden quality of modern capitalist society, Debord argued that the 'vague feeling that there has been a rapid invasion which has forced people to lead their lives in an entirely different way is now widespread'. But the encroachment of spectacular relations is 'experienced rather like some inexplicable change in the climate, or in some other natural equilibrium, a change faced with which ignorance knows only that it has nothing to say'. And what is more, he adds, 'many see it as a civilising invasion, as something inevitable, and even want to collaborate'.[12] Expressions of 'hypocritical regret' for the passing of real life and superficial concerns with the technological and cultural developments which accelerate the cycles of reproduction and simulation are voiced in an 'empty debate' conducted 'by the spectacle itself: everything is said about the extensive means at its disposal, to ensure that nothing is said about their extensive deployment'.[13]

Yet Debord still insists that an understanding of the consolidation of spectacular society is vital, for the sole reason that 'it is under such conditions that the next stage of social conflict will necessarily be played out'.[14] And, if we are to believe him, there is a great deal more to *Comments* than sits on the page. 'These comments are sure to be welcomed by fifty or sixty people', he observes at the outset: 'a large number given the times in which we live and the gravity of the matters under discussion'.[15] But 'a good half of this interested elite will consist of people who devote themselves to maintaining the spectacular system of domination, and the other half of people who persist in doing quite the opposite.'[16] Encouraging the air of mystique already surrounding him ('An anti-spectacular notoriety has become something extremely rare'[17]), Debord insists that he cannot therefore speak freely in the text. 'Above all', he declares, 'I must take care not to give too much information to just anybody.'[18] As a consequence, silences, secrets, and cryptic moments will have to prevail, with some elements 'intentionally omitted; and the plan will have to remain rather unclear'.[19] It is evidently up to the twenty-five or thirty revolutionary readers to put the text together for themselves. And although *Comments* is as pessimistic as the age in which it arises, the picture it paints is by no means closed and hopeless.

> If history should return to us after this eclipse, something which depends on factors still in play and thus on an outcome which no one can definitely exclude, these *Comments* may one day serve in the writing of a history of the spectacle; without any doubt the most important event to have occurred this century, and the one for which the fewest explanations have been ventured.[20]

It was clearly the conjunction of ubiquitous chatter about the spectacle with the complete absence of its serious critique which encouraged Debord to write still further. 'In other circumstances', he maintained, 'I think I could have considered myself altogether satisfied with my first work on this subject, and left others to consider future developments. But in the present situation, it seemed unlikely that anyone else would do it.'[21] But if no one has developed the situationist project, there has been no shortage of inversions, appropriations, and recuperations of the critique of spectacular society.

Baudrillard's trips through hyperreality take both situationist theory and poststructuralist discourse to an untenable extreme. Although Baudrillard's early nostalgia for some authentic relation between people and things left him vulnerable to the more strident rhetoric of Lyotard's *Economie Libidinale*, his more recent works have been beyond reproach from even the most insistent claims that reality, the human subject, and all senses of meaning, history, and purpose have forsaken the world. In Baudrillard's writing, we finally step into the postmodern with the same sense of giddiness and trepidation that accompanies the first step onto a boat. The deck shifts and sways beneath us; for a while there seems to be nothing to hold onto since everything is moving, and we look back with longing and fear as the land disappears. But after a while, we relax enough to turn our attention to the horizon, forgetting what dry land was ever like, so that the shore becomes as strange and mobile as the boat itself first seemed when we tread on it again. Baudrillard encourages us to believe that this is also the case for postmodernity. At first the postmodern world seems impossibly free and unbalanced, but soon we adapt so well to the perpetual motions that surround us that we can no longer remember how we ever lived on the solid foundations of the modern world. The only point at which the metaphor fails is that of the return to land. Both 'watchers and watched sail forth on a boundless ocean',[22] observes Debord: the postmodern voyager is doomed to be lost at sea.

In his writings of the late 1970s and 1980s, Baudrillard combined a sense of done-it-all-before world-weariness with a joyful enthusiasm for the disappearance of reality he discerns in every moment of contemporary life. The world of hyperreality and simulation is recorded and celebrated, and the possibility of making any sort of political intervention is happily dismissed. And this world is identical to the situationist spectacle: both are realms in which the real and the meaningful have slipped away amidst a confusion of signs, images, simulations, and appearances. But Baudrillard is content to take the spectacle at face value, removing all sense in which it can be considered as an inversion of the real. The spectacle must be believed: it has no mysteries, no secrets, and no underlying realities. Nothing is concealed, repressed, denied, or turned against itself; there is nothing to be represented, alienated, or separated, and mediations no longer stand between the subject and the world but circumscribe all meaning and reality. Baudrillard defined postmodernism as 'the characteristic of a universe where there are no more definitions possible';[23] a world in which everything has 'been done' and all that remains is to play with the fragments. 'Playing with the pieces – that is postmodern'.[24] The pieces with which the postmodernist toys are the theories, ideas, and vocabularies in which the remnants of the lost modernist belief in the possibilities of progress, liberation, and meaning remain. Postmodernity is 'a game with the vestiges of what has been destroyed. This is why we are "post" – history has stopped, one is in a kind of post-history which is without meaning.'[25] In a doubly ironic reversal of the situationists' argument that the choice of life over survival allows for the free construction of situations 'on the ruins of the modern spectacle', Baudrillard characterises postmodernity as the attempt 'to reach a point where one can live with what is left. It is more a survival among the ruins than anything else.'[26]

One of Baudrillard's central concerns is with the media; the realm of simulation and reproduction in which every aspect of contemporary life is forced to appear. Observing the accelerated reproduction of the real, he argues that postmodernity is the point at which the real, the meaningful, and the authentic are finally and irrevocably confused with representations which become more real than reality itself. Ubiquitous images, simulations, and reproductions no longer distort or conceal the real; reality has slipped away into the free-floating chaos of the hyperreal. But the representations of the hyperreal world are not without effect. Media representation gives events and experiences a power which they no longer carry in themselves while at the same time perpetuating our faith that there must be something behind the representation – a real event, a true moment, an authentic expression, a meaningful experience – which has only later been transmuted into the spectacular existence from which nothing seems able to escape. Representations seduce us into believing in a reality which has long since disappeared. Images encourage the conviction that they are images of something, rather than the components which entirely constitute the world.

Baudrillard certainly turns conventional wisdom about both the media and their audiences upside-down. Conjuring a bleakly passive and homogeneous picture of 'the silent majorities', he nevertheless offers some sort of defence of the stupid apathy he has already imputed to 'the masses'. *In the Shadow of the Silent Majorities* insists that the media impose imperatives of reason, communication, meaning, and reality on a mass which cares for nothing. 'They are given meaning: they want spectacle,'[27] he declares. In effect, they prefer pushpin to poetry or, in Baudrillard's terms, football to politics. The drama of the political cannot compete with the spectacle of football; continually cajoled into appreciating 'high culture' and discerning real meaning, the masses refuse point-blank to participate in the real world provided for them. For Baudrillard, this indicates that the media are actually overpowered by the mass, which absorbs and envelops them, accepting them with a proud and complete lack of interest or engagement. The masses are neither manipulated nor involved; their relation to the media is the entirely passive role of the object, and it is only in the ideology of the media itself that the insistent fears of manipulation and distortion are raised. 'Are the mass media on the side of power in the manipulation of the masses, or are they on the side of the masses in the liquidation of meaning?'[28] asks Baudrillard, overturning earlier radical convictions that 'resistance consists of reinterpreting messages according to the group's own codes and for its own ends. The masses, on the contrary, accept everything and redirect everything *en bloc* into the spectacular, without requiring any other code.'[29]

Far from signifying the extent of its alienation and domination, Baudrillard argues that the apathetic silence of the mass, which 'never participates', is its 'absolute weapon',[30] the means by which it continually verges on the destruction of all forms of power. Apathy is a problem only for those already in power or the revolutionaries who would seize it, both of whom are desperate to identify meaning, reality, and purpose in every aspect of social experience. 'Despite having been surveyed to death', however, the mass always refuses to answer: 'it says neither whether the truth is to the left or to the right, nor whether it prefers revolution or repression. It is without truth and without reason.'[31] This, Baudrillard argues, is the mass's answer to the overproduction of meaning which characterises the modern world and of which the Left is particularly guilty. 'Basically, what goes for commodities also goes for meaning,' he explains.

> For a long time capital only had to produce goods; consumption ran by itself. Today it is necessary to produce consumers, to produce demand, and this production is infinitely more costly than that of the goods. [...] For a long time it was enough for power to produce meaning (political, ideological, cultural, sexual), and the demand followed it; it absorbed supply and still surpassed it. Meaning was in short supply, and all the revolutionaries offered themselves to produce still more. Today, everything has changed: no longer is meaning in short supply,

it is produced everywhere, in ever increasing quantities – it is demand which is weakening. And it is the *production of this demand for meaning* which has become crucial for the system.[32]

In the absence of this demand, 'power is nothing but an empty simulacrum',[33] vainly insisting that it bears a significance which the masses, on whom it supposedly imposes its manipulations and oppressions, refuse to acknowledge. And whereas the demand 'for objects and services can always be artificially produced', the 'desire for meaning, when it is in short supply, and the desire for reality, when it is weakening everywhere, cannot be made good.'[34] In an apparent vindication of situationist observations on the transformation of the real into a distant spectacle, Baudrillard argues that we are 'already at the point where political, social events no longer have sufficient autonomous energy to move us, and hence unfold like a silent film'.[35]

It is this effect of distance and disappearance which brings us to postmodern declarations of the end of history, a moment which, as Marx, Lukács, and Debord insisted, is inevitably presented as a permanent feature of capitalist social organisation. The loss of memory, purpose, and meaning which the end of history implies is signified for Baudrillard by the empty vacuity of the masses, who 'have no history themselves, no meaning, no consciousness, no desire'.[36] In the face of this inert and silent force, 'history cools, it slows down, events succeed each other and vanish in indifference'.[37]

History stops here, and we see in what way: not for want of people, nor of violence (there will always be more violence, but violence should not be confused with history), nor of events (there will always be more events, thanks to the media and information!), but by deceleration, indifference, and stupefaction. History can no longer outrun itself, it can no longer envisage its own finality, dream of its own end; it is buried in its own immediate effect, it implodes in the here and now.[38]

And this disappearance of real experiences, events, and historical meanings is not a matter for regret. It is only the 'beautiful souls' of the revolutionary Left who still believe in the real and deplore the fact that 'the media are putting an end to the real event'.[39] Lamenting the ubiquity of the spectacle, the silence of the majorities, and the lack of interest in the meaningful, the revolutionaries of the modern world merely perpetuate the nostalgia for truth, meaning, immediacy, and liberation which has characterised the critical tradition.

'We have always had a sad vision of the masses (alienated), a sad vision of the unconscious (repressed),' writes Baudrillard. 'Upon our entire philosophy lies the heavy weight of these sad correlations.'[40] And against this collective melancholia, the spectacle must be celebrated for its refusal of reality, its ability to make meaning appear and disappear in one move. The postmodern age is one in which we must finally accept that the 'will to spectacle and illusion' is stronger than the 'will for knowledge and power' to which it is opposed:

> tenacious, deep in man's heart, it haunts nonetheless the process of events. There is, as it were, a desire for pure event, objective information, the most secret facts and thoughts, to be commuted into spectacle, to attain ecstasy in a scene instead of being produced as something really happening.[41]

The spectacle is not to be decried, but celebrated as the inevitable theatre of all existence. Events have no reality in themselves; there is no raw material of experience later subject to spectacularisation. Reality is something achieved by events and experiences only through their presentation in a scene. 'For something to be meaningful, there has to be a scene', he wrote, 'and for there to be a scene, there has to be an illusion, a minimum of illusion, of imaginary movement, of defiance to the real, which carries you off, seduces or revolts you.'[42] Meaning can only arise in the moment of its representation, when it assumes an appearance which immediately destroys its postulated reality. 'Without this properly esthetic dimension, mythical, ludic, there is not even a political scene where something can happen.'[43] Indeed, 'even Revolution can happen only if its spectacle is possible'.[44]

Such observations suggest that the real is only made possible in the moment of its reproduction, a position which Baudrillard reinforced with innumerable references to the copies and appearances ubiquitous in the postmodern world. Charting the historical movement of images from reflections to distortions and finally to equivalencies and perfections of the real, Baudrillard eventually identified a point at which it is no longer possible to speak of the image in terms of representation, but as a simulation which produces a reality more real than reality itself. Simulation 'threatens the difference between "true" and "false", between "real" and "imaginary"' with an unprecedented force. 'Since the simulator produces "true" symptoms, is he ill or not?'[45] he asks, challenging an increasingly untenable reality to assert itself in the midst of such confusion. Indeed, the image, he argues, has never merely threatened to distort or manipulate the real: rather, it has always been in danger of revealing the essential absence of that which it represents; it has always threatened to make the real disappear. Thus the iconoclasts' fear of images

> arose precisely because they sensed this omnipotence of simulacra, this facility they have of effacing God from the consciousness of men, and the overwhelming, destructive truth which they suggest: that ultimately there has never been any God, that only the simulacra exists, indeed that God himself has only ever been his own simulacrum.[46]

Today it is representations of the real world and the meaningful message which threaten their disappearance amidst an ecstasy of communication, information technology, screens, and virtual realities. Television, 'the most beautiful prototypical object of this new era',[47] is the medium in which simulation really comes into its own, confusing reality and its representation by becoming a reality in itself. The case of the Louds, a family whose life was filmed and broadcast on American TV in the early 1970s, is used to illustrate the eradication of the difference between fiction and reality, epitomising 'the dissolution of TV into life, the dissolution of life into TV'.[48] As Baudrillard points out, the Louds lived 'as if TV wasn't there', a claim which actually translates as 'as if you, the viewer, were really there'. The Louds became a hyperreal family: not only was their representation their entire reality, but the family without the cameras disappeared – in this case, more literally than the example requires, since the family broke up in the process. They really did sacrifice themselves to television: the cameras constructed and destroyed the family in one moment.

Examples such as this suggest that it is no longer sufficient to speak of television as spectacle, a medium which represents the real and provides for it a theatrical backdrop or mediation. The language of spectacle, theatre, and scene still conjure a sense of underlying reality, a world of meaning which is only later repre-sented and brought into the realm of meaning. For Baudrillard, this perspective is merely a step on the road to the full obscenity of the postmodern world; the era in which the scene is truly and finally all that there is. In the moment at which images make the real disappear, we have made an irrevocable leap over a border of simulation which brooks no return. It is no longer possible to seek out the real under the manipulations and distortions of the image and the apparent: reality, and the entirety of social, political, and historical meanings dependent on it collapses in on itself in an implosive disappearance. Just as we 'can no longer discover music as it was before stereo (unless by an effect of supplementary simulation)', so 'we can no longer discover history as it was before information and the media'.

> The original essence (of music, of the social . . .), the original concept (of the unconscious, of history . . .) have disappeared because we can never again isolate them from their model of perfection, which at the same time is their model of simulation, of their forced assumption in an excessive truth, which at once is their point of inertia and their point of no-return. We will never know what was the social, or what was music before their present exacerbation in useless perfection. We will never know what history was before its exacerbation in the technical perfection of information or its disappearance in the profusion of commentary – we will never know what anything was before its disappearance in the completion of its model . . . . Such is the era of simulation.[49]

And, in the absence of any referent of meaning and reality from which the spectacular world of scenes and appearances might be distinguished, the notions of spectacle and scene finally drop into obsolescence. Winding his way through the convictions of the avant-garde, situationist theory, the events of 1968 and poststructuralist philosophy, Baudrillard tells the story of this achievement.

> In the beginning was the secret, and this was the rule of the game of appearance. Then there was the repressed, and this was the rule of the game of depth. Finally comes the obscene, and this was the rule of the game of a world without appearance or depth – a transparent universe.[50]

'So the consumer society was lived under the sign of alienation, as society of the spectacle; but still the spectacle is only spectacle, it is never obscene.' It is only necessary to speak of the obscene 'when there is no longer a scene, when everything becomes inexorably transparent', when it is finally possible to say, 'We are no longer in the drama of alienation, we are in the ecstasy of communication'.[51]

Baudrillard presents the passage from the real to the scene and finally to the obscene as a consequence of power's long history of distorting reality, concealing the truth, and dominating the masses. In effect, he portrays a world in which this strategy has been destroyed by its own success. Continual denials of meaningful participation and subjective expression have finally eradicated the very possibility of their assertion. We are in a position in which the slaves, to return to Hegelian categories which Baudrillard has supposedly left far behind, completely undermine the power of their masters by refusing to recognise their dominion. So efficient has the exercise of power over meaning and subjectivity become, that these referents are no longer merely concealed and repressed, but actually eradicated. The masses no longer recognise or respond to the power relations which need them to participate as oppressed and manipulated victims. The master has destroyed the slaves and, with them, his own power. There is no longer any active force to be dominated or repressed, and power too is revealed as a chimerical simulation of itself: a vacuous, almost mystical category which only ever existed by virtue of its own ability to construct an effective and convincing image of power.

> The only weapon of power, its only strategy against this defection, is to reinject realness and referentiality everywhere, in order to convince us of the reality of the social, of the gravity of the economy and the finalities of production.[52]

The image which continually threatens to reveal the vacuity of the real must be invested with this strategy; used as a means to reinforce reality where it really eradicates it. And so, rather paradoxically, Baudrillard argues that the image now becomes the guardian of the real. This is a strategy epitomised by Disneyland, an imaginary America, which conveniently convinces us of the reality of everything outside it.

> Disneyland is there to conceal the fact that it is the 'real' country, all of America, which *is* Disneyland (just as prisons are there to conceal the fact that it is the social in its entirety, in its banal omnipresence, which is carceral). Disneyland is presented as an imaginary in order to make us believe that the rest is real, when in fact all of Los Angeles and the America surrounding it

are no longer real, but of the order of the hyperreal and of simulation.[53]

The imaginary worlds which threaten the real are therefore appropriated for its protection. But this too is a fictional scenario, in which it is merely the image of the real which is safeguarded while the real entirely evaporates. Just as subjectivity has been emptied from the masses, which finally stand revealed as the object they always were, so reality is emptied from the image, which now represents nothing but its own, and simulated, reality.

This circularity, in which the image is engaged in an eternal return upon itself, marks not only the ends of reality, meaning and history, but also signifies the impossibility of critical thought and all political engagement. Contradiction and negation are finally redundant in a world in which it is possible neither to distinguish between the real and the apparent, the true and the false, nor to privilege one term over another.

> Simulation, the generalised passage to the code and the sign-value, was at first described in critical terms, in the light (or shadow) of a problematic of alienation. It was still the society of the spectacle, and its denunciation, which was the focal point of the semiological, psychoanalytical, and sociological arguments. Subversion was still sought in the transgression of the categories of political economy: use-value, exchange-value, equivalence.[54]

All such possibilities of subversion are now removed if struggles for meaning and power persist only in simulated versions of themselves.

And yet Baudrillard, declaring the impossibility of opposition and critique, still insists on some sense of contradiction in his own work. His entire emphasis on the overwhelming matrixes of images, information, and communication systems in modern society is itself conducted in an effort to dispense with the metaphors of production which have characterised both Marxist and many poststructuralist philosophies. To production, a framework in which the world is always produced in some sense by some privileged and 'other' force – the subject, relations of power, or desire – Baudrillard counterposes seduction, a term which replaces all sense of fundamental relations at work in the world with strategies of disappearance and concealment engaged in a meaningless play. Production brings things into view, makes them real, meaningful, and purposeful; seduction comes into play at the moment when meanings and events are overproduced in the midst of accelerating circuits of image, message, and representation to the point at which they disappear. Seduced by the ubiquity of images to believe that the real still exists, the postmodern consciousness is then abandoned in a world from which any sense of reality has evaporated.

With the establishment of seduction as the new principle of the postmodern world, Baudrillard inverts the entire strategy of the old, modern, revolutionary project. In place of desires for truth and real experience, the '"liberation" of meaning and the destruction of appearances',[55] he promotes secrecy and mediation, artifice and objectification, arguing that the attempt to unveil the world's secrets and achieve some sense of immediate engagement with the world is misplaced and misguided. Positioning itself on the side of subjectivity, real events, meanings, and immediacy against commodified representations, images and experiences, the revolutionary tradition to which the situationists belonged has been fighting not merely a losing battle, but one which was always already lost. Struggles against recuperation were always doomed, argues Baudrillard: moments of authenticity have never preceded their recuperation, and the desire for their realisation has always been naïve. For such senses of acute reality are merely the seductive fictions which have deceived us into working and waiting for their fulfilment for more than a century. Still absorbed in the project to produce the world – to make it do, make, and mean more – and continuing to participate in linear and teleological conceptions of time and history which impute a purpose, direction, and sense of progress to every event, the revolutionary critique has merely contributed to the overproduction of meaning and reality which has finally made them disappear. The masses no longer pretend to be interested: objectified they have been, and objects they become. Things no longer presume to bear some use-value or purpose: commodified out of meaningful existence, they merely exist as dead weights, happily proclaiming their inert futility. In the face of simultaneous and simulating representations, ideas, events, and experiences can no longer be really felt, and even the most intimate emotions and the most radical gestures are irretrievably confused with their spectacular inversions. The great events of the day are subjected to endless media exposure,

but still we can't really imagine them. All of that, for us, is simply
obscene, since images in the media are made to be seen but not
really looked at, hallucinated in silhouette, absorbed – like sex
absorbs the voyeur: from a distance. Neither spectators, nor
actors – we are voyeurs without illusion.[56]

Such are the pessimistic reflections which mark Baudrillard's later
work, leading him to commend the honesty of the meaningless,
the superficial, the secret, and the artificial in a world saturated
with impossible searches for truth, revelation, depth, and authenticity. At least the surfaces and appearances of the world do not
pretend to be more than themselves, and it is in them that we
should place our faith.

Contrary to our residual faiths in an irreversible progress
towards resolution and realisation, history has turned back on
itself in a reversal which calls for a new and inverted strategy: 'For
critical theory one must therefore substitute a fatal theory, to bring
this objective irony of the world to completion.'[57] Like Lyotard,
therefore, Baudrillard insists that the 'only radical and modern
answer' to the ubiquity of the commodified image lies in 'the
deepening of negative conditions',[58] the attempt to 'potentiate
what is new, original, and unexpected in the commodity – for
example, its formal indifference to utility and value, the pre-
eminence given to circulation'.[59] Here ends the attempt to defend
the subject against the encroachment of commodity relations:
alienation and the entire world of appearances theorised by the
situationists is to be celebrated and encouraged; pushed beyond
itself and accelerated until it subverts and exposes itself. Subversion and dissent lie not in the subject but its reified form: the
object which refuses to bear meaning, the image which represents
nothing, the sign which fails to signify, the commodified and
silenced mass which refuses to participate.

This marks the complete inversion of situationist theory, with
which Baudrillard remains engaged throughout his work. Convinced that all desires for participation in created situations have
been replaced by the drive for spectacle, Baudrillard pours scorn
on the situationist dream. 'That things exhaust themselves in
their spectacle – in a magic and artificial fetishism – is the
distortion that serious minds will always oppose, in their utopian
expurgation of the world in order to deliver it exact, intact, and
authentic for the day of the Last Judgement.'[60] Against situationist

claims that struggles against alienation would reveal a new world of immediacy and participation, Baudrillard insists that the boredom of contemporary life, far from being counterrevolutionary, is not at all a problem. Rather, 'the essential point is the increase of boredom; increase is salvation and ecstasy'.

> How could we suppose that people were going to disavow their daily life and look for an alternative to it? On the contrary, they'll make a destiny out of it: intensify it while seeming to do the opposite, plunge into it to the point of ecstasy, seal the monotony of it with an even greater monotony.[61]

And against both the 'serious minds' and the 'beautiful souls' of the situationist tradition, Baudrillard implores us to throw in our lot with the winning side, abandoning all claims for the subject and accepting that the object has a power and irreducibility which subjectivity can never attain:

> the object does not believe in its own desire; the object does not live off the illusion of its own desire; the object has no desire. It does not believe that anything belongs to it as property, and it entertains no fantasies of reappropriation or autonomy.[62]

Why swim against the tide of commodification any longer, Baudrillard seems to be asking. 'Why privilege the position of the subject, why support this fiction of a will, a conscience, even of an unconscious for the subject?'[63] Years of defence and definition of the subject have called it into question to such an extent that it has become quite untenable. It is no longer possible to declare, with Vaneigem, that the subject is the unproblematic locus of desire, individuality, poetic experience, and creativity. 'We arrive then at this paradox, at this conjuncture where the position of the subject has become untenable, and where the only possible position is that of the object. The only strategy possible is that of the object.'[64]

In much of this work, Baudrillard assumes the role of the lone seer, desperately warning us of the hopelessness of our attempts to hang on to some conception of real life and meaningful experience. And because of this, there is a sense in which he continues the task of the critical theorist and still conveys some drive for opposition and negation. For although the substance of his work is quite alien to any critical tradition, Baudrillard admits his debt and attachment to situationist theory. 'I was very, very attracted by Situationism,' he declares. 'And even if today Situationism is past, there remains a kind of radicality to which I have always been faithful. There is still a kind of obsession, a kind of counterculture, which is still there. Something that has really stayed with me.'[65]

And while he scorns and inverts the situationist dream, Baudrillard continues, like generations of romantics and revolutionaries before him, to counterpose the world's self-image to some other, more real reality. His battle lines are drawn between all pretenders to truth, subjectivity, meaning, and the whole gamut of desiring and impassioned struggles for real experience on the one hand, and all blatant declarations of simulation, commodification, seduction, and artifice on the other. The world has in some sense shifted to this last camp, and it is here, in the surfaces and secrets of mediation, that the truly irrecuperable gestures are finally to be found. 'The present system of dissuasion and simulation succeeds in neutralizing all finalities, all referentials, all meanings, but it fails to neutralize appearances. It forcefully controls all the procedures for the production of meaning. It does not control the seduction of appearances. No interpretation can explain it, no system can abolish it. It is our last chance.'[66] Baudrillard insists that the struggle of the subject against the world of objects has finally been reversed purely as a consequence of its own history, by a simple twist of fate.

> Our all-too-beautiful strategies of history, knowledge, and power are erasing themselves. It is not because they have failed (they have, perhaps, succeeded too well) but because in their progression they reached a dead point where their energy was inverted and they devoured themselves, giving way to a pure and empty, or crazy and ecstatic, form.[67]

This sense of there being nowhere left to go and nothing new to say is a message which even the most optimistic readings of postmodernism are hard-pressed to avoid. For the postmodern age into which Baudrillard's work ushers us is above all characterised by a reworking of previous styles, vocabularies, ideas, and experiences; a representation of earlier moments from which all critical force and political momentum are excluded. Dada's cut-ups reappear in the fragmented texts of postmodern discourse, and surrealism's collages resurface on advertisement hoardings. Works of art more real than reality itself practise a struggle for the hyperreality of the over-commodified object and the disappearance of all aesthetic meaning, and many of those art forms characterised as postmodern appear as vacuous realisations of the situationist project. Boundaries between art and everyday life are eradicated, and distinctions between disciplines and styles are challenged with a new blossoming of discursive forms. Cultural references are glued, sometimes literally, onto the façades of factories and offices redundant even before their completion, and a curiously glamorous, classical, and superficial aesthetic, which is precisely that of the commodity, is painted over every remnant of the modern world. In gallery, street, and shop, the integrated environment has come into its own, and new technological developments continue to clear the way for holograms, laser lighting, and virtual reality to produce ever-more ecstatic forms of communication.

That situationist dreams of a freely constructed environment should be so subtly displaced comes as no surprise. 'The only thing that can be expressed in the mode of the spectacle is the emptiness of everyday life,' wrote Vaneigem. 'And indeed, what better commodity than an aesthetic of emptiness?'[68] Neither was it difficult to anticipate the re-emergence of the critical theory of the spectacle in Baudrillard's aimless excursions through a moment of history mistaken for its final realisation. Baudrillard's work is sophisticated and provocative: persuasive in the extreme, it is difficult to resist his exhortations and virtually impossible to contest them. But even at their best, his ideas are always and quite literally pointless. Devoid of both direction and origin, his most astute observations are mere descriptions made from some indeterminate realm too shifting and diffuse to constitute a critical perspective. As such, his texts are a perfect example of Debord calls 'lateral critique', a writing

> which perceives many things with considerable candour and accuracy, but places itself to one side. Not because it affects some sort of impartiality, for on the contrary it must seem to find much fault, yet without ever apparently feeling the need to reveal its *cause*, to state, even implicitly, where it is coming from and where it wants to go.[69]

Likening this kind of groundless criticism to 'those facsimiles of famous weapons, which only lack the firing-pin',[70] Debord awakens the notion of recuperation from the slumber induced by postmodern denials of its existence. Spectacular discourse 'isolates all it shows from its context, its past, its intentions and its consequences',[71] he writes. And from the pages of *Comments*, Baudrillard's work appears as a perfected and spectacular description of the spectacle, confirming its implicit insistence that history has ended, political action is futile, and subjective experience is always already commodified and recuperated.

Comments on the Society of the Spectacle observes many of the characteristics of the modern world described by Baudrillard. With and after situationist theory, Debord recognises the apparent impossibility of strategies of opposition, contradiction, or transgression with which the 'fragile meta-stability',[72] as Baudrillard describes American capitalist society, or Debord's conception of the spectacle as a state of '*fragile perfection*'[73] might be contested. For Debord, ours is a society which 'must no longer be exposed to attacks, being fragile; and indeed is no longer open to attack, being perfect as no other society before it'.[74] Baudrillard observes the 'evaporation of any real alternative', describing an 'uncontested and uncontestable' society to which there is 'no real opposition any more',[75] and Debord describes the spectacle's ability to dispense 'with that disturbing conception, which was dominant for over two hundred years, in which a society was open to criticism or transformation, reform or revolution. Not thanks to any new arguments, but simply because all argument has become useless.'[76]

But the similarities of their contemporary positions are underwritten and undermined by radical political differences. Debord's writing is purposeful and deliberate: he remains bitterly unhappy that simulations and appearances are emptying the world of meaning and reality and, still waiting for history to return to us, he decries the spectacular domination of the world as surely as in his earlier texts. For Baudrillard, however, it is not merely the case that we seem to have forsaken historical reality for a matrix of signs and simulations: this passage is complete, and the suggestion that history is at an end is 'by no means a despairing hypothesis, unless we regard simulation as a higher form of alienation – which I certainly do not'.[77]

From Baudrillard's perspective, Debord's laments are reactionary and nostalgic, still contained by struggles for production and the uncovering of more meaning, historical reality, and subjective experience. And to Debord, Baudrillard's work is based on a fundamental error, signalled, perhaps, by his specialised obsession with the media. Mistaking the appearances, simulations, and signs of reality for reality itself, Baudrillard has happily accepted the spectacle's own account of itself. As Debord had written in *The Society of the Spectacle*: 'Understood on its own terms, the spectacle proclaims the predominance of appearances and asserts that all human life, which is to say all social life, is mere appearance.'[78] And indeed, for Baudrillard, modern society is entirely circumscribed by its superficial characteristics. If we are led to believe that history has ended then it must be so; if dissent is always recuperated it must inevitably be lost; if events and experiences seem confused amidst a welter of spectacles and reproductions, they must truly have disappeared.

Like Baudrillard, Debord argues that 'the tendency to replace the real with the artificial is ubiquitous.'

> In this regard, it is fortuitous that traffic pollution has necessitated the replacement of the Marly Horses in place de la Concorde, or the Roman statues in the doorway of Saint-Trophime in Arles, by plastic replicas. Everything will become more beautiful than before, for the tourists' cameras.[79]

The growth of theme parks and the entire heritage industry substantiates Debord's claims that the false 'reinforces itself by knowingly eliminating any possible reference to the authentic', while the genuine 'is reconstructed as quickly as possible, to resemble the false'.[80] For Debord, this remains a matter for angry regret. The endless reproductions and representations of the spectacular world inspire no celebration, and privilege is still accorded to that which is spectacularised. There is still, in other words, a theatre into which real meanings and events are displaced and transported; a spectacle which remains an inversion of the real.

For Baudrillard, however, priority must now be given to appearance and artifice. And a nostalgic faith in the moment of liberation is not the only consequence of such pleas for the authentic. Taking nuclear war as his example, Baudrillard points out, as the situationists had also done, that the spectacle of war is more effective a display of power than its reality. And for Baudrillard, this merely proves that the appearance is infinitely preferable to the reality: 'this spectacle that the moralists disapprove of', he argues, 'is possibly the lesser evil. For God knows where unleashed meaning would lead to when it refuses to produce itself as appearance.'[81] This may be true of the nuclear spectacle, and coal mines converted for tourist appreciation are certainly safer than their earlier 'real' incarnations. But what of other realities and meanings? What of the love and poetry invoked by the situationists? Are mediations and simulations of the desires of Vaneigem's radical subject really preferable to struggles for their reality? Baudrillard clearly feels that they are. 'When nothing moves you any more', he writes, 'you must find a sign to stand in for passion.'

> I have played at passion, I have played at tenderness . . . . Some-
> times it even seems to me that I have never done anything but
> provide the semblance of ideas. But that is the one and only way
> out we have to take in a speculative world with no way out: to
> come up with the most successful signs of an idea. Or in an
> emotional world with no way out: to come up with the most
> successful signs of a passion.[82]

It is from a strangely misogynistic sexual experience and metaphor that Baudrillard derives much of his work on the seductive power of objects and artifice. The sexual object is said to be 'powerful in its absence of desire' just as the masses are 'powerful in their silence'.[83]

The extent of the differences between Baudrillard's endorse-ments of superficiality and the situationist perspective from which Debord still writes revolves around the question of whether the illusions encouraged by the spectacle have now become more real than the reality they once concealed, or whether, with Debord, they remain illusions to be unmasked. Does the modern world remain vulnerable to negation, merely appearing to make realities and meanings disappear by a sleight of hand to which commen-tators like Baudrillard fall happy victim, or have the spectacle's earlier denials of history really blossomed into a true end of history, bringing the absolute impossibility of meaningful change or social transformation? For Debord, the introduction of this last position into contemporary, and apparently radical, discourse, is a 'welcome break' for power, which is now guaranteed success 'in all its undertakings, or at least the rumour of success'.[84] The end of history is the eradication of any meaningful context in which the fragments of the contemporary world can be measured and assessed. 'History's domain was the memorable, the totality of events whose consequences would be lastingly apparent';[85] without historical knowledge, the possibility of judgement and evaluation is removed. 'When the spectacle stops talking about something for three days, it is as if it did not exist. For it has then gone on to talk about something else, and it is that which henceforth exists.'[86]

The precious advantage which the spectacle has acquired through the *outlawing* of history, from having driven the recent past into hiding, and from having made everyone forget the spirit of history within society, is above all the ability to cover its own tracks – to conceal the very progress of its recent world conquest. Its power already seems familiar, as if it had always been there. All usurpers have shared this aim: to make us forget that *they have only just arrived.*[87]

The end of history abandons us in an eternal present, in which events 'retreat into a remote and fabulous realm of unverifiable stories, uncheckable statistics, unlikely explanations and untenable reasoning'.[88] Devoid of meaning and purpose, events and experiences have neither past nor future, and significance is attributed 'only to what is immediate, and to what will be immediate immediately afterwards, always replacing another, identical, immediacy' in a media-generated 'eternity of noisy insignificance'.[89] The spectacle is sustained by the 'manufacture of a present where fashion itself, from clothes to music, has come to a halt, which wants to forget the past and no longer seems to believe in a future'; an eternity of meaninglessness 'achieved by the ceaseless circularity of information, always returning to the same short list of trivialities, passionately proclaimed as major discoveries'.[90]

The end of history facilitates the dissemination of an unverifiable discourse; a series of unanswerable lies and mystifications.

The spectacle proves its arguments simply by going round in circles: by coming back to the start, by repetition, by constant reaffirmation in the only space left where anything can be publicly affirmed, and believed, precisely because that is the only thing to which everyone is witness.[91]

This circularity of media, messages, and audience means that the spectacle skilfully 'organises ignorance of what is about to happen and, immediately afterwards, the forgetting of whatever has nonetheless been understood'.[92] And our entire society, writes Debord, is 'built on secrecy',

from the 'front' organisations which draw an impenetrable screen over the concentrated wealth of their members, to the 'official secrets' which allow the State a vast field of operation free from any legal constraint; from the often frightening secrets of shoddy production hidden by advertising, to the projections of an extrapolated future, in which domination alone reads off the unlikely progress of things whose existence it denies, calculating the responses it will mysteriously make.[93]

On one level, this secrecy is manifest in quite obvious areas. Debord points to areas of increasing inaccessibility – the quasi-military establishments and anonymous government departments which pepper the cities and countryside, and the prevalence of 'people trained to act in secret' – to suggest that 'under the rule of the integrated spectacle, we live and die at the confluence of innumerable mysteries'.[94] But Debord's secrecy is a more profound characteristic of spectacular organisation; one which, unlike Baudrillard's observations on the subject, continues to suggest that there are still things which are hidden. Insisting that secrecy is the exception to a free society of abundant information, the spectacle makes a virtue out of its concealed knowledges. 'Everyone accepts that there are inevitably little areas of secrecy reserved for specialists; as regards things in general, many believe they are *in on the secret*,' writes Debord. But this secrecy runs deeper still; it 'dominates this world, and first and foremost as the secret of domination',[95] since it is always the very existence of any system of domination which is perpetually denied.

Debord also suggests that our obsession with the media, surely epitomised by Baudrillard's work, is itself a distraction which precludes any critical engagement with the spectacle itself.

Rather than talk of the spectacle, people often prefer to use the term 'media'. And by this they mean to describe a mere instrument, a kind of public service which with impartial 'professionalism' would facilitate the new wealth of mass communication through mass media.[96]

The spectacle complains of its own abuses, criticises its spectators for being too stupid to see through its own propaganda, and organises a wonderful display of internal debate so that the excesses of particular spectacles conceal the ubiquity of spectacular life itself. The spectacle becomes 'merely the excesses of the media, whose nature, unquestionably good since it facilitates communication, is sometimes driven to extremes'.[97] But the spectacle is more than this: it is a world in which appearances are organised and lived experience eradicated. And likewise the media is much less: it is merely the realm in which orders are communicated 'with perfect harmony', for 'those who give them are also those who tell us what to think of them'.[98]

The apathy and stupidity of spectators is not the consequence of some ineluctable drive towards spectacle and reification, as Baudrillard would have us believe. It is the spectacle which stupefies and commodifies, forcing us to live in its truly 'global village', full of the 'conformism, isolation, petty surveillance, boredom and repetitive malicious gossip about the same families' which characterise every other sort of village.[99] When respect is demanded for the most banal of celebrities and stars, 'when they are held to be rich, important, prestigious, to be *authority itself*, it is little wonder that 'the spectators tend to want to be just as illogical as the spectacle'.[100] And meanwhile, 'news of what is genuinely important, or what is actually changing, comes rarely, and then in fits and starts. It always concerns this world's apparent condemnation of its own existence, the stages in its programmed self-destruction.'[101] Ours is a world in which '*everything which can be done, must be done*',[102] a society which has lost its reason[103] at the very moment in which thoughtful and strategic responses to enormous questions of environmental disaster, for example, are urgently required.

> It is indeed unfortunate that human society should encounter such burning problems [writes Debord] just when it has become materially impossible to make heard the least objection to the language of the commodity; just when power . . . *believes that it no longer needs to think*, and indeed can no longer think.[104]

Debord paints a scenario in which everyone is busily watching everyone else in a spiralling web of purposeless surveillance which 'spies on itself, and plots against itself'.[105] And so there is 'a contradiction between the mass of information collected on a growing number of individuals, and the time and intelligence available to analyse it',[106] until it becomes possible to 'speak of domination's falling rate of profit, as it spreads to almost the whole of social space and consequently increases both its personnel and its means'.[107] A host of 'professional conspirators are spying on each other without really knowing why . . . . Who is observing whom? On whose behalf, apparently? And actually? The real influences remain hidden, and the ultimate aims can barely be suspected and almost never understood.'[108] And the final contradiction of the all-pervasive surveillance of contemporary society is that it is 'spying on, infiltrating and pressurising *an absent entity*: that which is supposed to be trying to subvert the social order'.[109] This subversive force does not exist: 'Wherever the spectacle has its dominion the only organised forces are those which want the spectacle,'[110] and both revolutionary organisations and their theoretical developments appear to have exhausted themselves. 'Certainly conditions have never been so seriously revolutionary,' argues Debord, but, ironically, 'it is only governments who think so. Negation has been so thoroughly deprived of its thought that it was dispersed long ago. Because of this it remains only a vague, yet highly disturbing threat.'[111] Having taken the infiltration and provocation of negative forces to a limit at which it is no longer possible to distinguish the real elements of subversion from their simulated versions, the spectacle is now forced into the construction of its own enemies, developing 'an interest in organising poles of negation itself'.[112] But these manipulations, epitomised by the fabricated terrorist outrages in Italy, are no longer confined to such brutal manifestations. Now it is theoretical and ideological opposition which needs to be constructed and manipulated so that the reality of its disappearance is concealed.

Here Debord seems remarkably close to Baudrillard. Negation is absent; it has disappeared under the weight of discourses still desperately insisting on its existence. And Debord's penultimate observations in *Comments* reinforce this pessimism. The spectacle, he writes, has developed beyond the consciousness of those operating within it: spectacular society has still to become conscious of its own vacuity and meaninglessness.

> Not only are the subjected led to believe that to all intents and purposes they are still living in a world which in fact has been eliminated, but the rulers themselves sometimes suffer from the absurd belief that in some respects they do too . . . . This backwardness will not last long. Those who have achieved so much so easily must necessarily go further.[113]

But although Baudrillard's hyperreality seems to be waiting just around Debord's last corner as an ineluctable horizon at which the spectacle will one day meet its own image, there is still a sense in which Debord refuses to follow Baudrillard to the point at which the social world spirals off into a free-floating chaos of meaningless flux. There remains something confused by modern society; there are still realities to be secreted and revealed, gestures to be recuperated and recuperations to be subverted. The spectacle's obsession with surveillance may entrap itself in absurd webs of internal observation and the fabricated threat of subversion, but it still operates its fictional deterrence in anticipation of an outbreak of real dissent. The integrated spectacle has 'driven its critique into genuine clandestinity, not because it is in hiding but *because it is hidden* by the ponderous stage-management of diversionary thought', and 'provocation, infiltration, and various forms of elimination of authentic critique in favour of a false one . . . have been created for this purpose'.[114] And although memories of the past and hopes for the future have left the agenda of the integrated spectacle, the consequence of a perpetual present is that 'once the running of a State involves a permanent and massive shortage of historical knowledge, that State can no longer be led strategically'.[115] If the forces of negation are devoid of purpose, meaning, and reality, so too are those which support the spectacle. We return to the point at which 'order reigns and does not govern'[116] identified by Vaneigem; the moment at which all sense of strategy and direction is removed from spectacular organisation which endlessly and aimlessly reproduces itself.

For Baudrillard, this is all true, and there is nothing to be done about it. It is a comforting message, and postmodernism does of course relieve us of many exhausting burdens – not least the imperatives to seek the truth, to make the best, to create the new, and change the world – and frees us to enjoy the pleasures of the texts, the games among the vestiges. Without purpose and meaning, anything can be said and done. The cities look pretty, shopping is fun, commodities are friendly, and all sorts of dreams come true with barely a touch of a button. Superficially, everything is fine. And it is indeed tempting to assert the impossibility and undesirability of critical thought in such an apparently seamless world. In the face of the ubiquity of image and representation, unprecedented sophistications of the contemporary world, and the failure of a century of revolutionary critique, it is also far easier to swim with the tide and declare the end of all negation and dissent. Baudrillard's story fits like a glove; rather ironically, it is a faithful representation of the self-image promoted by capitalist social organisation.

And yet the seductive ease of such a world view is no reason to accept it. It has certainly become extremely difficult to introduce contradiction and negation into a discourse which has written out the possibility of a critical perspective or a world in which even the most radical gesture is immediately disarmed. But it is quite possible to assert that appearances are not, in fact, everything; that the spectacle has not spiralled off into an uncontrollable space; that the workings of contemporary society are not arcane; the masses continue to love, fight, work, and riot, and that history, contrary to decades of propaganda, is not dead, but merely sleeping. Nowhere, it is true, is there a critical project able to wield such observations as weapons of negation. But *Comments on the Society of the Spectacle* at least proves that it is possible to say all that Baudrillard has said without positioning oneself in the post-modern, and while there is no longer a flurry of revolutionary activity in which such a work can be received, it is also true that the age in which we live is far from the blind circularity of passive affirmation invoked by postmodern theory.

It fortunately remains the case that the networks of subversion which continue to arise in even the most postmodern pockets of the postmodern world are too numerous to detail here. And even in the midst of the 'aesthetic of emptiness' prevailing in the artistic milieu, recognition of the immense difficulties facing any critical engagement with an increasingly absorbent system of social relations has not led all cultural production to the aestheticisation of a spectacular environment. The radical trajectory begun by Dada has not accepted the petrifying conclusions of postmodern theory, and the awareness that even the most radical of gestures can be disarmed continues to encourage a search for irrecuperable forms of expression and communication. That a great deal of cultural agitation is hidden from the public gaze is sometimes indicative of its tactics rather than its absence. Radical artists have learnt from the 'horizontal' and anti-hierarchical networking characteristic of the contacts, with mail art networks establishing loose, transitory systems of information exchange which evade hierarchy and sidestep bureaucratic control. A flourishing samizdat tradition continues to produce music, magazines, performance, and political interventions in the spirit of ironic violence perfected by Dada; plagiarism, *détournement*, and provocation remain the hallmarks of a thriving and sophisticated world of agitation.

The 1980s were marked by a series of 'assaults on culture', culminating in calls for an art strike in 1990. Challenging all conventions of identity, originality, and the very nature of cultural production, the Praxis project convened a Festival of Plagiarism which reworked situationist notions of *détournement* and challenged the hypocrisy of high art distinctions between the plagiarism and evolutionary development of techniques and ideas. Plagiarism, wrote Stewart Home, 'saves time and effort, improves results, and shows considerable initiative on the part of the individual plagiarist. As a revolutionary tool it is ideally suited to the needs of the twentieth century.'[117] But Praxis distanced itself from the purposeless reproductions of postmodern culture with definitions of plagiarism as 'a collective undertaking far removed from the post-modern "theories" of appropriation .... Plagiarism is for life, post-modernism is fixated on death.'[118] And the pamphlet accompanying the Festival reinforced the plagiarists' distance from the postmodern insistence that progress is impossible and endless reiteration inevitable.

> Plagiarism in late capitalist society articulates a semi-conscious cultural condition: namely, that there 'is nothing left to say' .... The practitioners of much post-modern theory have tended to proclaim this feeling rather smugly; but if there is nothing to say, they yet demonstrate that there will always be something to sell. On the other hand, there are practitioners active in many disciplines who, recognising the necessity for collective action demanded by media such as film and electronic tape, engage in plagiarism in an attempt to expose and explode once and for all the individualistic attitudes which tend to make all current human activity seem redundant and increasingly alienated.[119]

The moves against individualism and originality made in the Festival of Plagiarism were underlined by proposals for multiple names. Karen Eliot, the most popular of these, was launched in 1985 as a name to be 'adopted by a variety of cultural workers at various times in order to carry through tasks related to building up a body of work ascribed to "Karen Eliot"' and so 'highlight the problems thrown up by the various mental sets pertaining to identity, individuality, originality, value and truth'.[120]

When one becomes Karen Eliot one's previous existence consists of the acts other people have undertaken using the name.

When one becomes Karen Eliot one has no family, no parents, no birth. Karen Eliot was not born, s/he was materialised from social forces, constructed as a means of entering the shifting terrain that circumscribes the 'individual' and society.[121]

Hundreds of people have adopted Karen Eliot for specific works and projects precisely because recognition and reward – so often the synonyms of commodification and recuperation – are provocatively evaded by the anonymity of a multiple name. 'Multiple names are connected to radical theories of play. The idea is to create an "open situation" for which no one in particular is responsible.'[122]

It goes without saying that few artists accepted the invitation to refuse creativity extended by those calling for an art strike between 1990 and 1993 to which these interventions led. Carrying a provocative ambiguity which incited confusion, the art strike reintroduced a whole range of issues around questions of strategy, recuperation, and the relation between culture and politics. Home argued that 'most "revolutionaries" have yet to realise the importance of fighting the bourgeoisie on cultural, as well as economic and political, fronts' and expressed the hope that 'the Art Strike will go some way towards correcting this oversight'.[123] Proposed as a means of 'intensifying the class struggle within the cultural, economic and political spheres', and aiming 'to demoralise a cross section of the bourgeois class',[124] the importance of the art strike was said to lie 'not in its feasibility but in the possibilities it opens up for intensifying the class war'.[125] For Home, art has never been a progressive political force, and the art strike was in part an attempt to demoralise those artists who believe their work to be oppositional or subversive. Situationist demands for a poeticised and freely created environment were only ever bourgeois dreams imposed on a disinterested proletariat by an over-enthusiastic avant-garde. Situationist hopes for an aestheticised daily experience have indeed come to 'reinforce the overall position of the bourgeoisie',[126] and situationist demands for the suppression and realisation of art in the name of free creativity, imagination, and pleasure are reactionary desires for a new cycle of mediations which, 'in the post-modern era . . . serve Power in the same way that honesty, truth, progress &c., served the capitalist system in the classical modern age'.[127]

To demand the destruction of art in the name of creativity is
merely a reform of Power. To trade off art against creativity is to
take back with one hand what has been rejected by the other.
Those who genuinely oppose alienated social relations will not
only break with art but affirm the refusal of creativity.[128]

Desires for authenticity were condemned as 'the most cynical of all
the pseudo-needs'. Offering 'the spectacle of its own inadequacy'
for mass consumption, capitalism 'uses this spectacle as the means
of reselling itself to those who "imagine" they have "progressed"
beyond bourgeois values in a "return" to the "authentic"'.[129]
Refusing all mediation and values, Praxis declared: 'ABOLISH
PLEASURE/REFUSE CREATIVITY/SMASH THE IMAGIN-
ATION/DESIRE IN RUINS/THE PRESENT IS ABSOLUTE/
EVERYTHING NOW!'[130]

Raising questions of authorship, responsibility, and authenticity, these adventures have contributed to debates dating back to
Dada's collaborations, Tzara's cut-up poems, Duchamp's ready-
mades, and surrealism's exquisite corpses. Surrealist arguments
about who, or what, constitutes the locus of artistic production and
responsibility were epitomised by an affair in which Louis Aragon,
threatened with prosecution for lines in *Red Front* which enthused,
'Kill the cops, comrades!', was unwillingly defended by Breton on
the grounds that poets can never be held responsible for their own
works when these are merely transcripts of an uncontrollable unconscious.[131] And it is in the cultivation of this sense of an anonymous, possibly ubiquitous, and uncontrollable surge of interrup-
tive and provocative desire that those associated with Karen Eliot
and the art strike have been most successful.

The strike itself, however, is a different matter. The interventions made around the Festival of Plagiarism were conceived
as 'the show-down that paved the way for the final conflict of Art
Strike',[132] a last attempt to subvert culture from within before the
tactics of sabotage come to an end with the recognition that any
participation inevitably enters into a relation of support with the
system of values and economic relations it seeks to undermine.
'Only total opposition, both theoretical and practical (i.e.,
silence), is irrecuperable,'[133] declares *The Art Strike Handbook* in an
apparent vindication of Baudrillard's claim that art 'no longer
contests anything, if ever it did. Revolt is isolated, the malediction
"consumed".' Art 'can parody this world, illustrate it, simulate it,

alter it', but 'it never disturbs the order, which is also its own'.[134] The only value of the art strike lay in its proposal of silence, rather than silence itself; the propaganda rather than the deed. It exposed the dangers of participating in a world to which it is implicitly opposed, but the noise with which it resisted recuperation was far more powerful than silence could ever have been.

Rather more optimistic responses to the circularity of all systems of signification are those which adopt tactics of occupation rather than strike. The possibilities of interrupting systems of communication and information exchange accelerate with the potential for forgery, abuses of copyright, anonymous production, and a whole new world of simulation and reproduction generated by the accessibility of new technology. 'The problems of tactics and strategy revolve around the question of how to turn against capitalism the weapons that commercial necessity has forced it to distribute,'[135] wrote Vaneigem in *The Revolution of Everyday Life*, and the relentless democracy imposed by commodity relations has indeed facilitated the appropriation of photocopiers, fax machines, screen printers, and desk-top publishers to a host of subversive, playful, and deterritorialising ends. Goods produced by high-prestige manufacturers are already faked by a booming industry of bootleggers whose reproductions of Rolex watches and Adidas T-shirts are often more prized than the mass-produced originals. 'People don't buy these things because they believe that they're real,' said one bootlegger. 'The shirts appeal to people because they *know* they're a rip-off. It's a matter of taking the piss out of the multinationals.'[136] On another front, the international Anticopyright network is busy collecting, distributing, and fly-posting provocative posters. 'When a piece of alien information is placed in the sheer banks of a shopping mall or office fax a fracture appears,' declare its propagandists. 'Instant and anonymous, splattered in a bus shelter or slipped into a magazine rack it is an economic crime – enjoyment without transaction.'[137] Attempts to interrupt the seamless circularity of equivalent signs continue to surface.

With both Baudrillard and the situationists, it has to be accepted that anything which is totally invulnerable to recuperation cannot be used in contestation either. The recognition that weapons can be turned against those who wield them is no reason to dispense with them altogether. 'Each word, idea or symbol is a double agent,' wrote Vaneigem. 'Some, like the word "fatherland" or the policeman's uniform, usually work for authority; but make no mistake, when ideologies clash or simply begin to wear out, the most mercenary sign can become a good anarchist.'[138] Nevertheless, calls for silence, disappearance, suicide, and refusals to participate in a game so difficult to play can have a powerful effect. The end of Dada, the death of Provo, the dissolution of both the SI and the Italian autonomists all testify that 'only the movements which were able to cease, to stop by themselves before dropping dead, have existed!'[139] Absences – of meaning, participation, reality, and identity – can constitute useful tactics in the struggle to unmask the social and economic relations of contemporary capitalist society. But their perpetration must be deliberate and intentional: although the drift into meaninglessness and the free acceptance of the commodification, silence, and apathy invited by capitalist social relations can be provocative and subversive, it cannot be turned into a universal principle which expresses, with Baudrillard, the inescapable state of the world. It is valid only as a meaningful gesture made against itself: Dada's absurdities were not performed without reason, and even its suicide was a last bid for autonomy. And knowing when to stop must not be confused with the tactics of despair: 'Let us have no more suicides from weariness, which come like a final sacrifice crowning all those that have gone before,'[140] wrote Vaneigem.

The despair invoked by the art strike has nevertheless engendered a variety of parodies of the intensified search for the irrecuperable, the truly radical gesture, introducing a measure of provocative humour to the world in which nothing can be said or done. Proposals by Karen Eliot for a 'thought strike' appeared in *Here and Now*, calling for 'all theorists to pour coke on their word processors and cease to think' between 3 January 1991 and 31 September 1994. 'Thought is a virus let loose on the world by a self-perpetuating elite in order to market the paraphernalia of the thinker – books, papers, pens, art films, word processors, whiskey,' the statement declared. 'Thought – who needs it? We proclaim the Thought Moratorium,' to be launched at the Festival of Stupidity. 'Events already planned include short personal statements of bewilderment by several passers-by. The Festival will be immediately followed by a retrospective exhibition at the ICA entitled "Thought: was it?"'[141]

The thought strike, actually taken seriously by some readers, was quickly superseded by the 'Post-Serious Internotional', a movement which 'becomes functionally inevitable at that point on the cruciality continuum when things have gone so far beyond a joke that all appropriate responses have ceased to be appropriate' and appeals for *more* thought. 'The mass Media will collapse in the face of a population intensively contemplating the possible implications of a magnetic potato for the future of furniture design.'[142] One of the most provocative of these *détournements* of calls for silence and suicide, 'Metastasis', was published in *Leisure* in 1990. Insisting that 'revolutionary proletarians' should 'encourage the growth of cancer in their bodies', it argues that good health 'is the technical realization of cellular creativity exiled into a beyond; it is separation perfected within the interior of the person' and calls for a 'fight against the capitalist recuperation of the creative cell. Don't let the rich get it all.'[143]

We cannot, of course, hope that postmodernism might make such witty or suicidal gestures. There is no movement, collectivity, or purpose in the postmodern project which would legitimate its disappearance, and since postmodernism has established itself as a social condition with neither history nor direction, demands for a postmodern suicide would be tantamount to asking the entire world to disappear, and not just apparently. But Baudrillard's insistence that all senses of originality, meaning, authenticity, and reality have abandoned us to a world of equivalent images and simulated experience invalidates all attempts to discriminate between the real Adidas logo and its copy, or the advertising hoarding and the flyposter. Asked whether his descriptions of circuits of signifiers without reference holds true not only for advertisements and TV images but all systems of signification, Baudrillard said 'Yes . . . all signs enter into such circuits – none escape.'[144] With the situationists, we can agree that everything arising in the spectacle assumes its characteristics: interventions will always be forced to assume the equivalence and vacuity of the commodity as long as an economic system dependent on production and consumption persists: 'when images chosen and constructed by *someone else* have everywhere become the individual's principal connection to the world he formerly observed for himself, it has certainly not been forgotten that these images can tolerate anything and everything; because within the same image all things can be juxtaposed without contradiction,'[145] writes Debord. But the recognition that even the most radical of gestures is implicated in this process cannot be allowed to lead to petrification and silence. It must, on the contrary, serve as a springboard for subversive strategies of interruption and provocation.

With both the situationists and the postmodernists, it is certainly true that we live in an age in which anything can be used for any purpose. But it is only in the absence of any purpose that the will to distinguish between plagiaristic *détournements* and recuperations disappears; only in a world with neither domination nor resistance can we give ourselves up to the endless ecstasies of purposeless communication. Meanwhile, *détournements*, subversions, and irreverent plagiarisms continue to match the assimilations, dissipations, and recuperations which strengthen and protect capitalist society.

An idiosyncratic path to the postmodern age has been followed in this book. Uncovering some political and cultural histories, it has neglected others: the passage through feminism, for example; or the more familiar debates about postmodernity conducted in the work of theorists like Jürgen Habermas and Frederic Jameson. The structuralist and poststructuralist ideas of Roland Barthes and Jacques Derrida, developments in and after Marxism by Althusserian theorists, and more conventional analyses of the media, consumerism, and the arts might all have been included. Psychoanalytic frameworks could have been treated more thoroughly, and a host of other themes, such as the influence of Antonin Artaud's maverick surrealism, or Alfred Jarry's pataphysical adventures, have been left out of this tale. It is, however, a book with a specific mission, which consideration of all these neglected figures would only have reinforced. In telling the story of the situationist influence on contemporary culture and insisting on the pivotal significance of the movement to a century of political, artistic, and philosophical debate, it has explored the possibilities of critical thought revealed by this history and tried to reintroduce some sense of meaning, purpose, and passion to a postmodern discourse of futile denial.

It is 'the destiny of signs', writes Baudrillard, 'to be torn from their destination, deviated, displaced, diverted, recuperated, seduced. It is their destiny in the sense that this is what always happens to them; it is our destiny in the sense that this is what always happens to us.'[146] This talk of destiny seems characteristic of the slumbering and reformist fatalism which seems to dominate the political atmosphere. In Britain, the Thatcher years have reinforced perceptions of a broader loss of freedom, alleviated only by rare moments of optimism such as the students' occupation of Tiananmen Square in 1988 and the dissolution of Stalinism in 1989, both of which seemed to herald a new age of refusal and dissent which might find a resonance in western Europe as well. But the massacre in China and the beginnings of eastern European assimilation into a strengthened capitalist order have merely reinforced Debord's claims for the integrated spectacle: a global order which conducts its wars and manages its famines with a blind adherence to economic survival. 'In a certain sense', writes Debord,

> the coherence of spectacular society proves revolutionaries right, since it is evident that one cannot reform the most trifling detail without taking the whole thing apart. But at the same time this coherence has eliminated every organised tendency by eliminating those social terrains where it had more or less effectively been able to find expression: from trade unions to newspapers, towns to books.[147]

It is difficult to dispel Debord's assertion that the situation is unique: this is 'the first time in contemporary Europe', he suggests, that 'no party or fraction of a party even tries to pretend that they wish to change anything significant.'[148]

But it is precisely here, with the question of what *is* significant in contemporary society, that the crises of critical thought and political action inscribed in postmodern theory have arisen. The issue of what really perpetuates existing social relations and, consequently, the form their negation might take, has been posed with increasing sophistication in every moment of twentieth-century contestation. Every possibility of contradiction has been tried and interrogated until the attempt to isolate a central contradiction between power and its other has itself been seen as the bearer of dogma and control. And out of this awareness comes the prevailing insistence that all attempts to transform the world are themselves responsible for the domination and impoverishment which continue to mark our society. We find ourselves in a morass, certain that there is nothing to be done, overwhelmed by the failures of the past, and convinced of the culpability of our theoretical frameworks.

With postmodernism, it is true that ours is a culture about which there is nothing more to say. Baudrillard's argument that the revolutionary movements of the past have in a sense been too successful, resulting in an overproduction of meaning, rings true. But the endless cycles of reversibility, reproduction, and simulation in which we play testify not to the redundancy of critical discourse, but that of the culture it contests. Ours is a culture about which there is nothing more to say precisely because it has outlived its discursive possibilities: art, literature, philosophy, and politics can only implode and return against themselves in spirals of ever-decreasing significance. And while everything is said about this imperative to repetition and return, the possibility of moving beyond it is rarely discussed. Postmodernity comes equipped with a refusal to countenance the possibilities of social transformation on which its supersession depends. Talk of revolution becomes embarrassing, and the suggestion that history has ended is embraced with open relief. Situationist desires for 'a rise in the pleasure of living'[149] have become the dreams of another age and no longer have anything to say to us.

But this drastic fall in expectations which seems to mark our approach to the end of the millennium is not something we are powerless to confront. Certainly it is no longer obvious that truth cannot be opposed to ideology, or life to survival; social groups and classes do not conveniently line up on opposite sides of the barricades, and the multitude of transgressive and often conflicting desires which constitute individuals and systems of social organisation can never again be ignored for the convenience of some revolutionary plan. But just as it is most useful to conspirators that the conspiracy theory of history is thoroughly discredited,[150] so it is very convenient for all those who would deny the possibility of social change to usher in a world in which subversion is impossible. Caught in a web in which all possibilities of dissent are countered by the immediate thought of their defeat, it is indeed more difficult than ever before to reintroduce any sense of negativity to the systems of power in which we live. No longer sure of the causes, we are more willing to dispense with them altogether than renew our search. But the scenario in which theorists trip over people asleep on the streets on their way to declare the impossibility of changing anything is merely the tip of an absurd and tragic iceberg with which we cannot continue to live. As the world spirals into senseless, devastating cycles of war, oppression, and environmental disaster, strategies which call for even less meaning, reason, and impassioned engagement seem increasingly redundant. It may be difficult to assert the possibility of wholesale change, but it is by no means certain that the necessity to do so has disappeared.

We have, of course, been warned off such a project – and not without reason – by poststructuralist suggestions that the search for causes and contradictions depends on an untenable world view populated by a teleological understanding of history, essentialist conceptions of the subject, and illegitimate references to something better, more real, more true, and more desired than the present. There are, indeed, huge dangers here. But those associated with the blanket refusal to develop a critical engagement with these positions are greater still, for they ultimately leave us unable to say, do, or speculate about anything. It is little wonder that the world appears chaotic and boundless when we have so thoroughly denied ourselves the critical tools with which to understand it.

So where can we look for the causes, the determining principles, of this apparently indeterminate world? For the situationists, the only place to look was to the spectacle, a space privileged above all others as the organising principle of the world and its critique. And for Debord, this remains true: in the midst of all our chatterings about codes, signs, and networks of purposeless domination, the one possibility we fail to confront is also that which might allow a renewed burst of negativity. It is the commodity, he writes in *Comments*, which is always 'beyond criticism'.[151] To be sure, the situationists were naïve and sometimes arrogant in their determination to find some 'other' to the ubiquity of commodity relations. And the proliferation of sites of complex domination and resistance which now characterise capitalist social relations may indeed have outstripped the usefulness of a critique of the spectacle. But albeit in circumstances very different from our own, they too were writing against a world of uncanny and petrifying circularity, similarly devoid of any locus of negation and all too aware of the failures of past revolutionary projects. And the over-riding merit of their project was its ability to develop a historical and material analysis of the world we now call postmodernity. Seduced only by the possibilities of challenging and negating capitalist social relations, the situationists were able to give some meaning to the apparently autonomous and incomprehensible dominion of its signs, the ubiquitous affirmation and fragmentation of its discourse, and the confusion and fragmentation of its rapid and purposeless change. For all its problems and absences, the identification of commodified relations in every area of social, individual, and cultural life threw up the possibility of new solidarities between social groups, desires, and experiences. It allowed the situationists to pose a freely constructed other to capitalist relations and inject an exuberant propaganda of the possible into a world of mundane despair and superficiality.

Spectacular discourse, writes Debord, 'isolates all it shows from its context, its past, its intentions and its consequences'.[152] Garbled versions of situationist imagery, attitudes, and theory pepper contemporary cultural discourse without a trace of their origins in the critique of commodity relations, and it is only too easy to characterise postmodernism – in art, philosophy, and politics – as a wholesale recuperation of the century's radical currents. And because the situationists were so aware of the dangers of recuperation, it is tempting to imagine that there are mines laid in the terrain which has been captured from them. They certainly fostered the idea that their critique would re-emerge regardless of the obstacles and recuperations it might face: 'like the proletariat', they wrote, 'we cannot claim to be unexploitable in the present conditions; we must simply work to make any such exploitation entail the greatest possible risk for the exploiters'.[153] In many respects, the arrogant confidence of such statements remains one of the movement's most attractive features. Perversely dogmatic, the situationists still wanted the world to have fun, and although their hostility to any of the qualities of spectacular society produced a tradition as glamorous and mystified as the commodified relations it opposed, there is still something inspiring about their declared faith in the imminence of revolution and the extravagance of their propaganda. And perhaps such arrogance is an inevitable feature of any intervention, be it in the form of political action, theoretical discourse, or transgressive deconstruction. At the extreme, it is always possible to ask with what right, rhyme, or reason anyone has for saying, doing, or imagining anything. Against doubtful poststructuralist and uncompromisingly negative postmodern responses to this question, the situationists have left a legacy of assertive confidence in the possibility of the collective construction not only of a playful discourse but impassioned forms of living too.

Notes

Note on Guy Debord, *The Society of the Spectacle*. An unpublished translation by Donald Nicholson-Smith has been used throughout this text in preference to the published translation, *The Society of the Spectacle*, Detroit, Black & Red, 1977. All references to this text refer the reader not to page numbers, but the numbered theses common to all editions.

Quotations from French texts are translated by the author.

'The most radical gesture' of the title of this book is a phrase from a comic strip advertising *Internationale Situationniste* 11. In French, the phrase is 'Il n'est pas de geste si radicale que l'idéologie n'essaie de recupérer'.

1 'NOW, THE SI'

'Now, the SI' is the title of an article in *Internationale Situationniste* 9, August 1964, and Ken Knabb (ed.), *Situationist International Anthology*, Berkeley, Bureau of Public Secrets, 1981.

1 Vaneigem's holiday is a completely unsubstantiated rumour which nevertheless captures the spirit of this debate.
2 Guy Debord, *Preface to the Fourth Italian Edition of The Society of the Spectacle*, London, Chronos, 1979, pp. 8–9.
3 Ibid., p. 24.
4 Guy Debord, 'Critique of Separation', Ken Knabb (ed.), *Situationist International Anthology*, Berkeley, Bureau of Public Secrets, 1981, p. 37.
5 Karl Marx, 'Economic and Philosophic Manuscripts of 1844', Karl Marx and Frederick Engels, *Collected Works*, vol. 3, London, Lawrence & Wishart, 1975, p. 274.
6 Guy Debord, *The Society of the Spectacle*, unpublished translation, 1990, 20.
7 Ibid.
8 Ibid., 12.
9 Ibid., 42.
10 Ibid., 212.

11 Ibid., 213.
12 Ibid., 1.
13 The Pleasure Tendency, *Life and its Replacement with a Dull Reflection of Itself*, Leeds, 1986.
14 *The Society of the Spectacle*, 30.
15 Ibid., 12.
16 Ibid., 47.
17 Karl Marx and Frederick Engels, 'Manifesto of the Communist Party', Karl Marx and Frederick Engels, *Collected Works*, vol. 6, London, Lawrence & Wishart, 1976, p. 490.
18 *The Society of the Spectacle*, 72.
19 Paul Cardan, *Modern Capitalism and Revolution*, London, Solidarity, 1974, p. 11.
20 *The Society of the Spectacle*, 26.
21 Raoul Vaneigem, *The Revolution of Everyday Life*, n.p., Left Bank Books and Rebel Press, 1983, p. 48.
22 Ibid., p. 50.
23 *The Society of the Spectacle*, 114.
24 Ibid., 115.
25 Ibid.
26 George Lukács, *History and Class Consciousness*, London, Merlin Press, 1983, p. 93.
27 Ibid., p. 86.
28 Ibid., p. 85.
29 Ibid., p. 93.
30 *The Society of the Spectacle*, 122.
31 Ibid., 84.
32 Ibid., 122.
33 Ibid., 119.
34 Ibid., 114.
35 Ibid., 121.
36 Ibid., 117.
37 *History and Class Consciousness*, p. 80.
38 Ibid., p. 89.
39 Ibid., p. 181.
40 Cf. Peter Wollen, 'The Situationist International', *New Left Review* 174, March/April 1989, pp. 67–95.
41 Ibid., p. 91.
42 Ibid., p. 197.
43 'Questionnaire', *Internationale Situationniste* 9, August 1964, and *Situationist International Anthology*, p. 138.
44 Jean-Paul Sartre, *Being and Nothingness: An Essay on Phenomenological Ontology*, London, Methuen, 1969, p. 489.
45 Ibid.
46 *Preface to the Fourth Italian Edition of the Society of the Spectacle*, pp. 23–4.
47 'Ideologies, Classes and the Domination of Nature', *Internationale Situationniste* 8, January 1963, and *Situationist International Anthology*, p. 101.
48 Guy Debord, 'Introduction to a Critique of Urban Geography', *Situationist International Anthology*, p. 6.

49 *The Society of the Spectacle*, 40.
50 Ibid.
51 Raoul Vaneigem, 'Basic Banalities I', *Internationale Situationniste* 7, April 1962, and *Situationist International Anthology*, p. 92.
52 Guy Debord, 'Perspectives for Conscious Alterations in Everyday Life', *Internationale Situationniste* 6, Aug. 1961, and *Situationist International Anthology*, p. 70.
53 *The Society of the Spectacle*, 44.
54 'Basic Banalities I', p. 90.
55 *The Society of the Spectacle*, 43.
56 Ibid., 42.
57 Ibid., 43.
58 Ibid., 1.
59 Ibid., 62.
60 Ibid., 69.
61 Ibid., 67.
62 Ibid.
63 Ibid.
64 Ibid., 69.
65 Ibid., 70.
66 Karl Marx, 'The Poverty of Philosophy', *Collected Works*, vol. 6, p. 174; *History and Class Consciousness*, p. 48; and *The Society of the Spectacle*, 143.
67 *The Society of the Spectacle*, 141.
68 Ibid., 143.
69 Ibid.
70 Ibid.
71 Ibid., 150.
72 Ibid.
73 Ibid., 155.
74 Ibid., 153.
75 Ibid., 152.
76 *History and Class Consciousness*, p. 90.
77 *The Society of the Spectacle*, 168.
78 Ibid., 173.
79 Ibid., 174.
80 Ibid., 177.
81 'Of Student Poverty, Considered in its Economic, Political, Psychological, Sexual, and Particularly Intellectual Aspects, and a Modest Proposal for its Remedy', *Ten Days that Shook the University*, London, Situationist International, n.d., p.11.
82 'Perspectives for Conscious Alterations in Everyday Life', *Internationale Situationniste* 6, Aug. 1961, and *Situationist International Anthology*, p. 74.
83 *History and Class Consciousness*, p. 181.
84 *The Society of the Spectacle*, 75.
85 Ibid., 203.
86 Ibid., 7.
87 Ibid., 8.
88 Ibid., 52.

89 Ibid., 68.
90 'The Decline and Fall of the Spectacle-Commodity Economy', *Internationale Situationniste* 10, March 1966, and *Situationist International Anthology*, p. 155.
91 Guy Debord, 'Report on the Construction of Situations and on the International Situationist Tendency's Conditions of Organization and Action', *Situationist International Anthology*, p. 25.
92 *The Society of the Spectacle*, 203.
93 'Instructions for Taking up Arms', *Internationale Situationniste* 6, Aug. 1961, and *Situationist International Anthology*, p. 64.
94 *Preface to the Fourth Italian Edition of The Society of the Spectacle*, p. 23.
95 Situationist International, *The Veritable Split in the International*, London, Chronos, 1990, p. 77.
96 *Preface to the Fourth Italian Edition of The Society of the Spectacle*, p. 9.
97 Ibid., p. 11.
98 Herbert Marcuse, *One Dimensional Man: Studies in the Ideology of Advanced Industrial Society*, Boston, Beacon Press, 1966, p. 9.
99 *The Society of the Spectacle*, 201.
100 Ibid.
101 Ibid., 202.
102 Ibid., 5.
103 Ibid., 4.
104 Ibid., 6.
105 Jean Baudrillard, *Le système des objets*, Paris, Denoel-Gonthier, 1968, p. 217.
106 Mark Poster (ed.), *Jean Baudrillard: Selected Writings*, Cambridge and Palo Alto, Polity Press and Stanford University Press, 1988, p. 31.
107 Ibid., p. 33.

2   '. . . A WORLD OF PLEASURES TO WIN, AND NOTHING TO LOSE BUT BOREDOM'

'. . . a world of pleasures to win and nothing to lose but boredom' is taken from Raoul Vaneigem, *The Revolution of Everyday Life*, n.p., Left Bank Books and Rebel Press, 1983.

1 A phrase taken from Charles Russell, *Poets, Prophets, and Revolutionaries: The Literary Avant-Garde from Rimbaud through Postmodernism*, Oxford University Press, 1985.
2 Raoul Vaneigem, *The Revolution of Everyday Life*, n.p., Left Bank Books and Rebel Press, 1983, p. 150.
3 Hugo Ball, in Hans Richter, *Dada: Art and Anti-Art*, London, Thames & Hudson, 1978, pp. 13–14.
4 Marcel Janco, 'Dada at Two Speeds', Lucy Lippard (ed.), *Dadas on Art*, Englewood Cliffs, NJ, Prentice-Hall, 1971, p. 36.
5 Tristan Tzara, 'Dada Manifesto, 1918', *Seven Dada Manifestos and Lampisteries*, London, John Calder, 1984, p. 12.
6 Maurice Nadeau, *The History of Surrealism*, Harmondsworth, Penguin, 1978, p. 47.

7 Arthur Rimbaud, *Collected Poems*, Harmondsworth, Penguin, 1986, pp. 10–11.
8 Guillaume Apollinaire, in Franklin Rosemont (ed.), André Breton, *What is Surrealism? Selected Writings*, London, Pluto, 1978, p. 373.
9 Jacques Vaché, in A. Alvarez, *The Savage God, A Study of Suicide*, Harmondsworth, Penguin, 1971, p. 248.
10 Tristan Tzara, 'Dada Manifesto on Feeble and Bitter Love', *Seven Dada Manifestos and Lampisteries*, p. 39.
11 Raoul Hausmann, in *Dada: Art and Anti-Art*, p. 118.
12 Hugo Ball, in Rudolf E. Kuenzli, 'The Semiotics of Dada Poetry', Stephen C. Foster and Rudolf E. Kuenzli, *Dada Spectrum: The Dialectics of Revolt*, Madison, Wis., Coda Press, 1979, p. 67.
13 Louis Aragon, in Robert Short, 'Paris Dada and Surrealism', Richard Sheppard, *Dada: Studies of a Movement*, Chalfont St Giles, Alpha Academic, 1979, p. 83.
14 Marcel Duchamp, in *Dada: Art and Anti-Art*, p. 88.
15 Anonymous, 'The Richard Mutt Case', *Dadas on Art*, p. 143.
16 Marcel Duchamp, in *Dada: Art and Anti-Art*, p. 90.
17 Gabrielle Buffet-Picabia, 'Some Memories of Pre-Dada: Picabia and Duchamp', Robert Motherwell (ed.), *The Dada Painters and Poets, An Anthology*, New York, Wittenborn Schultz, 1951, p. 255.
18 Hans Arp, 'Dadaland', *Dadas on Art*, p. 28.
19 Hans Arp, in Herbert Read, *Arp*, London, Thames & Hudson, 1968, pp. 38–9.
20 Hans Arp, 'Dadaland', p. 29.
21 Walter Mehring, in *Dada: Art and Anti-Art*, pp. 111–12.
22 Mustapha Khayati, 'Captive Words: Preface to a Situationist Dictionary', *Internationale Situationniste* 10, March 1966, and Ken Knabb (ed.), *Situationist International Anthology*, Berkeley, Bureau of Public Secrets, 1981, p. 172.
23 Pierre Canjuers and Guy Debord, 'Preliminaries Toward Defining a Unitary Revolutionary Programme', *Situationist International Anthology*, p. 309.
24 George Grosz and Wieland Herzfelde, 'Art is in Danger', *Dadas on Art*, p. 81.
25 Tristan Tzara, 'Monsieur Antipyrine's Manifesto', *Seven Dada Manifestos and Lampisteries*, p. 1.
26 'Dada Manifesto, 1918', pp. 10–11.
27 Ibid., p. 3.
28 Tristan Tzara, 'Monsieur AA the Antiphilosopher Sends us this Manifesto', *Seven Dada Manifestos and Lampisteries*, p. 28.
29 'Dada Manifesto, 1918', p. 13.
30 *Dada: Art and Anti-Art*, p. 61.
31 Cf. Roger Cardinal and Richard Short, *Surrealism: Permanent Revelation*, London, Studio Vista, 1970, and Alvarez, *The Savage God*, for discussions of Dada's 'suicide'.
32 Ben Vautier, 'The Duchamp Heritage', *Dada Spectrum*, p. 251.
33 Louis Aragon, *Paris Peasant*, London, Pan, 1987, p. 127.
34 Louis Aragon, in *The History of Surrealism*, p. 160.

35 André Breton, 'Second Manifesto of Surrealism', *Manifestoes of Surrealism*, Ann Arbor, University of Michigan Press, 1972, pp. 123–4.
36 André Breton, *Mad Love*, Lincoln, Neb., and London, University of Nebraska Press, 1987, p. 40.
37 Louis Aragon, in *Surrealism: Permanent Revelation*, p. 54.
38 André Breton, 'Manifesto of Surrealism', *Manifestoes of Surrealism*, p. 23.
39 *Mad Love*, pp. 13–15.
40 Walter Benjamin, 'Surrealism: The Last Snapshot of the European Intelligentsia', *One Way Street*, London, New Left Books, 1979, p. 230.
41 Lautréamont (Isidore Ducasse), *Poésies*, London and New York, Allison & Busby, 1980, p. 75.
42 André Breton, *Surrealism and Painting*, London, Macdonald, 1972, p. 288.
43 *Paris Peasant*, p. 64.
44 Louis Aragon, in *Surrealism: Permanent Revelation*, p. 60.
45 The last phrase of André Breton's *Nadja*, New York, Grove Press, 1960.
46 'Second Manifesto of Surrealism', p. 140.
47 André Breton, 'Legitimate Defence', *What is Surrealism?* p. 39.
48 Walter Benjamin, *Charles Baudelaire: A Lyric Poet in the Era of High Capitalism*, London, Verso, 1983, p. 14.
49 Robert Desnos, in J.H. Matthews, *Towards the Poetics of Surrealism*, New York, Syracuse University Press, 1976, p. 154.
50 André Breton, in *Surrealism: Permanent Revelation*, p. 122.
51 'Second Manifesto of Surrealism', p. 125.
52 André Breton, 'The Colours of Liberty', *Now* 7, Feb–March 1946, pp. 33–4.
53 André Breton, 'For Dada', *What is Surrealism?* p. 3.
54 'Second Manifesto of Surrealism', p. 139.
55 Henry Miller, 'Open Letter to Surrealists Everywhere', *The Cosmological Eye*, Connecticut, New Directions, 1939, pp. 159–60.
56 Ibid., p. 163.
57 Paul Hammond, 'Specialists in Revolt', an interview with Jean Schuster, *New Statesman*, 4 Dec. 1987, pp. 22–3.
58 Guy Debord, 'Report on the Construction of Situations and on the International Situationist Tendency's Conditions of Organisation and Action', 1957, *Situationist International Anthology*, p. 19.
59 'Ideologies, Classes and the Domination of Nature', *Internationale Situationniste* 8, Jan. 1963, and *Situationist International Anthology*, p. 106.
60 'Report on the Construction of Situations', p. 20.
61 'Preliminaries Toward Defining a Unitary Revolutionary Programme', p. 309.
62 Theo van Doesburg and Cor van Eesteren, 'Towards Collective Building', Ulrich Conrads (ed.), *Programmes and Manifestos on Twentieth Century Architecture*, London, Lund Humphries, 1970, p. 67.
63 Ivan Chtcheglov, 'Formulary for a New Urbanism', *Internationale Situationniste* 1, June 1958, and *Situationist International Anthology*, p. 1.
64 Attila Kotanyi and Raoul Vaneigem, 'Elementary Programme of the

Bureau of Unitary Urbanism', *Internationale Situationniste* 6, Aug. 1961, and *Situationist International Anthology*, p. 66.

65 Ibid., p. 67.

66 Guy Debord, 'Introduction to a Critique of Urban Geography', *Situationist International Anthology*, p. 5.

67 Ibid., p. 6.

68 Jacques Fillon, 'New Games', *Programmes and Manifestos on Twentieth Century Architecture*, p. 155. Surrealist drifts and situationist *dérives* clearly resonate with the whole tradition of the *flâneurs*, the idle saunterers of the European modernist city.

69 Guy Debord, 'Theory of the Derive', *Internationale Situationniste* 2, Dec. 1958, and *Situationist International Anthology*, p. 50.

70 'Report on the Construction of Situations', p. 24.

71 Ibid., p. 19.

72 'Intervention Lettriste', *Potlatch 1954-57*, Paris, Gérard Lebovici, 1985, p. 172.

73 André Breton, *Les Pas Perdus*, Paris, Gallimard, 1924, p. 12.

74 *The History of Surrealism*, pp. 106-7.

75 André Breton, 'Experimental Researches', *What is Surrealism?* pp. 95-6.

76 'Project d'Embellissements Rationnels de la Ville de Paris', *Potlatch 1954-57*, pp. 177-80.

77 'Report on the Construction of Situations', p. 25.

78 Guy Debord and Gil Wolman, 'Methods of Detournement', *Situationist International Anthology*, p. 11.

79 Attila Kotanyi and Raoul Vaneigem, 'Elementary Programme of the Bureau of Unitary Urbanism', *Internationale Situationniste* 6, Aug. 1961, and *Situationist International Anthology*, p. 67.

80 Cf. the reference to Manchester's Hacienda club in Chapter 4.

81 Ivan Chtcheglov, 'Formulary for a New Urbanism', *Internationale Situationniste* 1, June 1958, and *Situationist International Anthology*, p. 3.

82 Ibid., p. 4.

83 Ibid., p. 3.

84 'Report on the Construction of Situations', p. 17.

85 Ibid.

86 Ibid., p. 25.

87 *The Revolution of Everyday Life*, p. 183.

88 Ibid., p. 87.

89 Ibid., p. 15.

90 Ibid., p. 190.

91 Ibid., p. 183.

92 Ibid., p. 189.

93 Ibid., p. 150.

94 Ibid., p. 187.

95 Guy Debord, 'Perspectives for Conscious Alterations in Everyday Life', *Internationale Situationniste* 6, Aug. 1961, and *Situationist International Anthology*, p. 69.

96 Henri Lefebvre published 'La Signification de la Commune' in *Arguments* Nos 27-8, 1962; situationist accusations about its plagiarism appear in *Internationale Situationniste* 12, Sept. 1969, pp. 107-11.

97 Henri Lefebvre, *Everyday Life in the Modern World*, London, Allen Lane, Penguin, 1971, p. 204.
98 'Perspectives for Conscious Alterations in Everyday Life', *Internationale Situationniste* 6, Aug. 1961, and *Situationist International Anthology*, p. 75.
99 Ibid., p. 71.
100 Ibid., p. 72.
101 *The Revolution of Everyday Life*, p. 50.
102 Raoul Vaneigem, 'Basic Banalities II', *Internationale Situationniste* 8, Jan. 1963, and *Situationist International Anthology*, p. 122.
103 George Lukács, *History and Class Consciousness*, London, Merlin Press, 1983, p. 103.
104 'Basic Banalities II', p. 125.
105 Raoul Vaneigem, 'Basic Banalities I', *Internationale Situationniste* 7, April 1962, and *Situationist International Anthology*, p. 98.
106 Guy Debord, *The Society of the Spectacle*, unpublished translation, 1990, 60.
107 Ibid., 61.
108 Ibid.
109 *The Revolution of Everyday Life*, p. 103.
110 Ibid.
111 'Basic Banalities II', p. 129.
112 *Alcester Chronicle*, 4 July 1990.
113 *The Revolution of Everyday Life*, p. 85.
114 *The Society of the Spectacle*, 17.
115 Ibid., 59.
116 *The Revolution of Everyday Life*, p. 102.
117 Ibid., p. 97.
118 Ibid., p. 102.
119 Ibid.
120 'A New Idea in Europe', *Potlatch 1954–57*, p. 46.
121 'Introduction to a Critique of Urban Geography', p. 6.
122 André Breton, 'What is Surrealism?', *What is Surrealism?*, p. 113.
123 Ibid., p. 118.
124 Ibid.
125 *The Revolution of Everyday Life*, p. 189.
126 Ibid., p. 82.
127 Ibid., p. 202.
128 Ibid.
129 Ibid., p. 201.
130 'Report on the Construction of Situations', p. 24.
131 *The Revolution of Everyday Life*, p. 201.
132 'Basic Banalities II', p. 121.
133 *The Revolution of Everyday Life*, p. 59.
134 Ibid., p. 58.
135 Ibid., p. 59.
136 Ibid., p. 192.
137 Ibid., p. 194.
138 Ibid., p. 195.

139 Ibid., p. 91.
140 Ibid., p. 7.
141 *The Society of the Spectacle*, 52.
142 *The Revolution of Everyday Life*, p. 8.
143 Ibid., p. 149.
144 Ibid.
145 Ibid.
146 Ibid., p. 91.

3 '. . . A SINGLE CHOICE: SUICIDE OR REVOLUTION'

'a single choice: suicide or revolution' is the point to which Vaneigem leads readers of 'Basic Banalities I', *Internationale Situationniste* 7, April 1962, and Ken Knabb (ed.), *Situationist International Anthology*, Berkeley, Bureau of Public Secrets, 1981.

1 Herbert Marcuse, 'Repressive Tolerance', R.P. Wolf *et al.* (eds), *A Critique of Pure Tolerance*, Boston, Beacon Press, 1965.
2 Raoul Vaneigem, *The Revolution of Everyday Life*, n.p., Left Bank Books and Rebel Press, 1983, p. 74.
3 Guy Debord, *The Society of the Spectacle*, unpublished translation, 1990, 30.
4 'Instructions for Taking up Arms', *Internationale Situationniste* 6, Aug. 1961, and *Situationist International Anthology*, Berkeley, Bureau of Public Secrets, p. 63.
5 *The Society of the Spectacle*, 87.
6 Mustapha Khayati, 'Captive Words: Preface to a Situationist Dictionary', *Internationale Situationniste* 10, March 1966, and *Situationist International Anthology*, p. 173.
7 'Instructions for Taking up Arms', Internationale Situationniste 5, Dec. 1960, and *Situationist International Anthology*, p. 63.
8 *The Revolution of Everyday Life*, p. 127.
9 Richard Huelsenbeck, in Hans Richter, *Dada: Art and Anti-Art*, London, Thames & Hudson, 1978, p. 211.
10 Marcel Duchamp, in ibid., p. 208.
11 J-F. Dupois, in Henri Béhar and Michel Carassou (eds), *Le Surréalisme: Textes et Débats*, Paris, Librairie Générale Française, 1984, p. 69.
12 Philippe Soupault, in Dawn Ades, *Dada and Surrealism Reviewed*, London, Arts Council of Great Britain, 1978, p. 162.
13 'Basic Banalities I', *Internationale Situationniste* 7, April 1962, and *Situationist International Anthology*, pp. 97–8.
14 'Captive Words', p. 173.
15 Guy Debord, 'Report on the Construction of Situations and on the International Situationist Tendency's Conditions of Organization and Action', *Situationist International Anthology*, p. 20.
16 'Response to a Questionnaire from the Center for Socio-Experimental Art', *Internationale Situationniste* 9, Aug. 1964, and *Situationist International Anthology*, p. 144.

17 Raoul Vaneigem, 'Basic Banalities II', *Internationale Situationniste* 8, Jan. 1963, and *Situationist International Anthology*, p. 124.
18 Ibid.
19 'Captive Words', p 173.
20 'Basic Banalities II', *Internationale Situationniste* 8, Jan. 1963, and *Situationist International Anthology*, p. 123.
21 'Questionnaire', *Internationale Situationniste* 9, Aug. 1964, and *Situationist International Anthology*, p. 139.
22 René Viénet, 'The Situationists and the New Forms of Action against Politics and Art', *Internationale Situationniste* 11, Oct. 1967, and *Situationist International Anthology*, p. 213.
23 'Questionnaire', p. 139.
24 'Manifeste', *Internationale Situationniste* 4, Aug. 1961, p. 38.
25 'Questionnaire', p. 142.
26 Ibid., p. 140.
27 'The Countersituationist Campaign in Various Countries', *Internationale Situationniste* 8, Jan. 1963, and *Situationist International Anthology*, p. 113.
28 Attila Kotanyi and Raoul Vaneigem, 'Elementary Programme of the Bureau of Unitary Urbanism', *Internationale Situationniste* 6, Aug. 1961, and *Situationist International Anthology*, p. 65.
29 'The Countersituationist Campaign in Various Countries', p. 113.
30 Ibid.
31 'Basic Banalities II', p. 123.
32 Situationist International, *The Veritable Split in the International*, London, Chronos, 1990, p. 44.
33 Cf. Jean-Jacques Raspaud and Jean-Pierre Voyer, *L' Internationale Situationniste: protagonistes, chronologie, bibliographie (avec un index des noms insultés)*, Paris, Champ Libre, 1971.
34 Peter Stansill and David Zane Mairowitz (eds), *By Any Means Necessary: Outlaw Manifestos and Ephemera 1965–70*, Harmondsworth, Penguin, 1971, p. 39. An excellent article on Project Sigma is Howard Slater's 'Alexander Trocchi and Project Sigma', *Variant* 7, 1989, pp. 30–7.
35 'Instructions for Taking up Arms', p. 63.
36 'Ideologies, Classes, and the Domination of Nature', *Internationale Situationniste* 8, Jan. 1963, and *Situationist International Anthology*, p. 107.
37 *The Revolution of Everyday Life*, p. 127.
38 Ibid., p. 75.
39 'Basic Banalities II', p. 125.
40 'All the King's Men', *Situationist International Anthology*, p. 115.
41 *The Revolution of Everyday Life*, p. 137.
42 Cf. J.H. Matthews, *Languages of Surrealism*, Columbia, MO, University of Missouri Press, 1986, pp. 156–7.
43 *Internationale Situationniste* 9, Aug. 1964, p. 21.
44 Ibid., p. 36.
45 'Report on the Construction of Situations', pp. 18–19.
46 'Captive Words', p. 170.
47 Ibid.
48 Ibid., p. 174.

49 'All the King's Men', p. 114.

50 Ibid., p. 116.

51 Ibid., p. 115.

52 *Guy Debord and Gil Wolman*, 'Methods of Détournement', *Situationist International Anthology*, p. 9.

53 Ibid.

54 *The Society of the Spectacle*, 204.

55 Ibid., 206.

56 Ibid., 208.

57 Ibid., 205.

58 Ibid., 207.

59 'Détournement as Negation and Prelude', *Internationale Situationniste* 3, Dec. 1959, and *Situationist International Anthology*, p. 55.

60 Jean Barrot, *What is Situationism: Critique of the Situationist International*, London, Unpopular Books, 1987, pp. 23–4.

61 *The Revolution of Everyday Life*, p. 86.

62 *What is Situationism*, p. 26.

63 Ibid., p. 25.

64 Ratgeb, *Contributions to the Revolutionary Struggle Intended to be Discussed, Corrected and Principally Put into Practice without Delay*, London, Bratach Dubh Editions, 1977.

65 Chris Carlsson, with Mark Leger (eds), *Bad Attitude: The Processed World Anthology*, London, Verso, 1990.

66 *The Revolution of Everyday Life*, p. 98.

67 Cf. Guy Debord, 'The Situationists and the New Forms of Action in Politics and Art', *Situationist International Anthology*, p. 318, and 'The Spies for Peace Story', *Anarchy* 29, July 1963, pp. 197–229.

68 Roel van Duyn, *Message of a Wise Kabouter*, London, Duckworth, 1972.

69 Rudolf de Jong, *Provos and Kabouters*, Buffalo, NY, Friends of Maltesta, n.d., p. 11. This pamphlet is reproduced in David E. Apter and James Joll, *Anarchism Today*, London, Macmillan, 1971.

70 Ibid., p. 14.

71 Ibid., pp. 10–11.

72 The statue had been donated to the city of Amsterdam by the Imperial Tobacco Company.

73 *By Any Means Necessary*, p. 127.

74 Ibid., pp. 22–3.

75 *Provos and Kabouters*, p. 14.

76 *By Any Means Necessary*, p. 239.

77 'Of Student Poverty, Considered in its Economic, Political, Psychological, Sexual, and Particularly Intellectual Aspects, and a Modest Proposal for its Remedy', *Ten Days that Shook the University*, London, Situationist International, n.d., p.13.

78 'Basic Banalities I', p. 93.

79 *Dernières Nouvelles*, 4 Dec. 1966, quoted in *Situationist International Anthology*, p. 206.

80 'Of Student Poverty', p. 56.

81 Ibid., p. 7.

82 Ibid., p. 4.
83 This text is reprinted on the back cover of a number of editions of the pamphlet, notably *On the Poverty of Student Life*, Detroit, Mich., Black & Red, 1973.
84 'Our Goals and Methods in the Strasbourg Scandal', *Situationist International Anthology*, p. 207 (no author).
85 Ibid.
86 'The Beginning of an Era', *Internationale Situationniste* 12, Sept. 1969, and *Situationist International Anthology*, p. 228.
87 'Of Student Poverty', p. 23.
88 Henri Lefebvre, in 'The Beginning of an Era', p. 228.
89 Ibid., p. 229.
90 *Paris: May 1968, An Eye-Witness Account*, n.p., Dark Star Press and Rebel Press, 1986, p. 5.
91 *Observer*, 25 June 1968.
92 Roger Gregoire and Fredy Perlman, *Worker-Student Action Committees, France May '68*, Detroit, Mich., Black & Red, 1970, p. 61.
93 *Paris: May 1968*, p. 33.
94 Ibid.
95 *Paris: May 1968*, p. 26.
96 Ibid., p. 19.
97 *Le Nouvel Observateur*, 8 Feb. 1971.
98 Ibid., 8 Nov. 1971.
99 'The Beginning of an Era', p. 227.
100 Ibid.
101 René Viénet, *The Enragés and the Situationists in the Occupation Movement, May–June 1968*, York, Tiger Papers Publications, n.d., p. 14.
102 Ibid., p. 3.
103 Ibid.
104 Ibid., p. 15.
105 Ibid.
106 *Observer*, 2 June 1968.
107 *Observer*, 26 May 1968.
108 *The Enragés and the Situationists*, p. 15.
109 *Paris: May 1968*, pp. 24–5.
110 Cf. Harold Rosenberg, *The De-Definition of Art: Action Art to Pop to Earthworks*, London, Secker & Warburg, 1972.
111 Alain Jouffroy, 'What's to be done about Art?', Jean Cassou *et al.*, *Art and Confrontation: France and the Arts in an Age of Change*, London, Studio Vista, 1970, p. 199.
112 *The Enragés and the Situationists*, p. 15.
113 Ibid., p.16.
114 *Observer*, 19 May 1968.
115 Ibid., 2 June 1968.
116 Ibid., 26 May 1968.
117 *Worker-Student Action Committees, France May '68*, p. 63.
118 *Guardian*, 23 May 1968.
119 *The Enragés and the Situationists*, p. 7.

120 *News of the World*, 16 Feb. 1969.
121 For a comprehensive collection of 1968 graffiti, see Walter Lewino, *L'Imagination au Pouvoir*, Paris, Le Terrain Vague, 1968.
122 André Fermigier, 'No More Claudels', *Art and Confrontation*, p. 52.
123 Michel Ragon, 'The Artist and Society', *Art and Confrontation*, p. 27.
124 Ibid., p. 3.
125 Malcolm Imrie, in 'Say it with Cobblestones', supplement to the *New Statesman*, 18/25 Dec. 1987.
126 *What is Situationism*, p. 39.
127 'Slogans to be Spread Now by Every Means', *Situationist International Anthology*, p. 344.
128 Guy Debord, *Comments on the Society of the Spectacle*, London, Verso, 1991, p. 11.
129 Cf. Ferdinand de Saussure, *Course in General Linguistics*, London, Fontana, 1974.
130 Friedrich Nietzsche, *The Will to Power*, Walter Kaufman (ed.) New York, Random House, 1968, p. 550.

4 'VICTORY WILL BE FOR THOSE WHO CREATE DISORDER WITHOUT LOVING IT'

'Victory will be for those who create disorder without loving it' is in Guy Debord's 'Thèses sur la Revolution Culturelle', *Internationale Situationniste* 1, June 1958.

1 Michel Foucault, 'Preface' to Gilles Deleuze and Félix Guattari, *Anti-Oedipus: Capitalism and Schizophrenia*, London, The Athlone Press, 1977, p. xiii.
2 Jean-François Lyotard, 'A Memorial of Marxism: for Pierre Souyri', *Peregrinations: Law, Form, Event*, New York, Columbia University Press, 1988, p. 63.
3 Ibid., p. 50.
4 Jean-François Lyotard, *The Postmodern Condition, A Report on Knowledge*, Manchester University Press, 1984, p. 13.
5 Jean-François Lyotard, 'On Theory: An Interview', *Driftworks*, New York, Semiotext(e), 1984, p. 29.
6 'A Memorial of Marxism: for Pierre Souyri', p. 50.
7 Ibid.
8 Jean-François Lyotard, *Economie Libidinale*, Paris, Minuit, 1974, p. 117.
9 Jean-François Lyotard, 'Adrift', *Driftworks*, p. 13.
10 *Economie Libidinale*, p. 287.
11 Jean-François Lyotard, 'Nanterre: Ici, Maintenant', *Dérive à Partir de Marx et Freud*, Paris, Union Générale, 1973, p. 208.
12 Michel Foucault, 'Truth and Power', *Michel Foucault: Power/Knowledge: Selected Interviews and Other Writings, 1972–1977*, Colin Gordon (ed.), Brighton, Harvester, 1986, p. 115.

13 Michel Foucault, 'Theatrum Philosophicum', *Michel Foucault: Language, Counter-Memory, Practice. Selected Interviews and Essays*, Donald F. Bouchard (ed.), Oxford, Blackwell, 1977, p. 184.
14 Michel Foucault, 'The Eye of Power', *Power/Knowledge*, p. 158.
15 Michel Foucault, 'Two Lectures', *Power/Knowledge*, p. 98.
16 Michel Foucault, 'Body/Power', *Power/Knowledge*, p. 58.
17 Michel Foucault, 'Power and Strategies', *Power/Knowledge*, p. 142.
18 'Two Lectures', p. 94.
19 Ibid.
20 Michel Foucault, *Discipline and Punish*, Harmondsworth, Penguin, 1977.
21 Michel Foucault and Gilles Deleuze, 'Intellectuals and Power', *Language, Counter-Memory, Practice*, p. 207.
22 Michel Foucault, 'Polemics, Politics, and Problematizations: An Interview', *The Foucault Reader*, Paul Rabinow (ed.), Harmondsworth, Penguin, 1986, pp. 383–4.
23 'Adrift', p. 13.
24 'On Theory: An Interview', p. 29.
25 Cf. Jacques Lacan, *Ecrits: A Selection*, Alan Sheridan (ed.), London, Tavistock, 1977.
26 Gilles Deleuze and Félix Guattari, *A Thousand Plateaux, Capitalism and Schizophrenia*, The Athlone Press, London, 1988, p. 422.
37 *Anti-Oedipus*, p. 34.
28 Ibid., p. 378.
29 Félix Guattari, *Molecular Revolution: Psychiatry and Politics*, Harmondsworth, Penguin, 1984, p. 85.
30 Félix Guattari, 'The Proliferation of Margins', *Semiotext(e)* 9, *Italy: Autonomia: Post Political Politics*, Semiotext(e), New York, 1980, p. 109.
31 Ibid.
32 Gilles Deleuze, 'Nomad Thought', *The New Nietzsche: Contemporary Styles of Interpretation*, David B. Allison (ed.), Cambridge, Mass., MIT, 1985, p. 149.
33 Ibid.
34 Ibid.
35 Francis Picabia, in *The Dada Painters and Poets*, Robert Motherwell (ed.), New York, Wittenborn Schultz, 1951, p. 206.
36 *The Angry Brigade 1967–1984, Documents and Chronology*, London, Elephant Editions, 1985, p. 28.
37 Ibid., p. 31.
38 Stoke Newington Eight Defence Campaign, *If You Want Peace, Prepare for War*, London, n.d., p. 13.
39 *The Angry Brigade*, p. 32.
40 Ibid., p. 37.
41 Ibid., p. 29.
42 'La Pratique de la Théorie', *Internationale Situationniste* 12, Sept. 1969, p. 98.
43 *L'Europeo*, 6 Feb. 1976, quoted in Ken Knabb, *Situationist International Anthology*, Berkeley, Bureau of Public Secrets, 1981, p. 390.

44 Mario Tronti, 'The Strategy of Refusal', *Semiotext(e)* 9, *Italy: Autonomia*, pp. 28–34.
45 Cf. Chris Harman, *The Fire Last Time: 1968 and After*, London, Bookmarks, 1988, p. 218.
46 Bifo, 'Anatomy of Autonomy', *Semiotext(e)* 9, *Italy: Autonomia*, p. 156.
47 Maurizio Torealta, 'Painted Politics', *Semiotext(e)* 9, *Italy: Autonomia*, p. 102.
48 Ibid., pp. 102–3.
49 Ibid., p. 103.
50 'Anatomy of Autonomy', p. 156.
51 *Like a Summer with a Thousand Julys*, London, Blob, n.d., p. 43
52 'Anatomy of Autonomy', p. 156.
53 Collective A/Traverso, 'Radio Alice – Free Radio', *Semiotext(e)* 9, *Italy: Autonomia*, p. 131.
54 Ibid.
55 Ibid.
56 *Molecular Revolution*, p. 241.
57 'Radio Alice – Free Radio', p. 133.
58 Paul Virilio, 'Dreamers of a Successful Life', *Semiotext(e)* 9, *Italy: Autonomia*, p. 112.
59 'Anatomy of Autonomy', p. 166.
60 Félix Guattari, 'The Proliferation of Margins', p. 108.
61 Ibid.
62 Ibid.
63 Ibid., p. 109.
64 Toni Negri, 'Domination and Sabotage', *Semiotext(e)* 9, *Italy: Autonomia*, p. 63.
65 Jean Baudrillard, *For a Critique of the Political Economy of the Sign*, St Louis, Telos, 1975, pp. 176–7.
66 Jean Baudrillard, *Forget Foucault*, New York, Semiotext(e), 1987, pp. 114–15.
67 Jean Baudrillard, *The Mirror of Production*, St Louis, Telos, p. 164.
68 Ibid., p. 161.
69 Ibid., pp. 164–5.
70 Guy Debord, 'In Girum imus Nocte et Consumimur Igni', *Block*, 14, Autumn 1988, p. 36.
71 *The Mirror of Production*, p. 166.
72 Ibid., p. 165.
73 Ibid., p. 166.
74 Ibid., p. 165.
75 Ibid., p. 166.
76 Ibid.
77 'Nomad Thought', p. 146.
78 Ibid.
79 *Language, Counter-Memory, Practice*, p. 220.
80 Michel Foucault, *The History of Sexuality*, vol. I: *An Introduction*, Harmondsworth, Penguin, 1978, p. 159.
81 Jean-François Lyotard, 'Le 23 mars', *Dérive à Partir de Marx et Freud*, p. 306.

82 Ibid., p. 308.
83 Ibid., pp. 307–8.
84 *Economie Libidinale*, p. 133.
85 Ibid., p. 311.
86 Jean-François Lyotard, 'Notes sur le retour et le capital', *Des Dispotifs Pulsionnels*, Paris, Union Générale, 1973, p. 315.
87 Jamie Reid, *Up They Rise: The Incomplete Works of Jamie Reid*, London, Faber, 1987, p. 35.
88 Ibid., p. 38.
89 Ibid., p. 43.
90 Ibid.
91 *The End of Music*, Glasgow, 1978, pp. 32 3.
92 Ibid., pp. 12–13.
93 Ibid., p. 9.
94 Ibid.
95 *City Fun*, Manchester, May 1982. When the Hacienda was opened, *City Fun* also carried details of all the dimensions and colours of the club, the interior of which is reminiscent of a city street, and similar details were posted in Dry, a bar opened several years later in Manchester. Tony Wilson's Factory Records was one of the sponsors of the 1988 ICA Situationist exhibition. Among the exhibits there was a T-shirt with the logo: 'Well you've blown it now. You'll never see the Hacienda. It doesn't exist. Anywhere. THE HACIENDA MUST BE BUILT.' Chtcheglov's statement was made even more ironic by the threat of closure hanging over the Hacienda at the beginning of 1991. The club played no small part in the 'summers of love' which swept Manchester at the end of the 1980s, in which the 'psychogeographical' ambience of clubs, reinforced by the popularity of LSD and Ecstasy, grew in significance.
96 Sylvere Lotringer and Christian Marazzi, 'The Return of Politics', *Semiotext(e)* 9, *Italy: Autonomia*, p. 12.
97 George Branchflower, 'Oranges and Lemons', *Here and Now* 7/8, 1989, p. viii.
98 Ibid., p. vii.
99 Spectacular Times, *Buffo! Amazing Tales of Political Pranks and Anarchic Buffoonery*, London, n.d., p. 29.
100 'Oranges and Lemons', p. viii.
101 Ibid.

5 'FLEE, BUT WHILE FLEEING, PICK UP A WEAPON'

'Flee, but while fleeing, pick up a weapon' is a phrase from Gilles Deleuze and Félix Guattari, *On the Line*, New York, Semiotext(e), 1983.

1 Guy Debord, *The Society of the Spectacle*, unpublished translation, 1990, 203.
2 Guy Debord, *Comments on the Society of the Spectacle*, London, Verso, 1991, p. 7.

3 Ibid., p. 3.
4 Ibid., p. 7.
5 Guy Debord, *Preface to the Fourth Italian Edition of The Society of the Spectacle*, London, Chronos, 1979, p. 22.
6 *Comments on the Society of the Spectacle*, p. 82.
7 Ibid., p. 9.
8 Ibid.
9 Ibid., p. 10.
10 Ibid.
11 Ibid., p. 28.
12 Ibid., p. 4.
13 Ibid., p. 6.
14 Ibid., p. 4.
15 Ibid., p. 1.
16 Ibid.
17 Ibid., p. 18.
18 Ibid., p. 1.
19 Ibid., p. 2.
20 Ibid., p. 73.
21 Ibid.
22 Ibid., p. 79.
23 Jean Baudrillard, *L'Effet Beaubourg: implosion et dissuasion*, Paris, Editions Galilée, 1977, p. 24.
24 Ibid.
25 Ibid., p. 25.
26 Ibid.
27 Jean Baudrillard, *In the Shadow of the Silent Majorities . . . or The End of the Social and Other Essays*, New York, Semiotext(e), 1983, p. 10.
28 Jean Baudrillard, *The Ecstasy of Communication*, New York, Semiotext(e), 1988, p. 105.
29 *In the Shadow of the Silent Majorities*, p. 43.
30 Ibid., p. 22.
31 Ibid., pp. 28–9.
32 Ibid., pp. 26–7.
33 Ibid., p. 27.
34 Ibid., p. 28.
35 Jean Baudrillard, 'The Year 2000 Will Not Take Place', *Futur*fall: Excursions into Postmodernity*, E.A. Grosz *et al.* (eds), Sydney, Power Institute of Fine Arts, University of Sydney, and Futur*fall, 1986, p. 20.
36 Ibid.
37 Ibid.
38 Ibid., pp. 20–1.
39 Jean Baudrillard, *Fatal Strategies*, Semiotext(e) and Pluto, New York and London, 1990, p. 186.
40 Ibid., p. 99.
41 Ibid., p. 185.
42 Ibid., p. 65.
43 Ibid.
44 Ibid., p. 186.

45 Jean Baudrillard, *Simulations*, New York, Semiotext(e), 1983, p. 7.
46 Ibid., p. 8.
47 *The Ecstasy of Communication*, p. 12.
48 *Simulations*, p. 55.
49 'The Year 2000 Will Not Take Place', pp. 22–3.
50 *Fatal Strategies*, p. 65.
51 Ibid., p. 67.
52 *Simulations*, p. 42.
53 Ibid., p. 25.
54 *The Ecstasy of Communication*, pp. 77–8.
55 Ibid., p. 63.
56 *Fatal Strategies*, p. 65.
57 *The Ecstasy of Communication*, p. 83.
58 *Fatal Strategies*, p. 184.
59 Ibid., p. 117.
60 Ibid., pp. 185–6.
61 Ibid., p. 184.
62 Ibid., p. 113.
63 Ibid., p. 112.
64 Ibid., p. 113.
65 Judith Williamson, 'An Interview with Jean Baudrillard', *Block* 15, 1989, p. 18.
66 *The Ecstasy of Communication*, p. 74.
67 Ibid., p. 86.
68 Raoul Vaneigem, *The Revolution of Everyday Life*, n.p., Left Bank Books and Rebel Press, 1983, p. 85.
69 Guy Debord, *Comments on the Society of the Spectacle*, London, Verso, 1991, p. 76.
70 Ibid.
71 Ibid., p. 28.
72 Jean Baudrillard, *America*, London, Verso, 1989, p. 116.
73 *Comments on the Society of the Spectacle*, p. 21.
74 Ibid.
75 *America*, p. 116.
76 *Comments on the Society of the Spectacle*, pp. 21–2.
77 'The Year 2000 Will Not Take Place', p. 23.
78 *The Society of the Spectacle*, 10.
79 *Comments on the Society of the Spectacle*, p. 51.
80 Ibid., p. 50.
81 *Fatal Strategies*, pp. 185–6.
82 Jean Baudrillard, *Cool Memories*, London, Verso, 1990, p. 25.
83 *Fatal Strategies*, p. 114.
84 *Comments on the Society of the Spectacle*, p. 14.
85 Ibid., p. 15.
86 Ibid., p. 20.
87 Ibid., pp. 15–16.
88 Ibid., p. 16.
89 Ibid., p. 15.
90 Ibid., p. 13.

91 Ibid., p. 19.
92 Ibid., p. 14.
93 Ibid., p. 52.
94 Ibid., p. 55.
95 Ibid., pp. 60–1.
96 Ibid., p. 6.
97 Ibid., p. 7.
98 Ibid., p. 6.
99 Ibid., p. 33.
100 Ibid., p. 29.
101 Ibid., p. 13.
102 Ibid., p. 70.
103 Ibid., p. 39.
104 Ibid., p. 38.
105 Ibid., p. 84.
106 Ibid., p. 81.
107 Ibid., p. 84.
108 Ibid., p. 83.
109 Ibid., p. 84.
110 Ibid., p. 21.
111 Ibid., p. 84.
112 Ibid.
113 Ibid., p. 88.
114 Ibid., pp. 53–4.
115 Ibid., p. 20.
116 Raoul Vaneigem, 'Basic Banalities II', *Internationale Situationniste* 8, Jan. 1963, and Ken Knabb (ed.), *Situationist International Anthology*, Berkeley, Bureau of Public Secrets, 1981, p. 125.
117 Stewart Home 'Auto-Plagiarism', *Plagiarism: Art as Commodity and Strategies for its Negation*, London, Aporia Press, 1988, p. 6.
118 Praxis, 'Desire in Ruins', *The Art Strike Handbook*, Stewart Home (ed.), London, Sabotage Editions, 1989, p. 10.
119 Tex Beard, 'Plagiarism', *Plagiarism: Art as Commodity and Strategies for its Negation*, Stewart Home (ed.), p. 7.
120 'Art Strike: Karen Eliot interviewed by Scott MacLeod', *The Art Strike Handbook*, p. 5.
121 Karen Eliot, 'Orientation for the Use of a Context and the Context for the Use of an Orientation', *Plagiarism: Art as Commodity and Strategies for its Negation*, p. 9.
122 Stewart Home, 'Multiple Names', *Plagiarism: Art as Commodity and Strategies for its Negation*, p. 20.
123 Stewart Home, 'Introduction', *The Art Strike Handbook*, p. 1.
124 'Art Strike: Karen Eliot interviewed', *The Art Strike Handbook*, p. 7.
125 Stewart Home, 'Art Strike 1990–1993', *The Art Strike Handbook*, p. 3.
126 Stewart Home, 'Oppositional Culture and Cultural Opposition', *The Art Strike Handbook*, p. 13.
127 'Desire in Ruins', pp. 10–11.
128 Praxis, 'The Art of Ideology and the Ideology of Art', *The Art Strike Handbook*, p. 17.

129 Ibid., p. 16.
130 'Desire in Ruins', p. 11.
131 Cf. Maurice Nadeau, *The History of Surrealism*, Harmondsworth, Penguin, 1978, pp. 193–4.
132 Stewart Home, *The Festival of Plagiarism*, London, Sabotage Editions, 1989, back cover.
133 Karen Eliot, 'From Censorship to the Art Strike', *The Art Strike Handbook*, p. 24.
134 Jean Baudrillard, *For a Critique of the Political Economy of the Sign*, St Louis, Telos, 1981, p. 110.
135 *The Revolution of Everyday Life*, p. 206.
136 Vaughan Allen, 'Faking it', *The Face* 23, Aug. 1990, pp. 40–3.
137 'Flyposter frenzy', *Leisure*, 1990.
138 *The Revolution of Everyday Life*, p. 75.
139 Paul Virilio and Sylvere Lotringer, *Pure War*, New York, Semiotext(e), 1983, p. 81.
140 *The Revolution of Everyday Life*, p. 81.
141 Karen Eliot, 'Demolish Seriousness', *Here and Now* 9, 1989, p. 19.
142 'Second Thoughts on the Thought Strike', *Here and Now* 10, 1989, p. xv.
143 'Metastasis: Genetics and Ideology', *Leisure*, 1990.
144 'An Interview with Jean Baudrillard', p. 16.
145 *Comments on the Society of the Spectacle*, p. 27.
146 Jean Baudrillard, *The Ecstasy of Communication*, New York, Semiotext(e), 1988, p. 81.
147 Guy Debord, *Comments on the Society of the Spectacle*, London, Verso, 1991, p. 80.
148 Ibid., p. 21.
149 'Notice to the Civilized Concerning Generalized Self-Management', *Internationale Situationniste* 12, Sept. 1969, and *Situationist International Anthology*, p. 285.
150 *Comments on the Society of the Spectacle*, p. 59.
151 Ibid., p. 21.
152 Ibid., p. 28.
153 'Now, the SI', *Internationale Situationniste* 9, Aug. 1964, and *Situationist International Anthology*, p. 136.

Bibliography

SITUATIONIST TEXTS AND LATER PUBLICATIONS

Debord, Guy, *La Société du Spectacle*, Paris, Buchet-Chastel, 1967, and Paris, Editions Champ Libre, 1971. Translated as *The Society of the Spectacle*, Detroit, Black & Red, 1977, and by Donald Nicholson-Smith, unpublished, 1990.

—— *Oeuvres cinématographiques complètes: 1952–1978*, Paris, Editions Champ Libre, 1978. Of the scripts collected in this book, a translation of *In Girum imus Nocte et Consumimur Igni* is forthcoming from Pelagian Press, Leeds. A partial translation and introduction by Lucy Forsyth appears in *Block*, 14, Autumn 1988, pp. 27–37, and two other scripts, *On the Passage of a Few Persons Through a Rather Brief Period of Time* and *Critique of Separation* are translated in the *Situationist International Anthology*.

—— *Préface à la quatrième édition italienne de 'La Société du Spectacle'*, Paris, Editions Champ Libre, 1979, translated by Frances Parker and Michael Forsyth, *Preface to the Fourth Italian Edition of The Society of the Spectacle*, London, Chronos, 1979.

—— *Considérations sur l'assassinat de Gérard Lebovici*, Paris, Editions Gérard Lebovici, 1985.

—— *Commentaires sur la Société du Spectacle*, Paris, Editions Gérard Lebovici, 1988, translated by Malcolm Imrie as *Comments on the Society of the Spectacle*, London, Verso, 1991.

—— *Panégyrique I*, Paris, Editions Gérard Lebovici, 1989.

Debord, Guy, and Becker-Ho, Alice, *Le Jeu de la guerre (Relevé des positions successives de toutes les forces au cours d'une partie)*, Paris, Editions Gérard Lebovici, 1987.

Gray, Christopher (ed.), *Leaving the Twentieth Century: The Incomplete Work of the Situationist International*, London, Free Fall Press, 1974.

Internationale Situationniste, *La Véritable Scission dans L'Internationale*, Paris, Editions Champ Libre, 1972, translated as *The Veritable Split in the International*, London, Chronos, 1990.

—— *Internationale Situationniste 1958–1969*, complete facsimile edition, Paris, Editions Champ Libre, 1975.

Knabb, Ken (ed.), *Situationist International Anthology*, Berkeley, Bureau of Public Secrets, 1981.

De la misère en milieu étudiant, consideré sous les aspects economique, sexuel et notamment intellectuel et de quelques moyens pour y remedier, Association fédérative générale des étudiants de Strasbourg, 1966. Reprinted Paris, Editions Champ Libre, 1977, and published in English as 'Of Student Poverty, Considered in its Economic, Psychological, Political, Sexual, and Particularly Intellectual Aspects, and a Modest Proposal for its Remedy', *Ten Days that Shook the University*, London, Situationist International, n.d. There are many other translations of this pamphlet, including *On the Poverty of Student Life*, Detroit, Black & Red, 1973, and one which appears in the *Situationist International Anthology*.

Sanguinetti, Gianfranco, writing as Censor, *Rapporto Veridico sulle opportunita di salvare il capitalismo in Italia*, Milan, Ugo Mursia, 1975, translated by Guy Debord as *Véridique Rapport sur les Dernières Chances de Sauver le Capitalisme en Italie*, Paris, Editions Champ Libre, 1976.

—— *Del Terrorismo e dello Stato, La teori e la practica del terrorismo per la prima volta divulgata*, Milan, 1979. For a partial English translation, see *On Terrorism and the State: The Theory and Practice of Terrorism Divulged for the First Time*, London, Chronos, 1982.

Vaneigem, Raoul, *Traité de savoir-vivre a l'usage des jeunes générations*, Paris, Gallimard, 1967. Translated by John Fullerton and Paul Sieveking as *The Revolution of Everyday Life*, London, Rising Free Collective, 1979, and Donald Nicholson-Smith, n.p., Left Bank Books and Rebel Press, 1983.

—— writing as Ratgeb, *De la grève sauvage à l'autogestion généralisée*, Paris, Union Générale, 1974. Translated by Paul Sharkey as *Contributions to the revolutionary struggle intended to be discussed, corrected and principally put into practice without delay*, London, Bratach Dubh Editions, 1981.

—— writing as Jules François Dupois, *Histoire désinvolte du surréalisme*, Paris, Paul Vermont, 1977.

—— *Le Livre des Plaisirs*, Paris, Encre, 1979. Translated by John Fullerton as *The Book of Pleasures*, London, Pending Press, 1985.

—— *Le Mouvement du Libre-Esprit: Généralites et témoignages sur les affleurements de la vie à la surface du Moyen-Age, de la Renaissance, et, incidemment, de notre époque*, Paris, Editions Ramsay, 1986.

Viénet, René, *Enragés et situationnistes dans le mouvement des occupations*, Paris, Gallimard, 1968. Translated by Loren Goldner and Paul Sieveking as *The Enragés and the Situationists in the Occupation Movement, May–June 1968*, York, Tiger Papers Publications, n.d., and also published, with an afterword by Tom Ward, by Semiotext(e), New York, 1990.

GENERAL WORKS

Adorno, Theodor and Horkheimer, Max, *Dialectic of Enlightenment*, London, Verso, 1979.

Allen, Vaughan, 'Faking it', *The Face* 23, Aug. 1990, pp. 40–3.

Alquie, Ferdinand, *The Philosophy of Surrealism*, Ann Arbor, University of Michigan Press, 1965.

Althusser, Louis, *Essays on Ideology*, London, Verso, 1984.
Alvarez, A., *The Savage God, A Study of Suicide*, Harmondsworth, Penguin, 1971.
The Angry Brigade 1967–1984, Documents and Chronology, London, Elephant Editions, 1985.
Apollinaire, Guillaume, *The Poet Assassinated and Other Stories*, London, Grafton, 1985.
Apter, David E. and Joll, James (eds), *Anarchism Today*, London, Macmillan, 1971.
Aragon, Louis, *Paris Peasant*, London, Pan, 1987.
L'Archibras 4, June 1968. Includes surrealist comment on the May events.
Atkins, Guy, Alger John. *The Crucial Years 1954–1964*, London, Lund Humphries, 1977.
Bale, Jeffrey M., 'Right-wing Terrorists and the Extraparliamentary Left in Post-World War 2 Europe: Collusion or Manipulation?', *Lobster* 18, Oct. 1989, pp. 2–18.
Barrot, Jean, *What is Situationism: Critique of the Situationist International*, London, Unpopular Books, 1987.
Barthes, Roland, *Mythologies*, London, Paladin, 1973.
Baudelaire, Charles, *The Complete Verse*, London, Anvil Press, 1986.
Baudrillard, Jean, *Le Système des objets*, Paris, Denoel-Gonthier, 1968.
—— *For a Critique of the Political Economy of the Sign*, St Louis, Telos, 1975.
—— *The Mirror of Production*, St Louis, Telos, 1975.
—— *L'Effet Beaubourg: implosion et dissuasion*, Paris, Editions Galilée, 1977.
—— *In the Shadow of the Silent Majorities . . . or The End of the Social and Other Essays*, New York, Semiotext(e), 1983.
—— *Simulations*, New York, Semiotext(e), 1983.
—— 'The Year 2000 Will Not Take Place', *Futur*fall: Excursions into Postmodernity*, E.A. Grosz *et al.* (eds), Sydney, Power Institute of Fine Arts, University of Sydney, and Futur*fall, 1986.
—— *Forget Foucault*, New York, Semiotext(e), 1987.
—— *Selected Writings*, Mark Poster (ed.), Cambridge and Palo Alto, Polity Press and Stanford University Press, 1988.
—— *The Ecstasy of Communication*, New York, Semiotext(e), 1988.
—— *America*, London, Verso, 1989.
—— *Cool Memories*, London, Verso, 1990.
—— *Cool Memories II*, Paris, Editions Galilée, 1990.
—— *Fatal Strategies*, Semiotext(e) and Pluto, New York and London, 1990.
—— *Seduction*, Basingstoke, Macmillan Education, 1990.
Béhar, Henri and Carassou, Michel, *Le Surréalisme: Textes et débats*, Paris, Librairie Générale Française, 1984.
Benjamin, Walter, *Charles Baudelaire: A Lyric Poet in the Era of High Capitalism*, London, Verso, 1983.
—— *One Way Street*, London, New Left Books, 1979.
Bennington, Geoffrey, *Lyotard: Writing the Event*, Manchester University Press, 1988.
Berman, Russell, Pan, David and Piccone, Paul, 'The Society of the Spectacle 20 Years Later: A Discussion', *Telos* 86,1991,pp. 81–102.

Bernstein, Michèle, 'About the Situationist International', *The Times Literary Supplement*, No. 3262, 3 Sep. 1964, p. 781.

Berreby, Gerard (ed.), *1948–1957: Documents relatifs à la fondation de l'Internationale Situationniste*, Paris, Allia, 1985.

Blazwick, Iwona, *An Endless Adventure . . . an endless passion . . . an endless banquet*, London, ICA and Verso, 1989.

Bogue, Ronald, *Deleuze and Guattari*, London, Routledge, 1989.

Bonnett, Alastair, 'Situationism, Geography and Poststructuralism', *Society and Space* 7, 1989, pp. 131–46.

—— 'Art, Ideology and Everyday Space: Subversive Tendencies from Dada to Postmodernism', *Society and Space*, forthcoming.

Boorstin, Daniel J., *The Image, or What Happened to the American Dream*, London, Weidenfeld and Nicolson, 1961.

Bourges, Hervé (ed.), *The Student Revolt: The Activists Speak*, London, Panther, 1968.

Branchflower, George, 'Oranges and Lemons', *Here and Now*, 7/8, 1989, pp. vii–ix.

Brau, Elaine, *Le Situationnisme ou la nouvelle internationale*, Paris, Nouvelle Editions Debresse, 1968.

Brau, Jean-Louis, *Cours, camarade, le vieux monde est derrière toi! Histoire du mouvement révolutionnaire étudiant en Europe*, Paris, Albin Michel, 1968.

Breton, André, *Les Pas Perdus*, Paris, Gallimard, 1924.

—— 'The Colours of Liberty', *Now* 7, Feb.–March 1946, pp. 33–4.

—— *Les Vases Communicants*, Paris, Gallimard, 1955.

—— *Nadja*, New York, Grove Press, 1960.

—— *Ode to Charles Fourier*, London, Cape Goliard Press, 1969.

—— *Manifestoes of Surrealism*, Ann Arbor, University of Michigan Press, 1972.

—— *Surrealism and Painting*, London, Macdonald, 1972.

—— *What is Surrealism? Selected Writings*, Franklin Rosemont (ed.), London, Pluto, 1978.

—— *Mad Love*, Lincoln, Neb., and London, University of Nebraska Press, 1987.

Breton, André, and Soupault, Philippe, *The Magnetic Fields*, London, Atlas Press, 1985.

Brown, Bernard E., *Protest in Paris: Anatomy of a Revolt*, Morristown, General Learning, 1974.

Brown, Bruce, *Marx, Freud, and the Critique of Everyday Life: Toward a Permanent Cultural Revolution*, London and New York, Monthly Review Press, 1973.

Calle, Sophie, and Baudrillard, Jean, *Suite vénitienne* and *Please Follow Me*, Seattle, Bay Press, 1988.

Callinicos, Alex, *Is There a Future for Marxism?* London, Macmillan, 1982.

Cardan, Paul, *Modern Capitalism and Revolution*, London, Solidarity, 1974.

Cardinal, Roger, 'Soluble City, the Surrealist Perception of Paris', *Architectural Design*, vols 2–3, 1978, pp. 143–49.

Cardinal, Roger and Short, Richard, *Surrealism: Permanent Revelation*, London, Studio Vista, 1970.

Carlsson, Chris, with Leger, Mark (eds), *Bad Attitude: The Processed World Anthology*, London, Verso, 1990.
Cassou, Jean, *et al.*, *Art and Confrontation: France and the Arts in an Age of Change*, London, Studio Vista, 1970.
Caute, David, *Sixty-Eight: The Year of the Barricades*, London, Hamish Hamilton, 1988.
de Certeau, Michel, *The Practice of Everyday Life*, University of California Press, 1984.
Chadwick, Whitney, *Women Artists and the Surrealist Movement*, London, Thames & Hudson, 1985.
Chambers, Iain, *Border Dialogues: Journeys in Postmodernity*, London, Routledge, 1990.
City Fun, May 1982. Includes billing for 'The Hacienda'.
Cohn-Bendit, Gabriel and Daniel, *Obsolete Communism: The Left-Wing Alternative*, Harmondsworth, Penguin, 1968.
Conrads, Ulrich (ed.), *Programmes and Manifestos on Twentieth Century Architecture*, London, Lund Humphries, 1970.
Deleuze, Gilles, 'Nomad Thought', *The New Nietzsche: Contemporary Styles of Interpretation*, David B. Allison (ed.), Cambridge, Mass., and London, MIT Press, 1985, pp. 142–9.
—— *Nietzsche and Philosophy*, London, The Athlone Press, 1986.
Deleuze, Gilles and Guattari, Félix, *Anti-Oedipus: Capitalism and Schizophrenia*, London, The Athlone Press, 1977.
—— *On the Line*, New York, Semiotext(e), 1983.
—— *Nomadology: The War Machine*, New York, Semiotext(e), 1986.
—— *A Thousand Plateaux, Capitalism and Schizophrenia*, London, The Athlone Press, 1977.
—— 'City State', *Zone* 1/2, n.d., pp. 194–217.
Denevert, Daniel, *Theory of Misery, Misery of Theory: Report on the New Conditions of Revolutionary Theory*, Paris, Centre de recherche sur la Question Sociale, 1973.
Dews, Peter, *Logics of Disintegration: Post-structuralist Thought and the Claims of Critical Theory*, London, Verso, 1987.
Dubois, Pierre, *Sabotage in Industry*, Harmondsworth, Penguin, 1979.
Dumontier, Pascal, *Les Situationnistes et Mai 68: Théorie et Practique de la Révolution (1966–1972)*, Paris, Editions Gérard Lebovici, 1990.
van Duyn, Roel, *Message of a Wise Kabouter*, London, Duckworth, 1972.
Eagleton, Terry, *The Ideology of the Aesthetic*, Oxford, Blackwell, 1990.
Eco, Umberto, *Travels in Hyperreality*, New York, Harcourt Brace Jovanovich, 1986.
Eliot, Karen, 'Demolish Seriousness', *Here and Now* 9, 1989, p. 19.
The End of Music, Glasgow, 1978.
'Euroterrorism: Well, it's better than bottling it up', *Vague* 20, 1988, pp. 43–82.
Faurschou, Gail, 'Obsolescence and Desire: Fashion and the Commodity Form', *Postmodernism – Philosophy and the Arts*, Hugh J. Silverman (ed.), London, Routledge, 1990, pp. 234–59.
Fišera, Vladimir, *Writing on the Wall, France, May 1968: A Documentary Anthology*, London, Allison & Busby, 1978.

'Flyposter frenzy', *Leisure*, 1990.

Foster, Hal (ed.), *Postmodern Culture*, London, Pluto, 1985.

Foster, Stephen C. and Kuenzli, Rudolf E., *Dada Spectrum: The Dialectics of Revolt*, Madison, Wis., Coda Press, 1979.

Foucault, Michel, *Madness and Civilisation*, London, Tavistock, 1967.

—— *Discipline and Punish*, London, Allen Lane, 1977.

—— *Language, Counter-Memory, Practice. Selected Interviews and Essays*, Donald F. Bouchard (ed.), Oxford, Blackwell, 1977.

—— *The History of Sexuality*, vol. I: *An Introduction*, Harmondsworth, Penguin, 1978.

—— *The Foucault Reader*, P. Rabinow (ed.), Harmondsworth, Penguin, 1986.

—— *Power/Knowledge: Selected Interviews and Other Writings, 1972–1977*, Colin Gordon (ed.), Brighton, Harvester, 1986.

—— *Politics, Philosophy, Culture: Interviews and Other Writings 1977–1984*, Lawrence D. Kritzman (ed.), London, Routledge, 1988.

Fraser, Ronald, *1968: A Student Generation in Revolt*, London, Chatto & Windus, 1988.

Gombin, Richard, *The Origins of Modern Leftism*, Harmondsworth, Penguin, 1975.

—— *The Radical Tradition*, London, Methuen, 1978.

Gramsci, Antonio, *Selections from Political Writings 1910–1920*, London, Lawrence & Wishart, 1977.

—— *Selections from Cultural Writings*, London, Lawrence & Wishart, 1985.

—— *Selections from the Prison Notebooks*, London, Lawrence & Wishart, 1986.

Gregoire, Roger and Perlman, Fredy, *Worker-Student Action Committees, France May 1968*, Detroit, Black & Red, 1970.

Guattari, Félix, *Molecular Revolution: Psychiatry and Politics*, Harmondsworth, Penguin, 1984.

Guattari, Félix, and Toni Negri, *Communists Like Us: New Spaces of Liberty, New Lines of Alliance*, New York, Semiotext(e), 1990.

Habermas, Jurgen, 'Modernity versus Postmodernity', *New German Critique* 22, 1981, pp. 3–14.

Hammond, Paul, 'Specialists in Revolt', an interview with Jean Schuster, *New Statesman*, vol. 114, no. 2958, 4 Dec. 1987, pp. 22–3.

Hamon, Hervé and Rotman, Patrick, *Génération*, vol. I: *Les Années de rêve*, Paris, Editions du Seuil, 1987; vol. II: *Les Années de poudre*, Paris, Editions du Seuil, 1988.

Harman, Chris, *The Fire Last Time: 1968 and After*, London, Bookmarks, 1988.

Harvey, David, *The Condition of Postmodernity*, Oxford, Blackwell, 1989.

Hewison, Robert, *Too Much: Art and Society in the Sixties*, London, Methuen, 1988.

Home, Stewart, *The Assault on Culture: Utopian Currents from Lettrism to Class War*, London, Aporia Press and Unpopular Books, 1988.

—— (ed.), *Plagiarism: Art as Commodity and Strategies for its Negation*, London, Aporia Press, 1988.

—— (ed.), *Art Strike Handbook*, London, Sabotage Editions, 1989.

—— *The Festival of Plagiarism*, London, Sabotage Editions, 1989.
—— *Pure Mania*, Edinburgh, Polygon, 1989.
Isou, Isidore, *Réflexions sur M. André Breton*, Paris, Editions Lettristes, 1948.
—— 'The Creations of Lettrism', *The Times Literary Supplement*, No. 3262, 3 Sept. 1964, pp. 796–7.
Jameson, Frederick, 'Postmodernism, or The Cultural Logic of Late Capitalism', *New Left Review*, 146, July–August 1984, pp. 259–422.
Jarry, Alfred, *Selected Works of Alfred Jarry*, Roger Shattuck and Simon Watson Taylor (eds), London, Eyre Methuen, 1980.
Jencks, Charles, *Modern Movements in Architecture*, Harmondsworth, Penguin, 1985.
—— *What is Post-Modernism?*, London and New York, Academy and St Martin's Press, 1986.
Jong, Rudolf de, *Provos and Kabouters*, Buffalo, NY, Filienda af Maltesta, n.d.
Knabb, Ken, *Double Reflection: Preface to a Phenomenology of the Subjective Aspect of Practical Critical Activity*, Berkeley, Bureau of Public Secrets, 1974.
—— (ed.), *Bureau of Public Secrets*, 1, Jan. 1976.
Lacan, Jacques, *Ecrits: A Selection*, Alan Sheridan (ed.), London, Tavistock, 1977.
Lautréamont (Isidore Ducasse), *Maldoror and Poems*, Harmondsworth, Penguin, 1978.
—— *Poésies*, Alexis Lykiard (ed.), London and New York, Allison & Busby, 1980.
Le Brun, Annie, *Lâchez tout*, Paris, Sagittaire, 1977.
Lefebvre, Henri, *Critique de la vie quotidienne*, vol. 1: *Introduction*, Paris, L'Arche, 1947; vol. II: *Fondements d'une sociologie de la quotidienne*, Paris, L'Arche, 1958; vol. III: *De la modernité au modernisme (Pour une metaphilosophie du quotidienne)*, Paris, L'Arche, 1981.
—— *L'Irruption de Nanterre au sommet*, Paris, Editions Anthropos, 1968.
—— *Everyday Life in the Modern World*, London, Allen Lane, 1971.
—— *The Survival of Capitalism: Reproduction of the Relations of Production*, London, Allison & Busby, 1976.
Lemaitre, Maurice, *Toujours à l'avant-garde de l'avant-garde jusqu'au Paradis et au-delà*, Paris, Centre de Creativité, 1972.
Les Lèvres Nues 1954–1958, facsimile edition, Paris, Plasma, 1978.
Lewino, Walter, *L'Imagination au Pouvoir*, Paris, Le Terrain Vague, 1968.
Like a Summer with a Thousand Julys, London, Blob, n.d.
Lippard, Lucy, *Dadas on Art*, Englewood Cliffs, NJ, Prentice-Hall, 1971.
Lukács, George, *History and Class Consciousness*, London, Merlin Press, 1983.
Lyotard, Jean-François, *Dérive à Partir de Marx et Freud*, Paris, Union Générale, 1973.
—— *Des Dispotifs Pulsionnels*, Paris, Union Générale, 1973.
—— *Economie Libidinale*, Paris, Minuit, 1974.
—— *Driftworks*, New York, Semiotext(e), 1984.
—— *The Postmodern Condition: A Report on Knowledge*, Manchester University Press, 1984.

66

—— *Peregrinations: Law, Form, Event*, New York, Columbia University Press, 1988.

—— *The Lyotard Reader*, Andrew Benjamin (ed.), Oxford, Blackwell, 1989.

Marcus, Greil, *Lipstick Traces, A Secret History of the Twentieth Century*, London, Secker & Warburg, 1989.

Marcuse, Herbert, 'Repressive Tolerance', R.P. Wolf *et al.* (eds), *A Critique of Pure Tolerance*, Boston, Mass., Beacon Press, 1965.

—— *One-Dimensional Man: Studies in the Ideology of Advanced Industrial Society*, Boston, Mass., Beacon Press, 1966.

Mariën, Marcel (ed.), *Théorie de la Révolution Mondiale Immédiate*, Brussels, Les Lèvres Nues, 1958.

—— *L'Activité Surréaliste en Belgique (1924–1950)*, Brussels, Editions Lebeer-Hossmann, 1969.

Martos, Jean-François, *Historie de l'Internationale Situationniste*, Paris, Editions Gérard Lebovici, 1989.

Marx, Karl and Engels, Frederick, *Collected Works*, vol. 3, London, Lawrence & Wishart, 1975; vol. 6, London, Lawrence & Wishart, 1976; vol 29, London, Lawrence and Wishart, 1987.

Matthews, J.H., *Towards the Poetics of Surrealism*, New York, Syracuse University Press, 1976.

—— *Languages of Surrealism*, Columbia, University of Missouri Press, 1986.

Mauss, Marcel, *The Gift: Forms and Functions of Exchange in Archaic Societies*, New York, Norton, 1967.

'Metastasis: Genetics and Ideology', *Leisure*, 1990.

Miller, David, *Anarchism*, London, J.M. Dent, 1984.

Miller, Henry, *The Cosmological Eye*, Connecticut, New Directions, 1939.

Motherwell, Robert (ed.), *The Dada Painters and Poets, An Anthology*, New York, Wittenborn Schultz, 1951.

Nadeau, Maurice, *The History of Surrealism*, Harmondsworth, Penguin, 1978.

Neville, Richard, *Playpower*, London, Paladin, 1971.

Nietzsche, Friedrich, *The Will to Power*, New York, Random House, 1968.

Nuttall, Jeff, *Bomb Culture*, London, Paladin, 1970.

Ohrt, Roberto, *Phantom Avantgarde: Eine Geschichte der Situationistischen Internationale und der Modernen Kunst*, Hamburg, Editions Nautilus, 1990.

Paris: May 68. An Eyewitness Account, n.p., Dark Star and Rebel Press, 1986.

Pawson, Mark, 'Mail Art: The Eternal Network', *Variant* 7, 1989, pp. 9–12.

Péret, Benjamin and Munis, George, *Les Syndicats contre la Révolution*, Paris, Eric Losfeld, 1968.

Perlman, Fredy, *The Reproduction of Daily Life*, Detroit, Black & Red, n.d.

Pierre, José, *Surréalism et anarchie*, Paris, Plasma, 1983.

Plant, Sadie, 'The Situationist International: A Case of Spectacular Neglect', *Radical Philosophy* 55, Summer 1990, pp. 3–10.

—— 'When Blowing the Strike is Striking the Blow', *Here and Now* 10, 1990, pp. vi–vii.

Pleasure Tendency, The, *Desire-Value and the Pleasure Tendency*, Leeds, 1985.

—— *The Subversive Past*, Leeds, 1985.

—— *Life and its Replacement with a Dull Reflection of Itself*, Leeds, 1986.

—— *Theses Against Cynicism*, Leeds, 1987.

Poll Tax Riot: 10 hours that shook Trafalgar Square, London, Acab Press, 1990.

Posner, Charles (ed.), *Reflections on the Revolution in France: 1968*, Harmondsworth, Penguin, 1970.

Poster, Mark, *Existential Marxism in Postwar France*, Princeton, NJ, Princeton University Press, 1975.

Post-Serious Internotional, The, 'Second Thoughts on the Thought Strike', *Here and Now* 10, 1990, p. xv.

Potlatch 1954–1957 complete facsimile edition, Paris, Editions Gérard Lebovici, 1985.

Raspaud, Jean-Jacques, and Voyer, Jean-Pierre, *L'Internationale Situationniste: protagonistes, chronologies, bibliographie (avec un index des noms insultés)*, Paris, Editions Champ Libre, 1971.

Read, Herbert (ed.), *Surrealism*, London, Faber, 1936.

—— *Arp*, London, Thames & Hudson, 1968.

Reader, Keith A., *Intellectuals and the Left in France since 1968*, London, Macmillan, 1987.

Rebel Violence v. Hierarchical Violence: A Chronology of Anti-State Violence on the UK Mainland July 1985–May 1986, no publication details.

Reid, Jamie, *Up They Rise: The Incomplete Works of Jamie Reid*, London, Faber, 1987.

Richter, Hans, *Dada: Art and Anti-Art*, London, Thames & Hudson, 1978.

Rimbaud, Arthur, *Collected Poems*, Oliver Bernard (ed.), Harmondsworth, Penguin, 1986.

Riot not to Work Collective, *We Want to Riot not to Work: The 1981 Brixton Uprisings*, London, 1982.

Robertson, George, 'The Situationist International: its Penetration into British Culture', *Block* 14, 1988, pp. 38–54.

Rosemont, Franklin, *André Breton and the First Principles of Surrealism*, London, Pluto, 1978.

Rosenberg, Harold, *The De-Definition of Art: Action Art to Pop to Earthworks*, London, Secker & Warburg, 1972.

Ruins of Glamour, Glamour of Ruins, London, Unpopular Books, 1986.

Russell, Charles, *Poets, Prophets, and Revolutionaries: The Literary Avant-Garde from Rimbaud through Postmodernism*, Oxford University Press, 1985.

Sartre, Jean-Paul, *Being and Nothingness: An Essay on Phenomenological Ontology*, London, Methuen, 1969.

Saussure, Ferdinand de, *Course in General Linguistics*, London, Fontana, 1974.

'Say it with Cobblestones', supplement to the *New Statesman*, vol. 114, no. 2958, 18/25 Dec. 1987.

Seabrook, Jeremy, *The Leisure Society*, Oxford, Blackwell, 1988.

Seale, Patrick and McConville, Maureen, *Red Flag, Black Flag: The French Revolution 1968*, Harmondsworth, Penguin, 1968.

Semiotext(e) 9, *Italy: Autonomia. Post-Political Politics*, New York, 1980.

Sheppard, Richard, *Dada: Studies of a Movement*, Chalfont St Giles, Alpha Academic, 1979.

Shipway, Mark, 'Situationism', Maximilien Rubel and John Crump (eds), *Non-Market Socialism in the Nineteenth and Twentieth Centuries*, London, Macmillan, 1987, pp. 151–72.

Sichère, Bernard, *Eloge du Sujet: du retard de la pensée sur les corps*, Paris, Bernard Grasset, 1990.

Slater, Howard, 'Alexander Trocchi and Project Sigma', *Variant* 7, 1989, pp. 30–7.

Smile 10, *Sex without Secretions*, n.d. Includes articles on plagiarism and multiple names.

Smile 11, *Plagiarism special*, n.d. Includes an interview with ex-situationist Ralph Rumney and an article on Alexander Trocchi.

Spectacular Times, *The Bad Days Will End*, London, n.d.

—— *Bigger Cages, Longer Chains*, London, n.d.

—— *Buffo! Amazing Tales of Political Pranks and Anarchic Buffoonery*, London, n.d.

—— *Cities of Illusion*, London, n.d.

—— *The Spectacle: The Skeleton Keys*, London, n.d.

'The Spies for Peace Story', *Anarchy* 29, July 1963, pp. 197– 229.

Stansill, Peter and Mairowitz, David Zane, *By Any Means Necessary: Outlaw Manifestos and Ephemera 1965–70*, Harmondsworth, Penguin, 1971.

Stoke Newington Eight Defence Campaign, *If You Want Peace, Prepare for War*, London, n.d.

Thirion, André, *Révolutionnaires sans Révolution*, Paris, Editions Robert Laffont, 1972.

Timms, Edward and Kelley, David (eds), *Unreal City: Urban Experience in Modern European Literature and Art*, New York, St Martin's Press, 1985.

Turkle, Sherry, *Psychoanalytic Politics: Jacques Lacan and Freud's French Revolution*, London, Burnett Books and André Deutsch, 1979.

Tzara, Tristan, *Seven Dada Manifestos and Lampisteries*, London, John Calder, 1984.

Vague, Tom, 'The Twentieth Century and How to Leave It: The Boy Scout's Guide to the Situationist International', *Vague* 16/17, 1988, pp. 13–46.

Vague 22: *Media Sickness*, 1990. Includes interviews with Ralph Rumney, Margi Clark and Jamie Reid, and articles on the situationists.

Virilio, Paul, *Speed and Politics*, New York, Semiotext(e), 1986.

—— *The Aesthetics of Disappearance*, New York, Semiotext(e), 1990.

Virilio, Paul and Lotringer, Sylvere, *Pure War*, New York, Semiotext(e), 1983.

Ward, Tom, *Cultures in Contention*, Seattle, Wash., Real Comet, 1985.

Williamson, Judith, *Decoding Advertisements: Ideology and Meaning in Advertising*, London and New York, Marion Boyars, 1978.

—— 'An Interview with Jean Baudrillard', *Block* 15, 1989, pp. 16–19.

Wollen, Peter, 'The Situationist International', *New Left Review* 174, March/April 1989, pp. 67–95.

Wollen, Peter, *et al. On the Passage of a Few People through a rather brief Moment in Time: Situationist International 1957–1972*, Cambridge, Mass. and London, MIT Press, 1989.

Working Class Antonomy and the Crisis – Italian Marxist Texts of the Theory and Practice of a Class Movement 1964–1979, Red Notes and CSE Books, London, 1979.

Name index

Althusser, Louis 183
Apollinaire, Guillaume 42
Appel, Karel 54
Aragon, Louis 44, 47, 48, 50–1, 53, 179
Arp, Hans 45
Artaud, Antonin 183
Ascherson, Neal 101–2

Baj, Enrico 54
Ball, Hugo 41, 43
Bardot, Brigitte 80
Barrot, Jean 90, 105
Barthes, Roland 183
Bataille, Georges 135
Baudelaire, Charles 42
Baudrillard, Jean 5, 35–7, 109, 127, 134–8, 140, 141, 147, 148, 153–70, 172–6, 179–80, 182–4
Bernstein, Michèle 55, 60, 86
Branson, Richard 146
Breton, André 42–3, 47–53, 59–60, 70, 78, 87

Camus, Albert 94
Canjuers, Pierre 15
Cardan, Paul, *see* Castoriadis
Carr, Robert 126
Castoriadis, Cornelius 14–15
Censor, *see* Sanguinetti
Chalieu, Pierre, *see* Castoriadis
Chaplin, Charlie 55
Chtcheglov, Ivan 57, 61
Clausewitz, Carl von 83

Cohn-Bendit, Daniel 96, 102
Constant, (Constant Nieuwenhuys) 54, 57
Corneille, (Van Beverloo) 54

Debord, Guy 5, 8–10, 12, 15–17, 27, 29, 32–3, 34–6, 38, 55–6, 60, 66, 73, 79, 82–9, 96, 106, 127, 137–8, 150–4, 157, 167–74, 182, 184
Deleuze, Gilles 107, 124, 125, 129, 139, 140; and Guattari, Félix 108, 112, 122–3, 124–5, 142, 143
Derrida, Jacques 183
Desnos, Robert 52
Dotremont, Christian 54, 64
Ducasse, Isidore, *see* Lautréamont
Duchamp, Marcel 44, 49, 77, 104, 179
Duyn, Roel van 91

Eliot, Karen 177–9, 181
Engels, Friedrich 13

Fermigier, André 104
Fillon, Jacques 50
Foucault, Michel 107–9, 112, 116–21, 124, 132, 139–40, 148
Fourier, Charles 42, 101
Freud, Sigmund 49

Gaulle, Charles de 99
Geismar, Alain 102
Gide, André 78
Gramsci, Antonio 14

135, 165, 167, 170, 180, 181
Viénet, René 81, 100–3
Virilio, Paul 132

Wilson, Tony 146, 203n
Wolman, Gil 55, 60

Subject index